THE ANCESTRY OF DAVID BRACEWELL

Including the Allied Southern Families of Braswell, Brazil, Bay, Price, Passmore, Gage, Prillaman, and Allen

CAREY BRACEWELL

iUniverse, Inc.
Bloomington

The Ancestry of David Bracewell
Including the Allied Southern Families of Braswell, Brazil, Bay, Price, Passmore, Gage, Prillaman, and Allen

iUniverse books may be ordered through booksellers or by contacting:

iUniverse
1663 Liberty Drive
Bloomington, IN 47403
www.iuniverse.com
1-800-Authors (1-800-288-4677)

ISBN: 978-1-4502-9373-0 (sc)
ISBN: 978-1-4502-9375-4 (dj)
ISBN: 978-1-4502-9374-7 (ebk)

Printed in the United States of America

iUniverse rev. date: 05/26/2011

TABLE OF CONTENTS

INTRODUCTION

This book is dedicated to my son, David Bracewell, and other people who share any part of his ancestry. I wrote it trusting that in this new age where families play a lesser role in society than before, it may instill in them a greater respect for those who gave them life. It was written with three readers in mind: genealogists, David's relatives, or those interested in reading about a family of Southern spiritual leaders. I hope whatever your readership category you find this work worthwhile.

Overall, this book describes my findings on David's Yorkshire origins and research on each of the fourteen generations from his oldest known paternal ancestor, Edmund Bracewell, born about 1510, to David, born in 1964. The book also describes their wives and some of their families. In earlier generations, as we shall see, we're lucky to even know the given name of a male ancestor's wife, let alone her birth name. Fathers, expected to rule their families, decided among other things how to dispose of their wife's property, whom their children could marry, and what religion the family must follow. This book is about a male lineage but wasn't written to promote male chauvinism. I won't forget that "The hand that rocks the cradle rules the world."

This work started in the summer of 1958 when I was twenty-one. During a visit to a Hillian cousin in Lometa, Texas, he produced an old Bible that contained this inscription at the back:

> Richard Brazil
> his bible
> And his name wrote above
> and agee sett below is 69
> Richard Brazil was borne
> in the Yeare of our Lord 1759
> Richard Brazil and
> his wife Jemima was married
> the 15th day of May
> in the yeare of our Lord 1780

My cousin knew this Richard Brazil was related to us in some way but didn't know how. My interest piqued, I began searching for his identity. That curiosity has turned into this book.

Principles of genealogical research haven't changed in fifty years but access to the records has. When I began, fewer people were interested in their personal ancestry. In the South, genealogical research took place at the county courthouse or state archives either by mail or in person. Now, with the ease of the Internet, many more persons are interested in researching their roots. They find nearly all their records online including census data. Overall, these changes mark progress. But I never regret going to the places where my ancestors lived, seeing what they saw, gaining a better sense of what their lives were like.

Nor do I regret living on my Texas Hill Country farm for a few years after retirement, far from even the smallest towns, understanding what it was like to live in the country. There's no substitute for raising farm animals for sale or for one's own use, for growing a large garden and preserving its products for the winter or for the lonely, unending work of farming that was the life of most of David's ancestors.

As for references, I offer citations on all-important assertions down to the last few generations where the source reference is that ancestor's own statement--with one exception: federal census data. Census citations are repetitious and take up so much space, I omitted them except for giving the census' year and place. For returns from 1800 to 1840, I put males on the top line, females on bottom. I also omitted racial indicators since everyone I researched was white. If one needs census citations, they're available online or in any genealogical library.

About relatives not mentioned, again space limitation was the cause. Just to cover fourteen generations of one family seemed enough for one book. About content errors, I forgive myself since no one can write a book reflecting research on so many people without making a few mistakes, however regrettable. I only ask other researchers to follow a good genealogical authority and examine all resources before making any of their own corrections.

Finally, concerning all the many names and dates, I trust the non-genealogist reader will find my story of David's ancestry appealing enough at least to keep on reading despite having to wade through so many names and dates. It's the very stuff of genealogy.

My relatives made this book possible. Some were as close as my parents and my sister, Patti. Some distant ones I never met. Distant ones who became close friends and colleagues in solving David's lineage must include Pal Brasel Spencer, William C. Fields, Eunice Young, Jessie Wadley and Ann Braswell. My Aunt Laura Brazil (1869-1953), historian of her generation, her sisters, and her brother, Richard Allen Brazil (1877-1968), and Richard's children, especially Mary Dale Fornier, shared the earliest living memories.

More distant but helpful relatives were Dr. Hugh B. Johnston, Irene Kiker, Mrs. R. E. Heith, Katherine Zachei, Lois Hubbard, Leona Soliday, E.B. O'Neal, Katherine Edwards, Klute Braswell and many others. Two other researchers who helped greatly with this research but aren't directly related to me were Carole Mayfield and Nona Williams. I wish to thank the Church of the Latter Day Saints for collecting and sharing their comprehensive genealogical resources. I also wish to thank Mark Braswell in Cypress, Texas, for sharing the front cover picture. Finally, I wish to thank my loving wife, Nada, for her patience and editorial help.

Lib Jones, Carey, and Bill Fields, 1995

Pal Brasel Spencer and Carey, 1996

CHAPTER ONE

THE REVEREND ROBERT BRACEWELL (1611-1668)

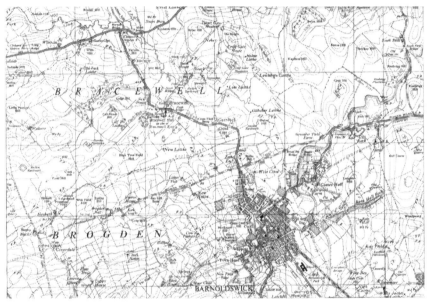

Bracewell, England (1954)

YORKSHIRE ORIGIN

Like more than half of English surnames, the Bracewell name came from a geographical feature, in this case, a village in Yorkshire named Bracewell. Even before they appeared on records, surnames were used to separate two people with the same given name. Early Bracewell's appear in *The Dictionary of English and Welsh Surnames:*[one]

"Bracewell: Local 'of Bracewell', a parish in County York and Bracewell, Brazwell: From Bracewell, West Riding of Yorkshire, Diocese Ripon.

Gilbert de Braycewell 1251- Assize Rolls, Yorkshire

1273 - John de Bracewell,   County Lincolnshire"

Using only written resources, I could never find enough information to connect David's third and fourth American generations let alone tying him back to medieval Bracewell. However, if "delays have dangerous ends," so too can they bring good fortune. Progress in solving David's paternal ancestry seemed dead-ended at that fourth American generation because I had so little information to go on. Then came DNA.

After working out the *human genome,* the complete set of human chromosomes, by the year 2000, DNA science became available to genealogists. In 2003, I launched the Braswell family DNA Project using the FamilyTree DNA program in Houston. With the help of more than one hundred volunteers willing to share their genetic samples, we discovered the *haplotype* or genetic code for all direct male descendants of our founder, the Reverend Robert Bracewell. Testing of other Bracewell men found that we all carry a variant of the same haplotype which could only have originated in Bracewell, a village already mentioned in the Doomsday Book in 1086. Even with so little information about that fourth American generation, the DNA match with other descendants of Reverend Bracewell proved our connection to him.

The clincher came when Gary Bracewell in Las Vegas got tested.   His oldest known Bracewell ancestor, Joseph Bracewell, born in 1751 in Colne, England, lived only seven miles south of Bracewell. Gary is a close genetic match to David Bracewell and others who descend from our immigrant ancestor even though the Reverend's family were already in Grantham, Lincolnshire, far to the south of Bracewell, as early as 1500. Gary and David, separated by at least twenty-five different human conceptions, yet their DNA is almost a perfect match.

Gary's results prove that he carries only one slight difference from Reverend Robert Bracewell's pattern, the one at genetic location DYS 449. It's a good match, proof that we all came from the same family in medieval

York. Evidently, only a single male ancestor who took the name *Bracewell* survived the Black Death of 1348 and all later calamities.

Genetic testing for paternity required an examination of certain "junk" DNA on the male chromosome. The parts geneticists look at here don't affect the baby. They are lazy genes, just part of ancient genetic baggage that have no real purpose nowadays. The segments we look at have the habit of repeating themselves on the gene. After we analyzed all the current markers, our particular DNA strain separates itself from other English families by the number of repeated segments.[2]

St. Michael's Church, Bracewell founded in 1153

LOCAL SOURCES

In a letter from William F. Bracewell in Doncaster, England, William told me:

"Our ancestral home is the village of Bracewell, England, located in Yorkshire, near the Lancashire border. The name Bracewell is a pure Saxon or Scandinavian name, meaning 'we well on the bray, or hill' and this feature is found in Bracewell where the water is derived from a well on the hillside above the village. . . .

After the Norman Conquest in the reign of Henry I, the family were dispossessed by the Normans and replaced by a family named Tempest, William le Tempest having come over with the Conqueror. When the English family were dispossessed by the Normans, they moved into the surrounding districts and references to the Bracewells are to be found in the Parish Records of the adjoining Parishes Thorton-in-Craven, Barnoldswick, Salterforth, and a little further afield in Colne and Burnley, where the name is quite common."[3]

A local English historian, Stanley Challenger Graham, in his series on the Bracewell's which he shared on his Internet page, explained why the Bracewells had already migrated from medieval Yorkshire to Lincolnshire as early as the thirteenth century--

"We have to go back quite a long way--1348 in fact. This was the year the Black Death reached England, a virulent infection carried by the rat fleas and was almost always fatal, sometimes within 24 hours. Our best estimate of the population of England in 1348 is about five or six million souls. In the years, 1348 and 1349 half of these died from the Black Death.

That was bad enough but the Black Death got worse. It recurred again five times between 1361 and 1413. Children were still being born and in economic and demographic terms the population should have recovered faster than usual because less people were competing for resources. The Black Death ate their increase faster than children could be born and the end result was that in 1450 there were only two to two and half million people left alive in England. Whole villages and estates were abandoned.

Modern Bracewell is a very good example of what a village looked like in the late Middle Ages. There was a church, a hall for the lord, and a loose collection of farmsteads each with a cottage or two for labourers. There were no more than 500 people in Bracewell. Everyone was self-sufficient in everything. Then the Black Death shook society to its foundations. In a feudal system, the peasants rely totally on the lord for sustenance and he controls how much they get. All this changed as the workers died off and labour itself became a commodity.

When the Normans took over England in the eleventh century they had two powerful tools for controlling the natives. They used the power of the barons in their castles—that was Clitheroe Castle in our case—to effect civil control. The church was the instrument of social and spiritual control. Bishop Odo of Bayeux was William the Conqueror's brother and fought alongside him during the invasion. Odo's secret ambition was to become Pope and as a means of enhancing his chances of doing this he encouraged the French monastic orders to set up daughter houses in England. The most successful of these were the Cistercians who started off as a very strict order which didn't encourage contact with the outside world but who were very active in farming and trade. For this reason they sought out thinly populated but fertile places to found their monasteries. England was ideal for their purposes and the artificial desolation produced by the Normans when they put down the Northern Barons was a perfect opportunity.

This was when Fountains Abbey and the daughter house at Barnoldswick were founded. Barlick {local name for "Barnoldswick"} proved too tough a nut for them and the monks moved to Kirkstall which was a good thing for the subsequent history of the town as the locals didn't have to compete with the highly organized Cistercians for trade. The monks had stifled competition until well into the sixteenth century and in most cases the surrounding areas never recovered and the enterprising yeomen moved on.

By 1500 the Cistercians were the biggest farmers and traders in wool in England. They, and other monastic orders were enormously wealthy and this attracted the attention of Henry VIII. By 1540 Henry had their assets. This removed monastic competition and was a massive boost to the wool textile industry as it opened it up to the army of entrepreneurial yeoman farmers and small land owners who were straining at the leash to get a toehold in the trade.

The Bracewell yeomen had been quietly trading in the absence of direct competition from the monks. The vacuum left by the Dissolution of the monasteries gave even more scope and this is where our story of the Bracewells really starts. Starting in the fifteenth century, the yeoman farmer's quest for independence led them into looking for ways to make money by trade. The domestic textile industry gave them that opportunity and they grabbed it with both hands. Sheep was the answer. It you can rear stock you can keep sheep and the most importantly, you don't have to kill them every winter. They grow their own overcoats so they can survive in the open and in spring, you can harvest the wool.

Wool is the key to the next leap forward. Another advantage of wool is that you can either simply sell the fleece or you can spin and weave it at home with family labour and, as a modern economist would say, add value. Using simple equipment you could convert the family's work into hard cash. Throughout the fifteenth and sixteenth century wool and cloth were the most important products of England and its biggest export.

Domestic spinning and weaving of wool was common in the farming families of the area but the place where the real money was to be made was in being a clothier. This was a man who traded in wool and cloth, putting wool out to cottagers and farmers to be spun and woven and selling the cloth, either in Colne or often by direct trade with Lincolnshire."[4]

In a message to me dated May 4, 2004, Graham said, "It's almost certain that the Bracewells at some point had connections with the wool trade as this was the major fibre up to the mid-18th Century. There was a thriving direct trade with Lincolnshire from this area and it would be no surprise if Bracewells had connections there."

In addition, in response to the information that one our London Bracewell's apprenticeship as a *fuller (*one who turns raw wool into fabric) Mr. Graham said "Fulling of woolen cloth was a major industry in this part of the country. Colne had fulling mills traceable back to 14th Century so Bracewells entry into this trade is not surprising..."[5]

Bracewell, Yorkshire, is in "W. Yorks" near the Lancaster ("Lance") border.
Grantham, Lincolnshire, is in the southeastern part of
the county. London is south of Grantham.

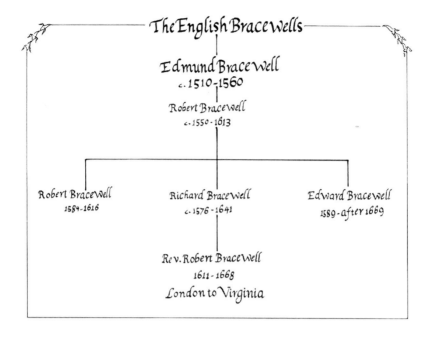

GRANTHAM, LINCOLNSHIRE

The oldest surviving Grantham Parish registers began in 1562 so our record of David's personal ancestry start there. Our oldest known ancestor was Edmund Bracewell, a saddler, born about 1510. The oldest probate records show he died in Grantham on March 27, 1560.

His son, Robert Bracewell, was born there about 1553 since he was aged thirty on a record dated May 14, 1583. Robert married a woman named "Jone." He was the local churchwarden in 1596-97. Robert was buried in Grantham on September 23, 1613. The inventory of his estate, dated September 30 described him as "Co-burgess of Grantham."[6]

Of Robert's several children, his son, Richard, immigrated to London about 1600. His will, written in 1641, appears below. His brother, Edward Bracewell, was witness and overseer to Richard's verbal will. Another brother, Robert Bracewell, Junior, of St. Bride's in London, a draper, also served as an overseer to his brother Richard's will...[7]

LONDON, 1600-1649

The go-getting age from the last decades of Elizabeth I's rule to nearly the end of the reign of James I is comparable to the era of expansion in America when bright, strong men grew very rich. The merchant who had come from a small town and made his money in London was a man of great initiative. The new gentry in London's business world were often minor merchants who attained gentility over the generations like the Bracewell's.

Richard Bracewell was designated a "gentleman" and had two sons. The records of St. Andrew Parish, Holborn, London show:

"Thomas the son of Richard Bracewell baptized VIIIth July. 1610- Anno James VIII

Robert the son of Richard Bracewell baptized October XIII 1611 –Anno James IX" [8]

This younger Robert Bracewell was our first American ancestor.

THE REVEREND ROBERT BRACEWELL'S EDUCATION: LATIN GRAMMAR SCHOOL

Although such records are long since lost, it's likely that Robert Bracewell attended the London Grammar School for the merchant class. "It was the aim of the grammar schools to instruct boys from seven or eight to fourteen or fifteen to read and write and speak Latin. The master was supposed to see to it that conversation in the school was carried on in Latin and to punish those who lapsed into English.

The student in his last years was put through a good selection of the writings of the ancients. The student gained facility in reading the language of learning, Latin. He was equipped to profit from the wisdom and observations of the ancients and of the medieval world. He was enabled to communicate with men of other countries, and to become a member of the international world. His training would prove indispensable if he went into public service. He was also prepared for the university if he looked in that direction.

Intellectual discipline was by no means all. The boys had to repeat prayers morning and evening, to recite the Lord's Prayer and the Ten Commandments, and to memorize catechisms. About moral behavior in general and about good manners, they learned much from the books they studied, from Lily's grammar, and from the many collections of extracts from the Latin writers.

It was a complaint of the Puritans that the boys were taught a pagan morality. Sons of gentlemen, except those of the very rich and of the great nobility, were taught in grammar schools, often in small ones, along with the offspring of parsons, yeomen, mercers, and masons. The man who had spent the formative years of his life in the grammar school of three hundred years ago was not likely to forget any of his fellow sufferers, even if lower born."9

Hart Hall, Oxford University

OXFORD, 1628-1631

Robert Bracewell, aged sixteen, son of Richard Bracewell, Gentleman, of London, matriculated at Hart Hall, Oxford University, on February 22, 1628.[10]

"The students came up to the university at a slightly earlier age than today. Boys of fourteen and fifteen were not unknown. They were of several categories, not always sharply marked off.   In general, at the top were the'fellow commoners' or gentlemen commoners, the sons of noblemen and great country gentlemen. The commoners were more in numbers. They paid lower fees, were often the sons of gentlemen or businessmen, and sometimes received scholarships that paid part of their expense. The family backgrounds of the students were almost as various as in the world outside.   So were the sons of well-to-do businessmen in London and country towns. There were more of them than any other group except sons of clergymen.

.For the four-year B.A. degree the backbone of the training was rhetoric and logic. In logic, the lectures were usually an exposition of Aristotle, and had been the staple of university training since the Middle Ages. As intellectual centers, the universities were still greatly concerned with theology. All studies in the liberal arts were considered proper prerequisites for the course in theology. The teachers had long been training students to be clergymen, and they were still at it, though in a less degree by the seventeenth century. To them the logic and rhetoric which they imposed upon their pupils were methods of arriving at the truth about divinity and expounding on it.

What the boys talked about in their off hours is seldom recorded. We may be sure that they talked religion for everyone did. That they worked long hours in their rooms would appear from the bills they incurred for candles. The arrangement for housing the students seem primitive to us. A fellow of the college would have about five students who would make up his 'company.' The five students would sleep on trundle beds underneath and around his bed."

On November 3, 1631, Robert Bracewell, aged twenty, graduated with a B.A. in holy orders at Oxford.[11]

LAST WILL AND TESTAMENT OF
THE REVEREND ROBERT'S FATHER,
RICHARD BRACEWELL

In the year of our Lord 1641

He being then Sicke and weake in body but of sound & perfect memory, did make and declare his last will & testament nuncupative, or by word of mouth in manner & form following or to the like effect viz:

He gave and or bequeathed to his sonne in lawe Mr. John Stiles twenty pounds which he the said John Stiles then ought {owed} him, for and because of his two children and to the two children of his said sonne in law he gave {12?} pence apeace.

And he made & appointed his sonne Robert Bracewell his executor, and to his wife he gave and bequeathed one third part of his estate and he nominated & appointed his two brothers Robert Bracewell and Edward Bracewell the overseers of his said will. There being then and there present Mr. Thomas Perry, Clerk, Edward Bracewell, Ann Grasvenor, and these credible witnesses.

Edward Bracewell

Ann Grosvenor

Proved December 13, 1641 on the oaths of Edward Bracewell and Ann Gravender {sic}12

THE REVEREND BRACEWELL'S
CHURCH IN ENGLAND

Victorious Puritans and the Great Fire of London of 1666 destroyed the records of Anglican ministers. Still, he must have been well experienced for the job. Robert, named his father's executor as surviving eldest son, yet Richard Bracewell named his two brothers as "overseers of the will." This suggests Reverend Robert Bracewell's parish was some distance from the Parish of St. Bartholomew-the-Great in London where his father died.

An English clergyman of the Established or national church during the 1630's held a position different from an American Anglican minister. Appointed to a "living," he was named vicar of a church with an income attached to it. He was not supported by the congregation. Named for life, he could not be removed except for grave cause, but he could be promoted to a better living at a larger church.

In the early seventeenth century his income was of several kinds. Lands were attached to the parsonage known as *glebe lands*, which he could lease or work with a servant or on his own. In addition he had the right to levy certain tithes, or tenths, from the farmers--tithes of crops, animals, poultry, eggs or garden produce. Some of the tithes might be commuted for money.

The collection of tithes was an embarrassment to the clergyman. It took time and involved business dealings with those to whom he ministered in a spiritual capacity. Members had to give one tenth of their annual income to the church. The parishioners often begrudged the parson his tenth hen and tenth calf, and found ways to get around him. He had a wife and children to support so he had to insist upon his rights. It was not easy to make demands upon those to whom one was preaching goodwill and forbearance. The parson also had fees for marriages, for the churching of women after childbirth and for burials.

The church had seen to it that the rector or vicar had a parsonage. Usually that building was not far from the parish church and was generally about the same size and grade as that of a fairly prosperous yeoman. A vicarage included a hall, a kitchen, which might be detached, a study, and a bedroom and possibly other small bedrooms. The furniture would be oak tables and cupboards as in a yeoman's house, and a little silver and some linen. The parson usually had farm implements and stock worth as much as his household equipment. As for help, the lucky clergyman had one or two laborers to farm the glebe; otherwise he would work his fields himself, with the aid of his sons. His wife in many instances had one helper in the kitchen. 13

The pulpit exercised a powerful influence, not only in religious matters, but also in the realm of party politics. In considering the work of those who took away Episcopal positions during the Puritan Revolution beginning in 1649, it must be remembered that the eradication of political 'disaffection' always held a big place in their minds. In the articles of accusation against the clergy we find that the charges of refusing the Covenant, speaking against the Covenant, refusing to read the Puritan Parliamentary proclamations were the most common accusations.

The question of the number of Episcopal clergy who were deprived of their living by the Parliamentary committees during the period of the Civil War and Commonwealth is impossible to arrive at. The sources from which an accurate list might have been compiled are no longer available, for the minutes of the Committee for Plundered Ministers are incomplete, and those of the local sequestration committees have, except in a very few cases, disappeared altogether." 14

Southside Virginia in the Seventeenth Century

THE REVEREND ROBERT BRACEWELL'S ARRIVAL IN VIRGINIA

King Charles I, executed by the Puritans in 1649, compelled Reverend Bracewell to join the company of loyalist Cavaliers and took ship for Virginia. His first surviving record, dated April 29, 1650, was the Bennett-Webb agreement:

Articles of Agreement concluded & agreed Between Ambross Bennett of the one partie & Thomas Webb of the other partie in manner & forme as followeth

Imprimis it is agreed between the parties aforesaid that the said Ambross Bennett doth give unto the aforesaid Thomas Webb & his heires forever, one acre of Land, that he shall erect a Mill upon, & the privilege of the Run that the said Mill doth stand upon, and it is further agreed between the parties aforesaid, that if in Case the aforesaid Thomas Webb be att any time disposed to make sale of the aforesaid Mill, or Acre of Land, the aforesaid Ambrose Bennett or his heirs for ever, shall have the refusall, of the aforesaid Mill & the Acre of Land, And it is further agreed between the parties aforesaid, that the said Thomas Webb is to grind the aforesaid Ambross Bennetts Corne toll free, & his heires & all them that doo belong to his owne family for ever, And it is further agreed between the parties aforesaid, that the said Ambross Bennett doth sett & lett unto the aforesaid Thomas Webb Sixty Acres of Land for the terme of Thirty years complett & ended, bounded on the other side, so farr as the aforesaid Ambross Bennetts Land doth runne & soe over the Runn, & soe bounded upon the Land of Mr Robert Bracewell, and from his Land A Cross over the path that goeth to the Church It is agreed between the parties aforesaid, that the said Thomas Webb, is to give the aforesaid Thomas Bennett in Consideration of the aforesaid Land three thousand pounds of tobacco & Cask & one hogshead of ground meal, to be paid ready downe, the Tobacco to be paid fifteen hundred in the year, of our Lord God One thousand Six hundred fifty & two, & for the true performance hereof we have Enforchangeably sett our hands & seales the 29th of Aprill 1650

Ambrose A Bennett (seal)

Thomas W Webb (his mark)

The word heires incerted in the first article was

done by the consent of Ambross Bennett being

onely forgotten att the first soe along

Teste Robert Bracewell

Ann A Bennett (her mark)

This was entered in the indyent

= water way . . . .

Signed Sealed & delivered in the presence of

Henry Preston

George Rawley

9th February I Ambross Bennett acknowledged the within written Articles In open court held for the Isle of Wight County & by him proved to be Recorded which is accordingly Ordered & done & Examined per me Johann Combe, Clerk" 15

This informal agreement dates Reverend Bracewell arrival to the New World before April 29, 1650. It also gives us a writing in his own words. That this agreement was written by a non-lawyer seems clear from its unusual language. Lawyers weren't welcome in early Virginia. Many came to America to escape them. And nowhere else can we find such terms in other colonial records as" *sett & lett, the terme of Thirty years complett & ended, to be paid ready downe"* and similar expressions.

No lawyer could admit in a post script to some important term " *being onely forgotten att the first."* So if a lawyer didn't write this agreement, who did? Bracewell is the likely choice since he had the same education as a seventeenth century lawyer. He also had close ties to Ambrose Bennett and the land in question.

Robert's neighbor, Colonel Joseph Bridger, owned White Marsh Plantation not far from the church. Bridger likely appointed Robert Bracewell vicar of St. Luke's Church. Bridger was a member of the king's Council of State, Sir William Berkeley's group that controlled Virginia affairs.

SIR WILLIAM BERKELEY, ROYAL GOVERNOR, 1642-1676

Sir William Berkeley created the Cavalier society in Virginia. "Cavalier" meant someone who supported Charles I of England in his struggles against Parliament. Berkeley granted them large estates to set up a ruling oligarchy that ran the colony for many generations. His model was his ancestral home in the south of England. The Cavalier migration continued throughout Berkeley's time as governor. Much of it occurred during the decade of the 1650's. Berkeley's Cavalier society set the stage for succeeding ruling classes throughout the South. Berkeley's plan modeled Gerald O'Hara's plantation society, "Tara," in the movie *Gone with the Wind*.

Of seventy-two families in Virginia's high elite whose dates of migration are known, two-thirds arrived between 1640 and 1669. A majority arrived between 1647 and 1660. The first Washington crossed the ocean in 1657. He was John Washington, the younger son of an Oxford-trained clergyman removed from his living by the Puritans.[16]

Sir William Berkeley's recruiting campaign was successful. Nearly all of Virginia's ruling families were founded by sons of eminent English families during his governorship. And like Robert Bracewell, the Cavaliers, if they had gone to a university, choose Oxford. One-third of the Cavaliers had lived in London before coming to America.

At the top of Virginia society were the Cavalier planters, who owned much of the land, most of the servants and nearly all of the slaves. Sir William Berkeley's "distressed cavaliers" at the top were only a small part of the total flow to Virginia. Below them was a group of yeoman who owned their own land and tilled it with their own hands, often with the help of a servant or two. This group of small freeholders was always a minority of Virginian population. The majority of Virginia's immigrants were humble people of low rank. Three out of four immigrants from this lowest class came as indentured servants.

St. Luke's Church built in 1632, the oldest church of English origin in America

MINISTRY AT ST. LUKE'S CHURCH

For more than a century, the religious life of Virginia developed along English Anglican lines. It was ceremonial, liturgical, hierarchical and ritualistic. No one had to share the same opinions but all had to join in the same rituals. The gentry who came from southwestern England had long favored "an uniform government of the Church in all points."

A minister was required to preach every Sabbath, gave communion three times a year, "examine, catechize and instruct'" all the children in his parish, and to "excel all others in puritie of life." Parishioners had to attend church on Sundays and holidays, or to pay a shilling for each absence. They also had to pay tithes, and couldn't openly criticize their minister.

Most Virginia gentlemen worked harder than they cared to admit. They raised crops for the market, and as a result found themselves engaged in trade. The great planters also acted as merchants and bankers for their neighbors. Many owned shops, stores, ships and warehouses.[17] A record dated September 24, 1652, showed the Reverend Bracewell was no exception. William Chapple, mariner, James Vawer, pilot, and John Fisher, carpenter, all of the ship *Mary* of Accomac in Virginia gave this account:

They were at Accomac last July, bound for Bristol, when they met one John Jones. This Jones died of fever, after saying that he had 40 hogsheads of tobacco in the hands of Robert Braswell, a merchant living on Pagan Creek on James River in Virginia. [18]

REVEREND BRACEWELL ELECTED TO THE HOUSE OF BURGESSES

In July 1653, Reverend Robert Bracewell, was elected to represent Isle of Wight County in the Virginia House of Burgesses but suspended after a time because it was contrary to English custom for an ordained minister to serve in a legislative body "since it is unprecedented and may produce bad consequences."[19]

A seat in the House was not an empty honor. This small body functioned as the governor's cabinet, the upper house of the legislature and the colony's supreme court. It controlled the distribution of land, and the lion's share went to twenty-five families who held two-thirds of the seats in that body from 1680 to 1775. One of them could have been Bracewell's, as we shall see.

ROBERT BRACEWELL'S WILL

Early Virginia was an unhealthy place to live. One part of the problem arose from the bay itself. Fecal pollution washed into swamps and stagnant pools. The estuary became the ideal breeding grounds for typhoid fever and amoebic dysentery, trapping deadly organisms that ravaged the sickly population in the summer months. No one then knew anything about bacteria. Robert Bracewell was likely sick many time before he died. This power of attorney likely marks his illness during the summer "sickness time" of 1664:

Know all men by these presents that I Robert Bracewell have appointed Mr William Thompson my Lawfull attorney, to answer the suit of Thomas Hipkins. and whatsoever my said attorney shall doe, I shall ratifie

Witness my hand June the ninth 1664.

Robert Bracewell

Robert Stoakes

Recorded 9th June 1664.20

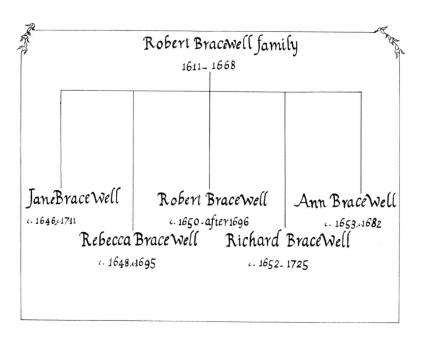

Then on February 15, 1668, he wrote his will:

In the name of God Amen, I Robert Bracewell beinge very weake & sicke of Body but of perfectt memorie, doe make this my last Will & Testament, Revockeinge all former Wills whatsoever, Imprimis I bequeath my Soule into the hands of my Redeemer, who gave it mee, And my body unto the ground from whence it came to be decently buried, And for those Temporall goods God hath given mee I dispose of them in manner as followeth, I give unto my daughter Jane Stockes her Children, three cowes, To Rebecca West my daughter one Cowe & Calfe And one Cowe & Calfe to the next child she shall have, And the rest of all my Estate unto my two sonns Robert and Richard whome I make my full & sole executors of this my Will, and the Mill I desire shalbe finisht, with what speed may bee And to be lett out, only reservinge corne for themselves, and the p.{ro} duse of the Mill to be equally divided betweene them both, And reserved to build a new mill hereafter And when built to be left wholly to my sonne Richard Likewise I give Seaven hundred Acres of land where I now live and sixe hundred Acres att the Western Branch of Nancemond County To be equally divided betweene my two sonnes Robert and Richard Likewise it is my desire that noe part or parcell of the estate shalbe disposed of, nor none of the land, untill they both are of full Age, nor no wayes divided But if it shall please God that either of them shall depart this life before he comes of Age, That then the Survivor shall enjoye the whole Likewise I give unto my Servant Elizabeth Hall when she shalbe free one heiffer of two yeares of Age And likewise it is my desire That my loveinge friends Mr Richard Izard and George Gwillam to be Guardians unto my Children in the time of theire Minoritie, And to see this my Will performed Likewise I give unto the said Richard Izard and George Gwillam, ffortie shillings to each of them, to buy them each one ringe, Likewise I give unto my Daughter Ann Bagnall one Cowe & Calfe And one Cowe & calfe to her first Child, if it please God she have any, And likewise it is my desire that my two sonnes, Robert & Richard shalbe putt to schoole untill they cann both write & read And this beinge my Will I testifie it with my hand this 15th of February 1667

Rob: Bracell

In Wittness of

George Gwillim

Richard {"x"} Izard

This will was proved in open Cort held for the Isle of Wight County this first Day of May 1668 And then RecordedTeste John Jennings Clr: Recordes"21

An Appraisement of the Estate of Mr Robert Bracewell - May 11th 1668

one pcell of young hoggs .... 1800 {pounds of tobacco}
Six Cowes wch values 3000
Two young Bulls of a year old 300

two Cowes att 800

one draught oxe att.......................... 700

one Mare & horse coult.................... 300

0one fether Bedd boulster one)

pillow 2 blancketts one rugg 1000

curtaines & vallens)

nine Shillings in money & 3 ringes 400

one silver Tankard one dram cupp)

and three silver spoones............................. 500

one Chest Drawers 250

Two Chests one cubberd drawers.................. 200

one Couch one warmeinge pann 100

one round Table 200

one old chaire & chest................................. 30

6 diap Napkins 1 table cloth 200

2 cubberd clothes & cushion...................... 300

one old Chest & Trunck 40

one glass att...................................... 500

one Table att 300

fivc paire of shoes at 100

one Coverlet for a bedd 400

one pcell of black broadcloth......................... 150

one pcell of qr ling broadcloth...................... 30

five yards Kerses att 100

one yard ¾ of flannin......................... 20

one pcell of weareing clothes 70

0one fether bedd 4 Coverings & one)

hamacke Curtaines & vallens)..................... 900

one pcell of beddinge att 100

two gunnes att 200

one old Chest & Trunck att 100

one old fether bedd pilloe 2 coverin............. 400

one pcell of old bedinge att 20

one Emptie bll att........................... 40

one parcell of Books at 500

one pcell of old pewter att 300

17,680

4 Iron potts & a brass Candelsticke............. 300

one old brass Kettell 50

one bell metell skillett at............................... 40
one morter frieinge pan dripping)
pan & one spitt at 80
one per Andirons tongs fire shovell............... 40
fower pott rackes & grandiron 100
one old brass Kettell att................................ 50
one pcell of earthern ware at......................... 60
one pcell of tubbs & lumber at...................... 200
one pcell of old Iron att................................ 200
one round table at 100
two bed steades at 10
0one Servant boy at...................................... 800
Summe in all is 19800
Debts good & desperatt in all .... 16000.

35800 (total)

Chattell belongine to the estate that are abroad att Severall places,

att Robert Stoakes 8 Cowes, 2 bulls 6 three yeare old heiffers and 5 two yeare old heiffers

1 Cowe at Coll Pitts
1 Cowe at Mr John Pitts
1 Cowe at Mr Nicholas Smithes
1 Cowe at Mr Thomas Taberers
1 Cowe at Mr John Hardy
1 Cowe att Mr Danniell Bouchers
1 Cowe att John Viccors
1 Cowe att William West
1 yearlinge att William West

An old Boate not appraised, neither the Cattell above named, But all things else that is Charged to Account is appraised by us

Gyles Driver
Benjamin Bealer
Robert Coleman
Ffrancis Ayres

Recorded 9th June 1668 P Mr Jno Jennings, Clr Court [22]

These records were buried during the Revolutionary War to prevent them being burnt by British soldiers. Some passages are hard to read but we are lucky to have the documents at all.

Reverend Robert Bracewell's will proved that he had at least five children—Jane Stokes, Rebecca West, Robert Bracewell, Jr., Richard Bracewell, and Ann Bagnall. The children, customarily listed first in their order of birth, were Jane and Rebecca who had married and had children of their own and mentioned ahead of their younger, unmarried brothers. Ann, mentioned last, and although she was also married, it's clear she married recently from the gift she was to receive, an additional cow and calf for her first child "if it please God she have any." Finally, Robert Bracewell, Junior, mentioned ahead of Richard, indicates he was older. Proof later came in a deed, James Bagnall to William West dated March 9, 1681, in which Robert is referred to as the "Eldest Sonne" of "Mr Robt Bracewell, Parson of ye Lower Parish."[23]

From the order of items listed in the inventory, it would appear Reverend Robert Bracewell's house contained five rooms with a chimney at each end of the house, much like the English glebe church described earlier. There were two rooms on the ground floor, a kitchen with library and master bedroom which included a dining nook. Upstairs, his inventory indicated he had bedrooms for his children and servants.

Rebecca Izard, wife of Richard Izard, rendered the following account current on January 10, 1669:

An Account of Mr Robert Bracewells estate both Creditor & Debitor/

Mr Robert Bracewells estate Credited as
By Appraisement in Goods & Chattel.. 19800

In Good and Separate Debts 16000
To one Cowe received of Mr Taberer
not appraised nor delivered & sould
Since by Mr Izard.. 600
To an old boate sould & ditto 350
To one Cowe more sould & ditto 470
To one Calfe sould 100
By a Crop of tob: made in Ann:o 1668 1440
{total} 38760

By one Cowe receaved of Col Pitt
not appraised nor delivered

Mr Bracewells estate Credited by the
profitt of the Mill from July 1668 to ....Bar: corne
the last of January last past
13 tn: barrells & ½ of meale & corne .... 13 – ½

To English grain the mill gott in the time aforesaid Wch
Remained in the Mill..Bushells 12

Mr Robert Bracewells estate Debitor
by severall disbursements in building the mill
& by severall paymts in debts & charges upon
the Children & Servants as p Acc.o approx 30968

Remaineinge in badd debts as they came
into Mr Izards hands...
4800

Rest in goods undisposed of...
11280

To a bill of Mr Drivers Since the ballance.................................. 380

                                                                Total   47428

Paid unto James Bagnall One Cow received of Col Pitt
as a legacie given by Mr Robert Bracewell unto Said Bagnall

Debitor by 3 barrells & ½ of meale paid John
Poole for a debt Mr Bracewell was indebted to bar: corne

the said Poole. .... 3 -
½

By 3 bar: of Corne the Mill was indebted unto

Mr Izard for the workmen & families
while the Mill did not go... 3

By Fower barr:l of Corne paid Mr Knowles
paid for the poision {boarding} of the Children
And 4 barells of Corne paid on: Wm Oldis
upon the aforesaid Account being... 8

—————————————
14 – 1/2

13 _ ½

Rest due to Mr Izard .... 1 bar Corne

To the Servants Corne..3 barrells

To Mary Parmentor...1 barrell
Ballance 8668

To Capt Greene.. 800
To Servants clothes.. 400
To Mary Parmentor for washing the children............................ 100
To Mrs Carter 200
To the Clk & Sher: for ffees unto Greene & Carter.................... 88
10256

A Just Acc:o errors excepted this10th Jany 1669
P me Rebeccah Izard
Recorded 10th January Ann:o 1669P me John Jennings Clr:
Recordes24

[January 30,1669] Disbursments made by Richard Izard &Sevrall
Debts by him paid on the estate of Mr Robert Bracewell Deceased

Tob(acco)

To 26 lb of brass 126. to mending the dam 80 206

To John _____ 160

To 1 thousand nails 50.. 215

To haleinge the Mill stones & Timber................................... 100

To 1___ of _____ 10 to Ann Madison 110

To 2 gall wine to take the stones out of the shep....................... 34

To Robt Smith for bringing the Mill sto................................... 500

To Tho: Clark & Ja: Bagnall to build the Mill........................ 600

To Jn:o _____ towards buildinge t ....
2930

To ditto pd more towards the buildinge of the Mill pd Cha
Tapladye..2100

To Majr Gent: Bennett for Millsto 5000

To Benj: Brals for goinge upp to receive the Mill stones............. 100

To Ambrose Bennett 700

To Geo: _____ for Smiths work 100

To making leasses & writeings for the lettinge out of the Mill..... 350

To John Gaurdinor for Saweinge planck for the Mill.................. 600

To John Coke for carring up of hoggs 100

To Cap: Jennings 222   to Tho: Greene 400 622

To Col Pitt... 246

To Maj: Hill by Col Pitt as apperith by Mr Skinners Accompt.... 800

To Tho: Greene paid More 400

To Jeremiah Marin pr order 1800

To the sheriff for ffees.. 103

To Majr Hill_____ pr order... 862

To Thomas Webb 225

To Wm Oldis pr order of Court
17 pounds ster: being in tobac 3200

To Doctor Ashley... 920

To Doctor Hiatt pr Ord & for fees.. 426

To Ffra: Ayers attey to Wm Wilson 1800

To Mr Ayers for a 150

To Capt Bridger assignee to Jno: Whit 880

To Capt. Jinings for ffees... 683

To bill to Mr Izard 128
To funerall chardges 795
To bill to Mr Driver 380

281651

Acc:o Errors excepted this 30th Janry An:o 1669　Rebecah Izard

(right-hand page)An acc:o of Disbursements for Mr Bracewells two Sonnes and the Servants
An:o 1668 & An:o 1669

To 1 paire of shoes 25: lb 4 lb soape 32 lb 57
To 2 hatts 44:lb Six pounds of Soape 48 lb 92
4 yards l/4 of blew lininge for drawers 48 & for pecketts & making.
Six shirts cont 15 ells att 15 lb pr ell 225
for making & thread 502
_____ 8 & to Tho: Moss for makinge closse 80 88
To making of fower shirtts & thred 30
To __ __ for Robt Bracewell & one Servant 304
to three hh {hogsheads?} & ½ to pack the Crop 96
To 2 pr shoes for the Servant 60
To 8 ells 1 yrd of Canvas for the boy E maide Servant 130
To ½ a ell of Canvas .... 5 ½
To makinge of drawers e thread 20
To 2 pr stockings for the boy 24
To 2 hoes 36
To 4 ells Canvas for the Serv.t boy making e thred 68
To Tho: Moss for makinge his two Sonnes two waisscoats
& buttons & thred 30
To 2 pr blew drawers cont 4 yards & ½ &
to makinge & thred 74
To 2 pr worsted Stockings 60
To 1 pr Canvas drawers for the Servant 20
To 5 yrds ¾ of Kerssy for his two Sonne 150

To ditto one yard ¾ flanninge...30
To 2 pairs of shoes...60
For ther boardinge & schooleing this year...............................1300
To two _____ waisscoats...60
To a prcell of _____...30
Som. 3157 ½ "
Recorded 10:th January An:o 1669"[25]

One can see from this account how the mill was rebuilt. Thomas Clark and James Bagnall had overall supervision of the project while Guardiner and Toplady did the actual work. The millstones arrived in Jamestown. Getting them hauled to the Bracewell Plantation was no small task. The mill was leased after it was rebuilt as spelled out in the will.

Bracewell Plantation was busy. Wine was used to take the stones out of the sheep. The plantation was still in the hog business as shown by the pay to Coke for "carring up of hogs." The "wether" bought from Ayres was for a castrated adult sheep.

Rebecca's disbursements for the clothing of the Bracewell boys and the household staff may interest some reader's more than castrated sheep or rebuilt mills. Seventeen pounds sterling paid out to William Oldis was tuition and board for the boy's schooling. We can follow the dressmaker's steps in assuring that the young men dressed to suit their class: waistcoats, blue-lined drawers and all.

REVEREND ROBERT BRACEWELL'S DAUGHTER, JANE STOKES ELEY ROBERTS

Robert Stokes joined up with the Bracewell family at least as early as June 9, 1664, when he witnessed Reverend Bracewell's power of attorney. Reverend Bracewell's inventory shows the bulk of his livestock, twenty-one head, were in Robert Stokes' hands.

After her first husband, Captain Robert Stokes, was hanged by Governor Barkeley following Bacon's Rebellion, Jane then married Robert Eley about 1678. Their marriage lasted only two years until he, too, died. She then married John Roberts by July 20, 1680. [26] Jane had children by each of her three husbands but it is hard to decide the paternity of her daughters. Her only child by Eley seems to have been Robert Eley III. John Roberts evidently died in Nansemond County as he does not appear in any Isle of Wight County records.27

Jane wrote her will on June 26, 1711, in what is now Southampton County, Virginia, then the southern part of Isle of Wight County. She gave one hundred acres each to her son, Robert Eley, "part of a patent of fourteen hundred and fifty acres granted to John Roberts and Jane his wife the 20ᵗʰ day of July 1680. . . all the Land on the Lower side of the Branch Called the Long Branch on the south side of the Beaver Dam swamp." To her grandson, Robert Scott, she gave one hundred acres on the White Oake Branch on the west side of Beaver Dam Swamp, "the said land lyeing between the White Oake Branch and the Cabbing Neck Branch—." To her daughter, Mary Parker, she gave one hundred acres on the west side of Beaver Dam Swamp "that was to her Husband William Parker deceased." To her granddaughter, Marthew Sanders, she gave another one hundred acres on Beaver Dam swamp "that was to her father and mother." Also, "unto Thomas Jones that land he now lives on according to the Bounds he Bought from my brother Richd Brasswell." She gave five shillings to Rebeckah Brinckley but the will left out their relationship. Her daughter, Jane Scott, got one shilling. To her son, John Roberts, she left "all my land on the upper side of the Reedy Branch" and to her son, Thomas Roberts, all the land on the lower side. She also gave Thomas Roberts all her land on the Lower side of Reedy Branch to the Long Branch. To her sons, John and Thomas Roberts, she gave equal shares in her "Removable Estate" and appointed them both her executors.28 Jane Bracewell was an ancestor to President Lyndon Baines Johnson.29

REBECCA BRACEWELL WEST

Rebecca Bracewell stayed married to William West for at least thirty years until her death. Unlike her sister Jane, Rebecca remained in their old neighborhood near St. Luke's Church.

William West was a fighter to the end of his life. An Isle of Wight County record dated April 10, 1703, "in the differences between William West and

John Drake, it appears that John Drake has abused him, William West, and his daughter, Ann West, and John Drake has begged forgiveness." [30]

Rebecca's last deed co-signed with her husband was dated April 28, 1694, in which they sold a tract of land.[31] William's will, signed October 20, 1708, mentions his wife but not by name. However, she is named as "Martha West" in his inventory taken later in 1709. West's children named in his will were William West, Junior, Richard West and Robert West, and daughters Mary Green and Rebecca West. Most if not all were born to Rebecca Bracewell.

West's will included--

"Item. I Give, & bequeath unto my daughter Mary Green my Indian Girl called Pinke.

Item. I Give, & bequeath unto my son Wm West my Indian Girl named Rose.

.Item. I Give & bequeath unto my Loving Wife, my negroes Tony, Jack, & my Indian woman Pegg, so long as she shall Live a Widd:w"[32]

ROBERT BRACEWELL, Jr.[33]

When in-depth Braswell research began, everyone assumed Robert Bracewell, Junior's children would be legitimate. After all, he was a minister's son. Then came this shocker: Richard Towle's 1692 Isle of Wight County will left

to my three youngest children of Susanna Braswell, Richard, William, and Elizabeth Braswell, all my whole and sole estate to be possessed of their parts as they shall attain to the age of seventeen years. Executor John Riggs.[34]

A dozen or so Braswell researchers including lawyers and even a college professor examined Towle's will and other of Susanna's documents and came to the same conclusion: her marriage to Robert Bracewell, Junior, wasn't a real marriage for long. DNA testing of descendants of her sons,

Richard and James, proved that neither one matches the genetic profile carried by descendants of Reverend Bracewell.

Towle's property at inventory was worth only thirteen pounds. One wonders why Susanna took up with a poor local farmer when she was legally married to Robert Bracewell, Junior, who at the time of her marriage stood to become a member of Virginia's F.F.V.'s, "First Families of Virginia," like the Washington's, Jefferson's, and Lee's. Whatever Towley got with Susanna, she was all he got. Her property legally belonged to her husband. Robert Bracewell, Jr. showed up in Surry County, the county just west of Isle of Wight, disposing of her inheritance during the 1680's.

No one knows why Robert Bracewell's marriage failed. Still, maybe one clue, given that daughters often grow up to be like their mothers, turned up in a record mentioning Susanna's mother, Mary. By 1694, Mary Burgess Colling, was John Colling's wife:

Order is granted Susanna Braswell against John Colling, Sr., for four hundred pounds of tobacco for looking after Colling's wife in her late extremity when she was beaten by Colling with costs.

It appearing to this Courte that John Collins Sr. hath lately most desperately beaten, bruised, & wounded Mary his wife, inasmuch that it was expected she would have lost her life. Thereby. . .for prevention whereof for the future, It is ordered that the said Collins pay & allow his wife five hundred pounds of tobo: forthwith, & one thousand pounds for her maintenanee (if she finde cause) To live separate & aparte from her husband.[35]

Why would a man severely beat his wife almost to death, especially in a remote colony where women were still scarce, where men still outnumbered women six to one?

Robert Bracewell disappeared from record after he gave his power of attorney to Susanna on March 27, 1696:

I Robert Braswell of the Isle of Wight County in verginia appoint my Loving wife Susana Braswell to be my Lawful attorney for me and in my name to produce and sue all such persones as are in debt to me and to answer all suits which I have depending in ye Isle of Wight Courts..[36]

It was normal for husbands to refer to their wives as "my loving wife" no matter the condition of their marriage.

ANN BRACEWELL BAGNALL

Ann, like her sister, Rebecca Bracewell West, stayed in the Tidewater Area of Isle of Wight County, while the rest of her family went on to Nansemond County. Ann's father-in-law, Richard Izard, in his 1669 will, mentioned Ann and her husband, James Bagnall, along with Izard's daughter, Mary, who was married to Ambrose Bennett. Ann's husband, James Bagnall, was mentioned in Rebeccah Izard's will dated October 15, 1675.

Ann had three children by James Bagnall, Rebecca, Mary, Joseph, and Robert Bagnall. Ann died at about age thirty. She left no will.[37] James Bagnall remarried Sarah Montague by May 29, 1683.[38]

CHAPTER TWO
RICHARD BRACEWELL (c.1652-1725)

BACON'S REBELLION: OUR LOST OPPORTUNITY TO BECOME A "FIRST FAMILY OF VIRGINIA"

The Bracewells lost their chance to become a "First Family of Virginia" like the Jefferson's, Madison's, and Custis's because Reverend Bracewell's family were leaders in a rebellion against royal authority. Two of the Reverend Robert Bracewell's sons-in-law led military companies in Bacon's Rebellion of 1676 and the rest of the family supported them.

The rebellion began in 1674 when Virginia militiamen murdered five Susquehannock Indian chiefs on the north bank of the Potomac River. The enraged Susquehannock broke into roving bands and attacked one plantation after another on the Virginia frontier. When Virginia's Governor Berkeley refused to "take a speedy course and destroy the Indians," the colonists got behind Nathanial Bacon. Bacon, a cousin to Lord Francis Bacon, the founder of scientific methodology, saw his father and the overseer of his upper plantation murdered by the Indians. When he appeared before a muster of militia to do something about these Indian outrages, he allowed their cry of "A Bacon! A Bacon!" to go to his young noble head.

He declared war on all neighboring Indians. Berkeley still refused to go after the Indians so Bacon marched on Jamestown, made the Governor run for cover, and set up a de facto government calling the Berkeley clique "sponges. . .who have sucked up the Publick Treasure" and "unworthy Favorites and juggling Parasites."

Bacon was a popular hero supported by the majority of the white population including a few wealthy planters like the Bracewells. That including Robert Stokes, husband of Jane Bracewell, eldest daughter of Reverend Bracewell, and William West, husband of Jane's sister, Rebecca. Both Bracewell sons-in-law recruited and led their own rebel companies.

According to historian John B. Boddie, "When Bacon's plantation was recaptured by Berkeley's forces, William West commanded a force that marched against him intending to surprise him but he in turn was surprised and captured by 'eighty horse and ninety foot' commanded by Colonel Bridger." Bridger--whose tombstone now lies on the floor in front of the high altar at St. Luke's Church, was a member on Berkeley's Council and a colonel in the Indian wars. His plantation at "White Marsh" was less than two miles from St. Luke's and not much farther from Reverend Bracewell's plantation.

Cromwell's revolt in England was too recent for anyone to challenge the king's governor and get away with it for long. The seventy-year-old Governor drove Bacon and his rag-tag army into a defensive position at Gloucester on the York River. At his last stand near Yorktown, Bacon came down with the "bloody flux" and died miserably on October 26, 1676. His pitiful army, which included indentured servants and even Negro slaves, quickly fell apart and the rebellion ended.

Following the usual procedure against defeated rebels, the Governor court-martialed and hanged all the gentlemen leaders on Bacon's side whom he could lay his hands on. That included Robert Stokes. William West was awaiting execution on a prison ship anchored in Hampton Roads when he somehow managed to escape.

When the English fleet arrived with 1,100 Redcoat regulars and a general pardon for the rebels, the Governor was surprised to find himself recalled to England to answer to the crown for his behavior. Besides favoring a clique of favorites with rich land grants and public offices and permanent vestry appointments, Berkeley was also guilty of not allowing the House of Burgesses to sit and solve colony problems since 1662.

The Governor returned to England in June 1677, and died there before having a chance to lay his case before the king. King Charles II, far from appreciating what his loyal servant had done, remarked, "That old fool has hang'd more men in that naked Country, than he had done for the Murder of his Father." Charles II referred to the beheading of King Charles I by Cromwell's Parliament in 1649, the act that prompted the Reverend Bracewell and other Cavaliers to come to Virginia.

In a letter from Henry West, William West's brother, to the Privy Council in London and Lord Culpepper dated Whitehall, November 21, 1677, the Council replied:

Upon reading this day at the Board the humble Petition of Henry West Planter a Native of his Majestys Colony of Virginia in behalf of himself and Brother, Setting forth, That his Brother William West having been seduced to accept of a Commission against the Indians under late Rebell Nathanial Bacon, and being sent by Colonel Bridger with Promise of free Pardon to lay down his commission, disband his men, and submit himself to the Governor, He was prevayled upon by the Petitioner so to do, upon the Petitioners Promise to go with him to the Governor, But so soon as they had surrendered themselves to Colonel Bridger, He contrary to his Promise sent them bound to the Governor Sir William Berkeley, who tryed them both by a Councill of Warr, and sentenced to Death the Petitioners Brother, who never acted to the prejudice of any one Person or Estate.

Another petition from Isle of Wight County sent to the Commission said:

A Petition of his Majesty's most loyal and obedient subjects of the Isle of Wight County in Virginia to his Majesty's Commissioner:

In behalf of William West 'a rebel absconding'. who took up arms against the Indians by whom his father was barbarously murdered, was taken prisioner, carried aboard a ship, from hence to prison and condemned to death, but has made his escape and, as yet, cannot be heard of. Pray for his life and the restitution of his estate to his wife and children.

The signers included Richard Bracewell.[3] West was forgiven and his son, William West, Junior, later became a member of St. Luke's vestry.

THE BRACEWELL BROTHERS MOVED TO NANSEMOND COUNTY, VIRGINIA

Robert Bracewell, planter, sold one hundred acres to James Bagnall, his brother-in-law, on February 3, 1673, for a "Valuable sum of Tob. & Cask." The tract began "att. . . the Dam side to A small branch of the said Dam close by said Bracewells Orchard & dwelling house that is now on his Land . . . .Upon reasonable request to him made he will acknowledge this present deed and Conveyance in this Isle of Wight County Court or Nanzimond Court."[4]

Four days later, on February 7, 1673, Richard Bracewell, planter, and wife Sarah, sold to Thomas Green, A parcell of Land lying on ye ffreshett side between Mr Izards and Thomas Pool by estimacon the one halfe of a Conveyance of four hundred Acres of Land from a patient of Capt John Uptons to Mr Bracewell my ffather, and by him given me by a Deed of Gift bearing date ye 16th day of Janry 1660....& promise for me my heirs & Assignes to prmit the sd Green...to have Timber of any of my land for to build houseing on the sd Greens Land aforesd not makeing any wast thereof. . . .

It is further concluded and agreed upon by said Richard Bracell and Sarah his wife...that if there be more than two hundred Acres of Land belonging to them on that side of Mr Bracewells Mill Runn that Mr Izard & Thomas Pool now liveth on wch wee have sould...That the sd Green shall have the sd parcell, more than two hundred Acres, payeing the same unto pporconable as is pd for ye two hundred Acres of Land wch is Six thousand pounds of Tob & Cask. And if it shall happen when surveyed that there be not on that side of Mr Bracewell's Mill Runn between Mr Izards and Thomas Pool two hundred Acres of Land as aforedf that yn the sd Richard Bracewell & Sarah his wife doe by these prsents bind ymselves...to make good the said two hundred Acres of Land on the other side of Mr Bracewells Mill Runn....Only Excepting Timber for ye building of Richd Bracewell soe long as ye sd mill remaines in his Custody.[5]

A year later, the Bracewell brothers went back in Isle of Wight County and sold off more of their inheritance. On March 14, 1674, Richard Bracewell, planter, and Sarah Bracewell his wife sold his brother-in-law, William West, for a valuable sum of Tob. & Cask, 100 acres runing upon the West side of the ffreshett upon Robert Bracewells Land & bounding upon the sᵈ Robt Bracewell, his Land, unto the woods for length according to yᵉ ancient patient & runing for breadth up the sᵈ West side of the ffreshett until ye sᵈ Complement of one hundred Acres of Land be compleated, whch sᵈ Land is now in yᵈ tenure of Anthony Hosier dureing his natural life it being part of a dividend of four hundred Acres by Mr Robert Bracewell deceased given to de sᵈ Hosier for his life Tyme.6

Then two weeks later, on March 31, 1674, James and Ann Bagnall swapped

the plantation that William Toley now dwelleth on & the Land thereunto belonging being by estimation one hundred Acres" to Robert Bracewell for "The plantation & Land thereto belonging that I now dwell upon & given to me by my deceased ffather Mr Roger Bagnall" which Robert Bracewell, planter, then sold his brother-in-law, James Bagnall, for 15,000 pounds of tobacco, it being by estimation one hundred Acres" the above Bagnall 100-acre tract plus "the whole divident of Land with all houseing fenceing houses orchards buildings & Edifices. . . That my late deceased ffather Mr Robert Bracewell Clerk lived on & gave unto me, as by deed of Guift & last Will may appear conteyning three hundred Acres.7

Finally, on "Xber 9" (October 9), 1674, Richard Bracewell and Sarah his wife sold their brother-in-law, William West, the remainder of his inheritance.

WHEREAS my ffather Robt Bracewell did in his life tyme by deed of Guift dated yᵉ 16ᵗʰ of Janry 1660 gave unto me Richd Bracewell his Sonne, one pcell of Land conteining about 400 acres, being pte of a Tract of Land conteining 1600 Acres lyeing in ye Isle of Wight County granted unto Lt Col Jno Underwood dated ye 16ᵗʰ of Novr 1638 & by said Upton sold to. . .my ffather Robt Bracewell & from him to me his Sonne, of wch four hundred Acres I . . .have by deed dated ye 7ᵗʰ of ffebry 1673 Sould unto Thomas Green two hundred Acres lyeing on ye ffreshett between Mr. Izards & Thomas Pooles Land, And have alsoe by another deed sould unto Wm West One hundred Acres lyeing on ye other side ye Runn adjoining to another tract of Land lately belonging to my sᵈ ffather Robert Bracewell

Now in consideration of 3000 pounds of good Marchantable tob & cask paid by sᵈ Thomas Green . . .one hundred acres of Land adjoining to that hundred acres sould Wm West being all ye mentioned 400 Acres sold by Lt Col Jno Upton wch sᵈ 100 Acres now by us sold is in the tenure or Occupation of Anthony Ogier. . .dureing his life. 8

Richard was born about 1652 in Virginia. On January 16, 1661, his father gave him four hundred acres, possibly a confirmation present.] About 1673, Richard Bracewell married a woman named Sarah. She was probably a Sarah Valentine, given they named a son "Valentine."²

Notice Richard's date of his father's gift, "1660/61." That was the Old Style calendar that changed years on March twenty-fifth. English-speaking countries adopted the Julian calendar in 1752.

RICHARD BRACEWELL TURNED QUAKER

Richard and Sarah turned Quaker. Note their deed dated "Xber 9, 1674," the radical new Quaker date. The Friends ridded themselves of the old pagan dates in favor of simply naming their months beginning with March as "first month." Thus, December ("Xber") became the tenth month. Richard's sister, Jane, and everybody else in Richard Braswell's family converted.

No one knows when or why Richard Bracewell's family made the switch to Quakerism. Changing one's religion in the seventeenth century was dangerous. Hundreds of thousands of people in the Western world died in defense of their faith in such conflicts as the Thirty Years' War (1618-1648). By custom, once Richard Bracewell converted, his children also switched from Anglican to the Society of Friends and, by the rules of their new faith, later married only Quakers.

When George Fox, mystic and founder of the Society of Friends, visited Virginia in November 1672, he found many Friends already living in Isle of Wight County. In Fox's journal, he mentioned going to "…a very good meeting at William Yarrow's on Pagan Creek which was so large. . . the house not being large enough to contain the people." Maybe it took the spellbinding speeches of mystic George Fox to persuade Richard Bracewell to abandon the Church of England. We don't know.

George Fox, a man with little education, son of a weaver and apprenticed to a shoemaker, left his master and his relatives "at the command of God" and began his preaching that ended only with his death in 1691. All the virtues of the Puritans were reflected in their offshoot, the Quakers. The fear of God and Satan was so strong in them that sometimes it set their bodies trembling and gave them their name, "quakers." They accepted the basic tenants of the Puritans—the divine inspiration of the Scriptures, the fall of Adam and Eve, the natural sinfulness of man, the redeeming death of Christ the Son of God, and the possibility of the Holy Ghost or Spirit coming from heaven to enlighten and ennoble the individual soul. To perceive and feel the Inner Light, to welcome its guidance, was to the Quaker the core of religion. If a man followed the light, he needed no preacher or priest and no church.

Different from other religions, Quakers allowed no ornaments on their clothing and refused to take off their hats to any person of whatever rank, even in church or palace or at court. They addressed all persons by the singular "thou" or "thee" instead of by the ordinary "you." They worshiped as readily outside as indoors. Invited to tell what the Holy Ghost had inspired a Quaker to say, then all practiced a reverent silence when he spoke. Women worshiped and preached on the same terms as men.

Otherwise the Friends were model Christians. They gave as they could to all who asked. Their married life was beyond reproach. However, their rule against marrying any but another Quaker limited their growth. Their reputation for honesty, courtesy, industry, and thrift raised them from their humble English origins in which they first appeared up to the middle classes.

A God of love and light whose benevolent spirit harmonized the universe stood at the center of Quakerism. A central tenant of Quaker theology was the doctrine of the inner light, which held that a beam of divine goodness and virtue passed from Jesus into every human soul. They believed that this "light within" brought the means of salvation within the reach of everyone who awakened to its existence. Most Quakers rejected the Calvinist principle of limited atonement. They believed that Christ died not merely for a chosen few but for all humanity. They rejected all sacraments, ceremonies, churches, clergy, ordinations and tithes, and maintained no ministers, only lay missionaries and exhorters whom they sometimes called ministers.

In the words of George Fox, the Quakers, believed that the family should "outstrip and exceed the world, in virtue, purity, in chastity, in godliness and in holiness; and in modesty, civility, and in righteousness and love." They tended to think of the family as a spiritual entity, a sanctuary of goodness and love in a world full of sin and hatred.

Quakers named first-born children after their grandparents. Unlike Virginia Anglicans, they were careful to honor maternal and paternal lines in an even-handed way. Thus Valentine Bracewell was likely named for his maternal grandfather. Quaker families also made occasional use of grace names for their daughters, with particular favorites being Obedience, Patience, Grace, Mercy, and Chastity. Quaker families were more child-centered than home life in other cultures. Travelers of other faiths were shocked that a child reared among the Quakers could say "I will not" to his parents and get away with it. Quaker parents made heavy use of rewards rather than punishments, and promises rather than threats.

Also important was an attitude which encouraged extreme austerity. The Quakers, more than a major Protestant denomination, fostered a style of life called *worldly asceticism*, the idea of living in a world but not a part of it. Work itself became a sacrament, and idleness a deadly sin. Wealth was not to be consumed in rich display, but rather to be saved, invested, turned to constructive purposes. Restraints were placed upon indulgence. A Quaker's honor was far removed from the code of chivalry that existed among Virginia gentlemen. Instead it was a reputation for Christian love, peace, "good neighborhood," godliness, and doing good to others.

Quakers had become the third largest religious denomination in the British colonies by 1700, third only to Congregationists and Anglicans. But by 1750 they had dropped to fifth and by today, sixty-sixth. The Society of Friends always maintained an official hostility to formal doctrine, and never required subscription to any set of beliefs.

When Quakers began to appear the Virginia authorities moved quickly against them. A law in 1658 ordered all Quakers to be banished from Virginia. Quakers were reduced to a few small meetings such as the Chuckatuck meeting in Nansemond County. By the end of the seventeenth century, nearly everyone in the Virginia Colony counted themselves as Anglican. By 1705, the dissenters weren't more than five churches, namely three small meetings of Quakers like the Chuckatuck meeting. Quakers headed south into North Carolina, the new Southern Quaker stronghold.[9]

Richard Bracewell and family remained in Nansemond County, Virginia, for twenty years, from 1674 until 1694, before returning to the southern part of part of Isle of Wight County. The area became Southampton

County in 1749. Through a succession of courthouse fires, all the records in Nansemond County were burned up to 1866.[10]

Richard Bracewell's removal to Nansemond County and Nansemond's first loss of records is mentioned in this Isle of Wight County deed dated August 9, 1681:

Richard Bracewell & Sarah his wife, have formerly given a Conveyance of ye Mill Dam pool & two acres of Land adjoining to ye Mill unto William West of ye Isle of Wight County. . .the wch former Conveyance was acknowledged by Mr Richard Bracewell & Sarah my Wife in ye Cort of Nansemond & there entered on ye Records since wch the Records are burnt & ye Convenyance lost. Wherefore now Know thee that I the abovesd Richd Bracewell & Sarah my Wife do convey unto ye abovesd William West, all my right Tytle & interest of ye Mill dam & pool wth the two acres of Land . . .ye same as it was given to me by my Deceyed father Mr Robt Bracewell the sd Mill being now in ye possession of the sd William West.[11]

Note how Richard and Sarah said "...now Know thee..." in Quaker fashion.

On February 9, 1694, Richard Bracewell reemerged in the records of the southern part of Isle of Wight County. He witnessed the assignment of James and Elizabeth Corley's land patent to Thomas Kirby.[12] By August 7, 1697, Richard had assigned to him a royal deed for land "on ye Maine black Water"—Beaverdam Swamp.[13] A "swamp" then meant " a lowland along a water course," not today's meaning of an area covered with shallow water.

Richard's land was mentioned again in a deed from Owen Bourn and wife Hannah to Thomas Mandue, Junior, dated February 28, 1702, for a tract "situate on ee Maine Blackwater River. . . .Bounded thus beginning in ye fork of a Branch Called Richard Bracewells Branch. . . ." It was witnessed by Richard's son, Robert Bracewell.[14] Then on March 5, 1709, Richard and Sarah Bracewell signed their last deed, a one hundred acre tract, part of their original patent from Gyles Linscott for 6,600 pounds "of good Sound Merchantable tobo & Caske. . .lying and being upon ye Maine Blackwater..."[15]

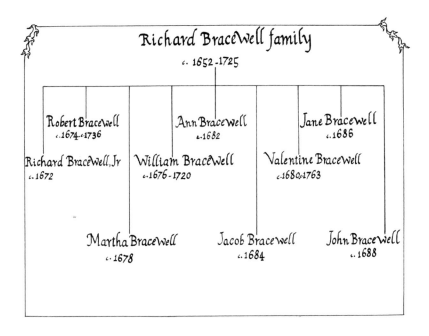

RICHARD BRACEWELL'S WILL

July 28, 1725

IN THE NAME OF GOD. AMEN. This being the last Will & Testament of Richard Braswell being Sick & Weak but in perfect Mind & Memory thanks be to God for it. FIRST I Give and Bequeath my Soul to Almighty God hoping to find Mercy.

2dly. I Give my Body to the Earth therein to be Buried after a decent Christian manner and all my Worldly Goods as followeth after my Debts being paid.

1st. I give unto my well beloved Son Richard Brasewell one shilling and no more.

2dly. I give unto my Son Robert Brasewell Ten Shillings worth of my Estate and no more at present.

3dly. I give unto my Son Valentine Braswell Ten Shillings and no more at present.

4thly. I give unto my Son Jacob Ten Shillings worth and no more at present.

5thly. I Give unto my Son John Braswell Ten Shillings worth and no more at present.

6thly. I give unto my Daughter Martha Murfy Ten Shillings worth and no more at present. { Martha married first William Browne who died in N.C. by 1724}

7thly. I give unto my Daughter Ann Strickland Ten Shillings worth and no more at present. {Wife of Matthew Strickland, Jr. of Isle of Wight County}

8thly. I Give to my Daughter Jane Williams Ten Shillings worth and no more at present. {Wife of Samuel Williams, Jr. who died in Edgecombe County, N.C. c. 1749}

9thly. I give to my Grandaughter Susanah Braswell one cow and Calf.

10thly & LASTLY I give unto my loving wife Sarah Braswell all the rest of my Estate to her and to her disposing appointing her my whole & sole Executrix of this my last Will & Testament whereof I do here-unto set my Hand & Seal this 28 day of July 1724/5.

Richard (mark) Braswell (seal)

SIGNED SEALED & DELIVERED in psence of us

Edw:d Powers sen.r Edwd powers

Examd & truly Recorded16

John Bracewell returned from North Carolina to look after his mother following his father's death in 1725. In Virginia, this patriarchal system of respect for seniority made a major difference in family relations, particularly between fathers and sons. As fathers grew older, they commonly kept at least one son near them. In a series of four deeds between April 20,

1730, and July 14, 1733, John Bracewell and wife Alice sold 640 acres in Southampton County's Beaverdam Swamp area.17

Following common usage among researchers, most Braswell genealogists refer to family members living in Virginia before 1700 as *Bracewell,* thereafter as *Braswell.* The family must be called something and *Braswell* is the most common variant of Bracewell. But fifty-six different Bracewell spellings have turned up so far in records with *Brazil* one of the more popular, accounting for about ten percent of the total.

SARAH BRACEWELL'S WILL

IN THE NAME OF GOD AMEN. The 20th day of March in the Year of our Lord 1733/34. I Sarah Braswell of the Isle of Wight County being very sick & weak of body but of perfect Mind & Memory thanks be to God for the same

ffirst & Cheifest I Give & Bequeath my Soul to the Hand of Almighty God who gave it me. Secondly my body to be decently Buried at the Discretion of my Executors, and as for my Worldly Estate as it pleased God to endow me with I Give & Bequeath in manner and form as followeth.

I Give & Bequeath my whole Estate in General to my Grandson John Braswell junr that's Cattle Hoggs household-Goods and all manner of Implements whatsoever to me belonging EXCEPT one Negro Man named Limehouse I give him the said Negro to my Daughter Jane, and him to be hers any person or person after my decease AND I make & ordain my Son John Braswell and my said Grandson John Braswell Junr my whole Executors of my afores Estate, and my Son John Braswell to have the Care of look after the said Estate 'till the said John Braswell junr shall come to the Years of Twenty one my said Grandson to have the aforesd Estate in his own possession and my said Son John Braswell to sell such Cattle & Hoggs out of the same as shall be necessary And for what is Sold out of the said Estate my Son John to have the one Half for his Trouble and the other Half to be laid out for the Use of my said Grandson

And Benjamin Braswell my Grandson shall have the first Mare Colt that a Mare shall bring which said Mare is part of the said Estate and Given to my Grandson John Braswell junr as aforesd but if in Case the said John Braswell junr should decease without Heir the same shall be equally divided amongst the other of my said John's Children namely Mary Benjamin William & Sampson Braswell and to either of them if in case the other deceaseth without Heir

And I own this to be my last Will & Testatment denying all other Wills & Testaments ever made before by me and this to stand and no others. AS WITNESS whereof I have hereunto put my Hand & Seal the Day and Year above written.

Sarah X Braswell (Seal)

Richard Blow junr   Samuel X Smith   Samuel X Willis

At a Court held for Isle of Wight County May the 26: 1735

THE last Will & Testament of Sarah Braswell deceased was Proved by the Oath of Samuel Willis one of the Witnesses thereto and it is admitted to Record.[18]

After his mother died, John returned to Quaker North Carolina.[19]

RICHARD'S SON, WILLIAM BRASWELL (c.1676-1720)

William was born before October 9, 1682, as shown by a 1703 deed proving he was of legal age by that later date.[20] In 1703, William Bracewell witnessed his brother-in-law, William and Martha Browne's deed to Richard Bracewell, Junior, for thirty-five acres on the south side of the main Blackwater River near Beaverdam Swamp.

William Bracewell was among the first of his brothers to pioneer North Carolina. He patented many land grants and became wealthy. His last patent before his death in 1720 was for another one hundred acres on Cypress Swamp on the Meherrin River. After he died, his widow, Mary, kept on acquiring property. For example, she bought one hundred ninety acres on the north side of Meherin River as early as "8ber" (October) 21, 1721.

Mary married Moses Ginn in North Carolina by November 4, 1726. Joshua Ginn, likely Moses' son, sold Valentine Bracewell three hundred acres at the head of Cape Fear River in 1744. Then on the 1755 Orange County tax list, nine names below Valentine's was Moses Ginn.

Mary's son by her marriage to William Bracewell, William Bracewell, Junior, settled in the western part of Edgecombe County that became Nash County in 1777. William, Junior, a wealthy landowner, was in turn father to several planter-class Braswells whose descendants settled throughout the region and later on in Tennessee. William must have been considered a hero to early Braswells since almost every branch had at least one son named *William* down to my father's generation.

Richard Bracewell's 1725 will named five sons: Richard, Robert, Valentine, Jacob, and John. William was not mentioned in his father's will. William's association with the other five Bracewell sons indicates he was Richard's sixth son. William died in 1720, five years before his father. Moreover, William's documented descendants match Reverend Robert Bracewell's DNA profile. *(See Reference 1, Chapter One)*

RICHARD'S SON, RICHARD BRASWELL, Jr. (c.1672-1758)

Richard Braswell, Junior, proved an account against the estate of William Carver in Chowan County, North Carolina, in 1715. Ann Carver, William's daughter, was granted letters of administration on Carver's estate in 1714-15. By 1720 or earlier, Richard Braswell took Ann as his de facto wife.[21] Richard signed several deed records throughout his long life including one in 1728 in which had previously sold 640 acres "to my father Richard Bracewell."

Richard married Eleanor late in the seventeenth century and had several children by her. He then left her to take up with the younger Ann Carver in North Carolina. Those days, none but kings could get a divorce. As the law required, Richard and Eleanor continued to sign Richard's deeds of sale well into the 1720's in North Carolina even though they no longer lived together as man and wife.

Ann's last recorded signature appeared on the Bertie County will of Thomas Wimberly dated October 22, 1731, which she proved in February 1732.[21] After that, she disappeared from record. According to Bill Fields, "At the time Thomas Wimberly was living on Fishing Creek. One of Wimberly's bequests was 150 acres to daughter Sarah Wimberly...'and my desire is for Jacob Braswell & young Rich Braswell for to Devide it amongst them.'[22] No doubt 'young Rich Braswell' was Richard Junior, so called to distinguish him from his father. Another mystery is what the connection was between the Wimberley's and Braswells. It seems evident that it was a close one but no amount of speculation will reveal the truth and there is absolutely no hint in any record I've found thus far. At any rate, the bequest to 'young Rich' provides evidence that Eleanor was the wife of Richard Braswell, Senior. In 1747, Richard, Senior, made deeds of gift to his four Carver children: William, 'born of the body of Anne Carver commonly called by the name of William Braswell'; Robert, 'commonly called Robert Braswell,'; David Braswell; and Sarah Braswell."[23]

RICHARD BRASWELL II'S COUNTERFEITING CASE

Ann Carver is next identified in1745 in a counterfeit case as "Mrs. Braswell." That year, Richard Braswell, Senior, narrowly escaped death for counterfeiting. On May 22, 1745, this record appeared at the capital, Edenton, North Carolina:

Mr. Haywood one of the Members of this Court acquainted the Bench that he hade issued Search Warrant against one Richard Braswell for passing and uttering false Coine and had accordingly ordered Hardy Cane a Sworn Constable to apprehend the said Braswell and to search his house for Counterfeit money & the materials for making it, & that the Constable Hardy Cane had executed the Warrant and had also brought the said Braswell here to be Examined thereupon and that the Constable had also found some Counterfeit money and he believed some materials for making of it in the said Braswells House. . . .

Accordingly the said Richard Braswell was ordered before this Court & appeared and Hardy Cane the Constable who Executed the Warrant also appeared and brought with him a small Cagg or Barrel which contained several little Wooden Moulds with some Brass & Pewter Mettle, some Chalk & Borax. . . .It is thereupon Considered and Ordered by the Court on hearing the said Canes Deposition. . .is that the said Richard Braswell stand Committed and Sheriff is hereby Ordered forthwith to convey the said Richard Braswell to the Publick Goal at Edenton and deliver the said Richard Braswell to the Keeper thereof to be kept until he shall be thence discharged by due Course of Law. [24]

Edgecombe County – The Deposition of Hardy Cane Constable Sworn Saith that he received a Search Warrant from John Haywood Esquire one of His Majestys Justices in Commission of the Peace for Edgecombe County aforesaid the Twentyeth of this Instant May against One Richard Braswell   That this Deponent Executed the said Warrant the next day on the said Richard Braswell who told this said Deponent that he was right welcome to Search his house, and accordingly this Deponent went into said Braswells house where said Braswell took Keys out of his Pocket and told this Deponent he might search every where & any Chest he had in the House, the said Braswell accordingly opened his Chests & bid this Deponent look into them, he did & found nothing in them concerning what he searched for, Then this Deponent went to said Braswells storehouse but found nothing in the lower Room, the said Braswell then asked this Deponent whither he would not go up in the loft above and accordingly brought a Ladder, & the said Braswells wife came into the Store & told the Deponent She would go up first and this Deponent because there was some Honey and he might spil it, and accordingly she went up first and this Deponent followed her and as soon as Mrs Braswell got up in the loft he the Deponent saw the said Mrs Braswell put her foot against the little barrel (now produced on the Table) and Slide it away & put some old thing up & threw upon the barrel, and there was a Chest in the loft which he felt it, being very dark but found nothing, but having a Mistrust this Deponent went to the Barrel and asked Mrs Braswell what it was & felt in the Barrel, & felt a parcel of wooden Moulds & other stuff in it, and then handed it down it to one Thomas Price who was below in the Store, & he Immediately went down and Examined what was in the barrel which the said Richard Braswell looked strange at and admired how these things came there, & looking further into the barrel he, this Deponent found Three Counterfeit peices commonly called Georgia Peices & Four Counterfeit pieces in likeness of Portuguese money, one in likeness of a

Spanish peice of Eight & two small peices in likeness of Pistereens which he now produced. . . .The said Braswell also told this Deponent that he sometime agoe asked one Hughs and one Clift whither they could make any money Genteely, That Clift answered he could and accordingly he made some which said Braswell did not like, and that one of them said they could make money as good as any if they had Ingredients, upon which the said Braswell sent his Son to Williamsburgh and gave him forth shillings to buy Ingredients to run this silver money seemingly by his discourse but that his Son could not get any. [25]

The jury's verdict: "Case No. 33 – Dom: Rex vs. Richard Braswell – Recognized for his appearance for uttering false Coin. Defendant pleads Not Guilty. . . .Say we of the Jury do find the Defendant Not Guilty." [26]

Despite his guilt, Richard Braswell was found not guilty by his peers. Conviction meant death by hanging. Some colonials resorted to counterfeiting because the British "mercantile policy" drained her colonies of hard currency. That's why colonials resorted to Portuguese or Spanish coinage for trade. Our *dollar* came from that practice.

CARVERS SPLIT FROM THEIR BRASWELL HALF-BROTHERS

In 1758, Richard Braswell III filed a lawsuit over the estate of David Braswell Carver. David's estate included fourteen Negro slaves and forty head of "Black Cattle." Letters of Administration granted to another person on the estate of David Carver had his letters revoked. Letters ad colligend now went to David's mother, Ann Braswell alias Carver. Richard Bracewell, Senior, died during this lawsuit, which fixes his date of death between David's death and the appointment of his mother, Ann.[27]

According to Bill Fields, "Richard Braswell Senior--described in the Isle of Wight deeds of 1703 and 1706 as Junior to distinguish him from his father--was, unquestionably, son of Richard Braswell of Isle of Wight, will 1725, and his wife Sarah. He moved to North Carolina about 1710. His wife, Eleanor, is a valuable clue to his identity as she figures in a number of his deeds between 1706 and 1729.

Richard Braswell, Junior, must have been born very early in the century, probably ca. 1705. The earliest reference to him so designated is in 1725, when he patented land. He need not have attained his majority to accomplish that but it is probable that he was nearly twenty-one anyway, if not a little older. Deeds indicate that by about 1730 he had moved on into what was to become Edgecombe and it would appear that his mother, Eleanor Braswell, was with him as she witnessed the will of Thomas Wimberly, who was living nearby. Richard Braswell, Senior, was described as 'of Bertie' in a 1735 deed but, according to the deed by which Robert Carver sold his Edgecombe land, had patented that land in 1728.

In the 1747 deed of gift Richard described it as 'the plantation whereon I now dwell,' giving the location as west of Fishing Creek and on Crooked Branch, that being in the eastern part of the county near the Halifax line about 10 or 12 miles above the town of Tarboro. His other land was in the same general area: White Oak Swamp, Maple Swamp. Richard Braswell, Junior, was in the same area but last lived on the south side of Tar River near Hatcher's Swamp, where most of his sons settled also. This is about five miles west of Tarboro.

The Carver children of Richard Braswell, Senior, were born in the 1720's at latest. The suit of Benjamin Willis vs. Richard Braswell indicates that David Braswell-Carver had died before September 30, 1758, and that Richard Braswell, Senior, died after that date but by November 28, 1758, when the Council granted letters ad colligend to Ann Carver."

The family of Richard Bracewell II and the Carvers produced many outstanding Southern citizens since the 1700's. I repeated Richard Braswell's counterfeiting story to reflect Valentine Braswell's times, not to disrespect this largest branch of American Braswell's.

Two other sons of Richard and Sarah, Robert and John Bracewell, also have descendants in America as shown by research backed up with DNA evidence. Still, William and Richard Braswell, Junior, have the largest number of living descendants.

More than 30,000 Americans can claim Richard Bracewell as their direct immigrant ancestor. Tens of thousands more can claim him as at least one of their ancestors, if not direct. Most of his descendants still live in the South.

CHAPTER THREE

VALENTINE BRACEWELL (c.1685-c.1766) AND HIS SON, RICHARD, (c.1707-AFTER 1755)

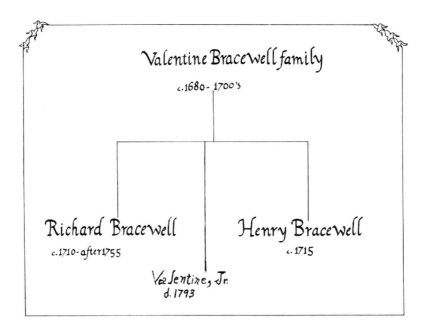

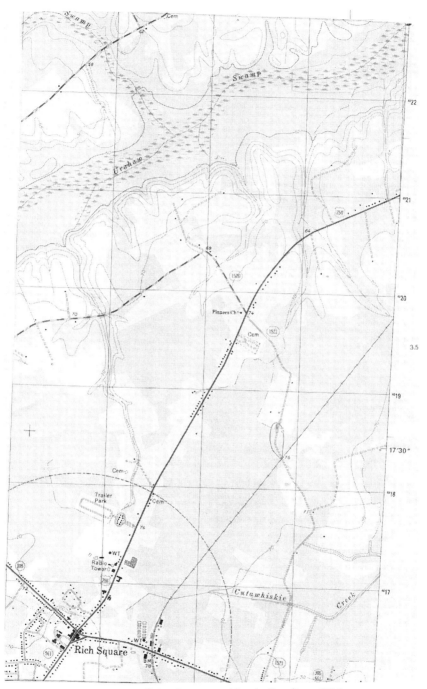

First Braswell Settlement in North Carolina, 1715

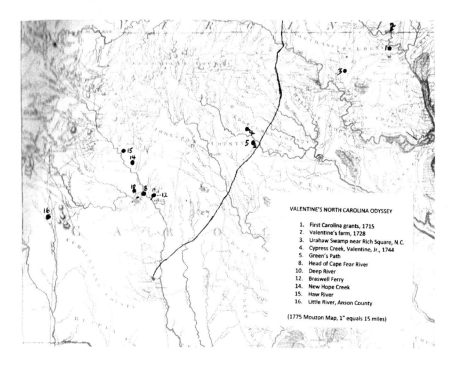

VALENTINE'S NORTH CAROLINA ODYSSEY

1. First Carolina grants, 1715
2. Valentine's farm, 1728
3. Urahaw Swamp near Rich Square, N.C.
4. Cypress Creek, Valentine, Jr., 1744
5. Green's Path
8. Head of Cape Fear River
10. Deep River
12. Braswell Ferry
14. New Hope Creek
15. Haw River
16. Little River, Anson County

(1775 Mouzon Map, 1" equals 15 miles)

THE POPES

Valentine Bracewell married Jane Pope in Virginia early in the early 1700's. Henry Pope, born in Virginia "on the last of the 11th month 1663," made his will on May 28, 1728, in Isle of Wight County. His seventh bequest was "unto my Daughter Jane Brassell One Cow & Calf She having had her part before."1 Henry Pope owned land near the Richard Bracewell's on Beaverdam Swamp.2

In a Quaker manuscript, Henry Pope was named as a son in the list of children of William and Mary Pope. From that same source, proof that Henry Pope married Sarah Watts around 1684 is in John Watts' will, dated January 20, 1698. In addition, evidence that Alice was a daughter of Englishman Captain John English is seen in his 1678 will.3

QUAKERS IN NORTH CAROLINA

The Quaker church or the Society of Friends, its official name, was the only important religious sect in North Carolina before 1730. Quakers continued to be the most potent force in the religious life of the colony until then. The Friends had a great appeal to the "unchurched" masses because of their regularity of their lives, hospitality to strangers, and kindness to strangers.

Quaker power and influence in the Albemarle region declined after 1730 but there were new settlements of Friends in the central part of the colony, especially after 1750 when many migrated from Pennsylvania and New Jersey and settled in the present counties of Guilford, Randolph, Alamance, and Chatham County where the Valentine Bracewell family lived.   The growth of Quakerism continued until the outbreak of the Revolution, when Quaker immigration practically stopped. Quaker opposition to war caused the Friends to lose favor in North Carolina and they experienced a decline in membership.

After the earliest North Carolina grants on Meherrin River, Richard Bracewell's sons decided upon the area east of Rich Square at the head of Bridgers Creek and Urahaw Swamp in present Northampton County as their new family seat. Valentine's first Carolina record, dated July 16, 1715, was a deed for 150 acres from James and Sarah Bryant.[4] Three years later, on March 9, 1718, Valentine Braswell received a grant for 640 acres at the head of Bridgers Creek next to William Bryant.[5]

Valentine's first stay in North Carolina lasted only seven years. He was the first of his brothers to leave the new family center near Rich Square. On April 15, 1721, "Valentine Brasswell & wife Jeane" gave John Cotton, Esquire, their power of attorney to sell his land on Urahaw Swamp, "the manor plantation of Valentine Brasswell."[6] Three months later, July 13, 1721, they sold 200 acres of his patent to John Pope, Jane's brother.[7] Their Quaker friend, Barnaby McKinney, handled the sale. Then on September 3, they sold their original 150 acres from the Bryant's to John Blackman[8] who then bought out the rest of their 640-acre grant on December 3, 1722.[9]

Valentine and family returned to what is now Southampton County, Virginia, where he settled on the road to John Cheshire's Ferry near the

Meherrin River. Surrounded by Williams families, he lived only a few hundred yards inside the North Carolina-Virginia border. We don't know why Valentine abandoned his brothers' new family station near Rich Square. Was he injured? He was never able to work as hard as his brothers after returning to Virginia.

Valentine left some debts behind in North Carolina. John Speir sued Valentine Brasswell in North Carolina's Chief Justice Court in March, 1723, saying that "Valentine oweth to him the said John and from him unjustly detaineth two hundred and ten pounds of porke and one five year old steer . . .and that he suspects the aforesaid Valentine is removing in order to conceall and withdraw himself out of the Government."[10] By the July court, the case was dismissed "per plaintiffe."[11] Whatever the cause, Valentine was always in debt.

Valentine's farm was mentioned in Governor William Byrd's journal for settling the boundary between the colonies of Virginia and Carolina. On April 1, 1728, Byrd noted

". . .from the head of Indian Town Creek is a main road, bearing N. 20o E. of the line, it leads from James William's on Nottoway River three miles from the line to John Cheshires on the north side of Meherrin seven miles from the Line. James Williams's is two miles and a half from Nottoway river mouth.

At 150 chains from Do Valentine Brasswel bore N. 100 yds.

At 150 chains from Do is a small branch of Indian Town Creek.

At 240 chains from Do is John William's bore S. ¼ of a mile."[12]

Governor William Byrd noticed how little these Quakers had any use for his Anglican chaplain: ...it was Strange tht none came to be marry'd in such a Multitude if it had only been for the Novelty of having their Hands Joy'd by one in Holy Orders. Yet so it was, that. . .our chaplain. . .did not marry so much as one Couple during the whole Expedition. But marriage is reckon'd a Lay contract in Carolina, as I said before, and a Country Justice can tie the fatal Knot there, as fast as an Arch-Bishop.

Byrd went on to describe his contempt for North Carolinians whom he considered far beneath him socially:

Surely there is no place in the World where the Inhabitants live with less Labour than in N Carolina. It approaches nearer to the Description of Lubberland than any other, by the great felicity of the Climate, the easiness of raising Provisions, and the Slothfulness of the People. Indian Corn is of so great increase, that a little Pains will Subsist a very large Family with Bread, and then they may have meat without any pains at all, by the Help of the Low Grounds, and the great Variety of Mast that grows on the High-land. The Men, for their Parts, just like the Indians, impose all the Work upon the poor Women. They make their Wives rise out of their Beds early in the Morning, at the same time they lye and Snore, till the Sun has run one third of his course, and disperst all the unwholesome Damps. Then, after Stretching and Yawning for half an Hour, they light their Pipes, and, under the Protection of a cloud of Smoak, venture into the open Air; tho' if it happens to be never so little cold, they quickly return Shivering into the chimney corner. . . .Thus they loiter away their Lives, like Solomon's Sluggard, with their Arms across, and at the Winding up of the Year Scarcely have Bread to Eat. To speak the Truth, tis a thorough Aversion to Labor that makes People file off to N Carolina, where Plenty and a Warm Sun confirm them in their Disposition to Laziness for their whole Lives. [13]

After returning in the fall, on September 20, 1728, Governor Byrd showed how notorious were he and his men in comparison to his pious Quaker guests:

Mr. Kinchin had unadvisedly sold the Men a little Brandy of his own making, which produced much disorder, causing some to be too cholerick, and others too loving; insomuch that a Damsel, who assisted in the Kitchen, had certainly Suffer'd what the Nuns call Martyrdom, had she not capitulated a little too soon. This outrage would have call'd for some severe Discipline, had she not bashfully withdrawn herself early in the Morning, & so carry'd off the Evidence. [14]

The Anglican Church was never very strong in North Carolina. It was unpopular because it had been established by the royal government and had a close relationship to it. Non-Anglicans resented its support by public taxes, its control of education, and its other special privileges, particularly the law which permitted only Anglican clergymen to perform the marriage ceremony. Prospective ministers had to go to England for ordination so there was always a shortage of ministers.

CHATHAM COUNTY

Years of frustrating delay dragged by for me trying to figure out how Valentine's grandson, Richard Braswell (c.1732-1799) connected to him. Our Quakers practiced modesty and aestheticism so well they hardly left any records. We are only left tantalizing clues like Richard Smith's diary. Smith told us that his mother Diana Braswell Smith's father was Richard Braswell. He then scratched out "father" and substituted "grandfather." I believe both father and grandfather were named Richard Braswell. (See *James Smith Bible*, Chapter 4 references).

We have no record of Valentine Bracewell's family for the next sixteen years after Governor Byrd's 1728 expedition. His son, Valentine, Junior, appeared again in an Edgecombe County deed dated March 4, 1744, in which Sampson Williams sold his 320-acre farm on the north side of Tar River and both sides of Cypress Creek to Samuel Williams, a tract "whereon Valentine Braswell now lives." Witnesses were William Williams and Mourning Braswell, Valentine, Junior's wife.15   A year later, March 13, 1745, Valentine Braswell and John Pope, Junior, witnessed another Edgecombe deed from Samuel Williams to John Pope, Valentine's brother-in-law.[16]

By April 8, 1746, Valentine Braswell and his family moved down Green's Path and settled in Chatham County. A map drawn for Earl Granville on that date showed a "Path from Brasswell to Goodrick," just east of Parker's Creek near present Moncure, North Carolina.[17]

Then, on October 6, 1746, for only ten pounds, Valentine bought a 350-acre tract from Joshua Ginn " on the S W side of Deep River beginning at the lower end of the Great Falls running down…"[18]   at the head of Cape Fear River. Moses Ginn also lived in the area.

THE GRANVILLE DISTRICT

Lord Granville's District included Chatham County.   Granville alone among the British lords refused to sell his one-eighth fraction of North Carolina to the Crown in 1729. This sale by the other nobles changed the province from a proprietorship to a crown colony.

As compensation, the Crown allowed Granville to charge *quitrents* to his settlers. Quitrents were an ancient form of taxation paid by a feudal tenant in lieu of customary labor or services. Private proprietary grants from Granville within a royal colony meant a loss to the government of badly needed royal revenue and introduced more discord into the already troubled situation.

The Granville District proved to be unsatisfactory to all parties concerned. Granville failed to realize much revenue from his holdings, partly because of the conduct of his agents, mainly Sheriff Francis Corbin. In many cases, his agents, accused of charging illegal fees and rents, acts that resulted in several mob actions. The only solution seemed to be purchase by the crown, a proposal advanced by Governor Tryon in 1767. However, the king did not act, the Revolution broke out, and within a short time, and the new state of North Carolina solved the problem by confiscating all the ungranted lands in the Granville District.

The quitrent problem troubled Granville's settlers. Scarcity of Granville records trouble genealogists. Valentine and Richard Bracewell were farmers and land speculators. All of Orange County deed records were lost for the period 1753 to 1778, a critical period for the Braswells.

Disease also caused many families to disappear. According to genealogist Malcolm Fowler, author of *The Valley of Scots,* "In 1761, the year the Black Death swept the Cape Fear country, the disease wiped out river families by the dozen." Valentine's son, Richard, may have been among the victims.

A colonial record indicates that on January 30, 1748, Valentine Bracewell had surveyed for him a 200-acre tract "beginning at a pine in the fork of Middle River on the south side of Poplar Branch" in what became Orange, later Chatham County. Richard Bracewell was a chain bearer.[19] In 1752, Orange County, created from western portions of Granville, Bladen, and Johnston counties in turn divided in 1770 to form Chatham County.

Valentine farmed the frontier land he squatted on but seemed to have no permanent address for very long. He simply stayed on the land until someone met his price. On November 22, 1751, a Thomas Davis was granted 640 acres "in the fork of Middle Creek including the Place Valentine Bracewell now lives on." [20]

In September 1753, Valentine and Richard Braswell were sued in the General Court by a William Burk. Court officials looked hard for them but they were "not to be found."21 Meanwhile, at work on the Carolina frontier, Richard served as a chain bearer for John Smith's survey of 300 acres on the north side of Buckhorn Creek.[22]

A few days later, November 13, 1753, "Volentine Brasswell Senior on New Hope" applied for a grant in Orange County on the side of Walnut Branch.[23] On the backside, Colonel Haywood and Thomas Davis paid for the survey and Davis received the patent in 1756.[24] A companion entry, subsequently crossed out, read "Richard Braswell Son of Volentine" entered for a 640-acre grant in Orange County beginning on the North Side of New Hope including the Dogwood Creek." [25] Another pioneer, granted 456 acres on Bear tree Creek on June 2, 1755, was adjacent Richard Parker and "Valentine Braswel's Line."[26]

It was necessary to specify "Richard Son of Volentine" because Valentine's brother, Henry Braswell, living at the eastern end of the county, also had sons named Richard and Valentine. Henry's family owned Valentine's original 1746 tract he bought from Joshua Ginn at the head of the Cape Fear River. There they operated Braswell's *Ordinary*—a tavern and inn for travelers along Green's highway and owned a ferryboat operation on Cape Fear River. The few early Braswell records genealogists have from Chatham County refer mainly to the Henry Braswell family.

Orange County officials drew up a tax list of its citizens in 1755. Richard Braswell was counted with himself and his son and one Negro.[27]   I believe this was Richard Braswell and his son, Richard Brazil (c.1732-1799). It may seem odd that Richard, a Quaker, owned a Negro. But the Society of Friends had slaves in those days. Even William Penn had them. The turning point with Quakers came in 1758 in Philadelphia, the year when Quakers began their first movement for the abolition of slavery, the first anywhere in the Western world.

In November, 1756, "Valentine Brazill, Senr., late of Orange County, Planter otherwise called Valentine Brazill Senr of the Province of North Carolina and County of Johnston Planter" was summoned to answer James Willet to render him fifty pounds Virginia Currency "which he owes . . . the said Valentine the twentieth day of September in the Year of

our Lord one thousand seven hundred and fifty four at Rowan County .
. . acknowledged in writing."[28]

In May 1757, Richard Brassell and Sampson Williams were named
securities in this case, James Willett vs. Valentine Brazill[29]   the case was
"put off the docket by September, 1766, after aliases had been issued to
Orange, Anson and Rowan with no effect."[30] This was the last record we
can confirm as referring to the senior Valentine Braswell. Neither can
we determine what happened to his son, Richard Braswell, after the 1755
Orange County tax list. Did he die in that great plague in 1761? We
simply don't know.[31]

Richard, son of Valentine, fathered the family who first spread the Braswell
name west into Tennessee, Illinois, and Arkansas. They learned subsistence
farming in the North Carolina Piedmont and practiced it beyond the
Alleghenies. They took with them their habit of Baptist leadership.

CHAPTER FOUR

RICHARD BRASWELL, JR. (c.1732-1799)

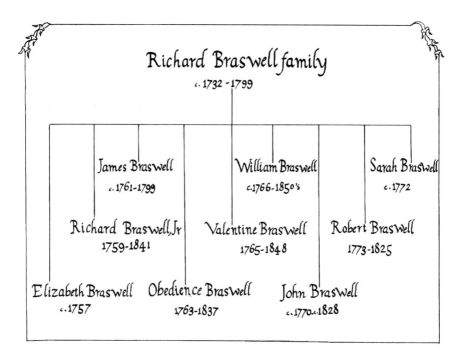

Richard Braswell family
c. 1732 -1799

James Braswell
c. 1761-1799

William Braswell
c.1766-1850's

Sarah Braswell
c. 1772

Richard Braswell, Jr
1759-1841

Valentine Braswell
1765-1848

Robert Braswell
1773-1825

Elizabeth Braswell
c. 1757

Obedience Braswell
1763-1837

John Braswell
c. 1770-c.1828

Richard Braswell, born about 1732, married Obedience in Orange County, North Carolina, about 1755. Their issue:
Elizabeth Braswell, born c. 1757, married James Butler

Richard Braswell, born 1759, married Jemima White in 1780, died in Saline County, Arkansas, in 1841

James Braswell, born c.1761, married Nancy Hall, murdered in Roane County, Tennessee, on July 29, 1799

Obedience Braswell, born c.1763, married David Hall in Wilkes County, North Carolina, on January 20, 1784

Valentine Braswell, born in 1765, married second Nancy Journey; died in Jo Daviess County, Illinois, on November 27, 1848

William Braswell, born in 1766, died in Carroll County, Arkansas, about 1856

John Braswell, born c. 1770 in Anson County, North Carolina, married Rebecca Pruitt in Greenville District, South Carolina about 1790, died in Tennessee

Nancy or Sarah Braswell, born about 1772, "never married"

Robert Braswell, born about 1773 in Anson County, died in Madison County, Illinois, on May 17, 1825[1]

BAPTISTS AND THE SANDY CREEK ASSOCIATION

Reverend Shubal Stearns migrated from Boston in 1755 and founded the Sandy Creek Church in Guilford County, North Carolina. This church, "the Mother of all the Baptists," had a fast growth, increasing from sixteen to six hundred and six members within a few years. By 1772, forty-two churches and one hundred twenty-five ministers had sprung from the parent church. By the outbreak of the Revolution with more than forty churches, the Baptists of one variety or another came to be the largest religious sect in North Carolina.[2]

Baptists made North Carolina's Anglican rulers suspicious. In the March Court, 1759, the Orange County officials "ORDERED that the Sherriff take into his custody Stephen Howard he having refused in open Court to Qualify as an Evidence on pretence of Tenderness of Conscience, being one of the sect that calls themselves Baptists—"

Quakers, present from the start of North Carolina and more of them at first than Baptists, still got treated with contempt and suspicion by Anglican officials: "John Dennis proved on his Solemn Affirmation-- he being one of the people called Quaker--that a Certain Bay horse having one Wall Eye and a Blaze in his face. . .Supposed to be taken away by the Indians some time agoe- - - -"[3]

The Great Awakening of spirituality that swept New England in the 1740's spread to North Carolina with the Baptists and was too strong for Anglican rulers to control. Baptists ministers required no formal training, only the "call of the Holy Spirit" and local ordination to take up preaching. They emphasized the "doctrine of the new birth, believer's baptism, free justification" and the autonomy of each congregation.

The Baptists celebrated the nine following rites: baptism--the Lord's Supper--love feasts--laying on-of-hands---washing feet--anointing the sick--right hand of fellowship--kiss of charity--and devoting children. The Baptists also emphasized weekly communion or Sunday services and evangelical religion. They established camp meetings for convenience and necessity but gave them up as soon as they weren't needed after they built their own churches.

Reverend George Pope, a famous Baptist minister, observed ".... falling down under religious impressions was frequent among them. Many were taken with these religious epilepsies . . . not only at the great meetings where those scenes were exhibited which were calculated to move the sympathetic affections, but also about their daily employment in the fields, some in their houses, and some when hunting the cattle in the woods." [4]

After such dramatic beginnings, some Baptist groups started splintering away and formed new sects like the Disciples of Christ and the Church of Christ. But the majority of Baptists became Southern mainstream types and settled on a set of doctrines based on the following set of Calvinistic principles:

I.   We believe that the Holy Bible, written by men divinely inspired, and the full unmixed truth is a perfect rule of faith and practice.

II.   We believe in one God, Father, Son, and Holy Ghost.

III.   We believe that man, once holy, fell by voluntary Jesus Christ. transgression from that happy state, and is now utterly void of holiness.

IV.   We believe that sinners are saved by grace alone.

V.   We believe that men are justified by faith in the Lord Jesus Christ.

VI.   We believe that salvation is free to all who will accept the Gospel.

VII .   We believe that, except a man be renewed by the Holy Spirit, he is not qualified or prepared for the Kingdom of Christ on earth, or to enjoy his glory thereafter.

VIII.   We believe that repentance toward God and faith in the Lord Jesus Christ are the duties of everyone who hears the Gospel.

IX.   We believe that election is the eternal purpose of God, by which he preciously reigns by the power of God through faith unto salvation regenerates, sanctifies, and saves sinners.

X.   We believe that sanctification, begun in regeneration, and ever progressive, is the process by which we are made to partake of God's holiness.

XI.   We believe in the preservation of the saints {converts}; that they are kept.

XII.   We believe that God's law is the only, the eternal and unchangeable rule of his church and moral government

XIII.   We believe that a Church of Christ is a congregation of baptized believers, united in the faith and fellowship of the Gospel, observing the ordinances and obeying the laws of Christ; and that its officers are pastors and deacons.

XIV.   We believe that Christian baptism is the only immersion of a believer in water, by a properly qualified administrator, into the name of the Father, Son, and Holy Ghost.

XV.   We believe that only such as have been properly baptized and received into the fellowship of a regularly organized Baptist Church, should partake of the Lord's Supper.

XVI.   We believe that the Lord's day or Christian Sabbath should be devoutly observed, and sacredly devoted to religious services.

XVII.   We believe that civil government is of divine appointment, and that the governors of states and nations should be obeyed, when the laws they seek to enforce do now conflict with the Gospel.

XVIII.   We believe in the future resurrection of the dead.

XIX.   We believe in the final judgment; and that in that day, the righteous and the wicked will be separated forever

XX.   We believe that the righteous will be made happy forever in heaven, and the wicked miserable in hell."[5]

Reverend Philip Mulkey, one of the most successful and active of the early Baptist preachers, baptized in 1756 at Sandy Creek Church and ordained in October 1757. Afterward, he took charge of the Deep River church in Orange County. Mulky continued in that church until it was dissolved and moved as an organized church to Little River in North Carolina in 1759.[6] Within the next decade, Richard Braswell and his brother, George, left Orange County and joined the Deep River Baptist commune on Little River in present Montgomery County, North Carolina.[7]

PEACEABLE FARMING IN THE DEEP RIVER BAPTIST COMMUNE IN ANSON COUNTY, NORTH CAROLINA

Richard Braswell always made his living as a farmer and land speculator. North Carolina farmers produced and exported a great variety of foodstuffs of which corn, wheat, peas and beans were the most important. Wheat, broadcast by hand, and cut with reap-hooks or sickles, thrashed with flails or treaded on by oxen, and ground in water-driven mills, was produced in all parts of the colony, but in large amounts only in the Cape Fear Valley and later in Piedmont counties like Anson. Honey, wine, sorghum, hops, timothy grass, white potatoes, sweet potatoes, and a wide variety of fruits and vegetables were also produced, mainly for home use.

The major crops were wheat, corn, tobacco, peas, and beans. Tobacco became the leading "money crop." The culture of tobacco--seeding, transplanting, worming, priming, suckering—required a great deal of farm labor. After the harvest, the leaves were cut into stalks, assorted, and packed into hogsheads.

Oxen, the main draft animals, were used for such heavy work as plowing and hauling. The farmer had horses for riding, milk cows, beef cattle, hogs, chickens, geese, and other kinds of poultry. Most of the cattle and livestock had a "lean and hungry look." Horses and cattle were branded by their owners and turned loose to fend for themselves. Great numbers of hogs, usually of the "razor-back" species, their ears notched with the owner's mark, roamed the unfenced woods, growing fat on mast until a few weeks before "killing time" when they were penned and fed corn to improve the quality of their meat. Farmers ate large amounts of hog meat. Huge droves of hogs were driven on foot to Virginia to be sold.

The Bracewell brothers, like other North Carolina farmers, were self-sufficient jacks-of-all-trades. They were a combination of farmer, engineer, hunter and trapper, carpenter, mechanic, and businessman. `The colonial farmer supplied himself with nearly all foodstuffs--bread, dairy products, pork and beef, and many other articles for the table. Surplus grains and fruits were manufactured into beer, wine, brandy, whiskey, and other "intoxicating beverages" by the people who believed them to be good for health.

Cloth making, a major household industry, meant every home had cards, spinning wheels, and looms, which converted wool and flax into cloth. Farmers tanned cattle hides and turned them into shoes, breeches, and harness. Deerskins became leggings, caps, and moccasins. Most farmers made their own furniture, farm implements, and household utensils from local timber. Firewood from the forest provided the fuel for heating and cooking. Every household molded its own candles and made its own soap.[8]

TROUBLES BEGAN: THE REGULATORS

Richard and George Braswell joined the Baptists and moved to the Piedmont but troubles in the Granville District followed them anyway. The common people resented the fact that not a single officer at their seat of government in Hillsboro got picked by popular vote. The county court, consisting of justices of the peace, controlled almost every aspect of local government and administration. It appointed the sheriff, constables, and overseers of roads. In effect, the election machinery was in the hands of the "courthouse ring."

The land policy of the Granville District caused charges of corruption, illegal fees, and excessive rents and taxes. As early as 1755 a legislative committee reported that Francis Corbin, Lord Granville's agent in the province, and his subordinates were "exacting fees on all grants," but nothing was done to relieve their grievances. Corbin was finally dismissed but too late to prevent riots.

The first organized effort to redress these abuses took place in August 1766 at a mass meeting at Sandy Creek in Orange County, with the issuance of "Regulator Petition Number 1." This document appealed to all the people of North Carolina to resist local oppression and to put an end to county official's extortions. The turning point came in 1768 and marked the formal organization of the Regulator movement. "Regulator Advertisement Number 6," written March 22, 1768, used the word "Regulator" for the first time and stated in plain language what these aggrieved people proposed to "regulate."

Cousins Benjamin Braswell and James Brantley signed Orange County "Regulator Petition Number 9" in May 1768. The Regulation agreement said "An officer is a servant of the publick, and we are determined to have the officers of this county under a better and honester regulation than any have been for some time past."

Some of the sheriffs failed to turn in their tax collections for many years especially in Rowan and Anson counties. The situation became so bad in Anson that the people took matters into their own hands and pledged themselves not to pay taxes for the current year.

Richard and George Braswell were among the hundreds of signers of this 1769 Anson County Regulator petition:

Anson County Petition Mr Speaker and Gent of the Assembly The Petition of the Inhabitants of Anson County, Being part of the Remonstrance of the Province of North Carolina, HUMBLY SHEWETH That the Province in general labour under general grievances, and the Western part thereof under particular ones; which we not only see, but very sensibly feel, being crouch'd beneath our sufferings: and not withstanding our sacred privileges, have too long yielded ourselves slaves to remorseless oppression Permit us to conceive it to be our inviolable right to make known our grievances, and to petition for redress. A few of the many grievances are as follows (Vizt)

1. That the poor Inhabitants in general are much oppress'd by reason of disproportionate Taxes, and those of the western counties in particular as they are generally in mean circumstances.

2. That no method is prescribed by Law for the payment of the Taxes of the Western counties in produce (in lieu of a Currency) as is in other Counties within this Province; to the Peoples great oppression.

3. That Lawyers, Clerks, and other pentioners; in place of being obsequious Sarvants for the Country's use; are becoming a nuisance, as the business of the people is often transacted without the least degree of fairness, the entention of the law evaded, exorbitant fees extorted, and the sufferers left to mourn under their oppressions...

12. That the assembly in like manner make known that the governor and Council do frequently grant Lands to as many as they think proper without regard to Head Rights, notwithstanding the Contrariety of His Majesties Instructions; by which means immense sums have been collected, and numerous Patents granted, for much of the most fertile lands in this Province, that is yet uninhabited and uncultivated, environed by great numbers of poor people who are necessitated to toil in the cultivation of bad Lands whereon they hardly can subsist; who are thereby deprived of His Majesties liberality and Bounty: nor is there the least regard paid to the cultivation clause in said Patent mentioned, as many of the said Council as well as their friends and favorites enjoy large Quantities of Lands under the above-mentioned circumstances....

16. That every denomination of People may marry according to their respective Mode Ceremony and custom after due publication or license

17. That Doctr Benjamin Franklin or some other known patriot be appointed Agent, to represent the unhappy state of this Province to his Majesty, and to solicit the several Boards in England: Dated October ye 20th 1769 ⁹

Disorders erupted at the Hillsboro Court on September 24, 1770, when about 150 Regulators marched into the courthouse, assaulted a lawyer, dragged land agent Fanning through the streets, and caused the judge to run for safety. The next day the Regulators conducted a mock court, filling the dockets with many bitter, sarcastic, and profane remarks, usually ending with "plaintiff pays costs." One "trial" was Case #86, Valentine Braswell versus Duncan McNeal, administrators of the estate of Hector McNeal. The verdict, "Restrain and be darned."¹⁰

THE BATTLE OF ALAMANCE

Governor Tryon decided to take drastic action. He called out the militia in March 1771 to suppress the Regulators. About 1500 militiamen responded, mostly from the Eastern counties. Tryon marched from New Bern to Hillsboro and camped on Great Alamance Creek a few miles from Hillsboro where he was met by a force of about 2,000 Regulators. The Regulators petitioned the Governor for an audience but he refused to talk with them "as long as they were in arms against the government." He gave them one hour to lay down their arms and go home. At the end of the hour, he gave the order to fire, and after a two-hour battle the Regulators were defeated and scattered. Tryon's losses were nine killed and sixty-one wounded. The Regulators lost nine killed and an unknown number wounded.

Tryon tried twelve Regulators for treason and all were convicted. Six were hanged and the rest were pardoned by the Governor. Tryon offered to spare all Regulators who would lay down their arms and submit to authority. Within six weeks 6,409 submitted and later received pardons from the King, [11] including Richard and George Braswell.[12]

Many Regulators moved to the Tennessee country soon after their defeat at Alamance. Morgan Edwards, a noted Baptist preacher, traveler, and author, said that these people "despaired of seeing better times and therefore quitted the province. It is said that 1,500 families have departed since the battle of Alamance and to my knowledge a great many more are only waiting to dispose of their plantations in order to follow them."

We will never know all the mischief the Regulators inflicted on the crown, but it is clear from their retreat from Anson County to the upper Yadkin country after Alamance that they had cause to put distance between themselves and royal authority. Again church history provides a clue: according to Morgan Edwards, Edmund Fanning, the hated royal land agent, was particularly hostile towards Reverend Joseph Murphy who was "first a member of the Deep River church in the present county of Chatham, then of the Little River church in that part of Anson since erected into the county of Montgomery."

Paschal quotes Edwards saying the Deep River Church scattered after Alamance, "from its membership of five hundred they were reduced to a handful owing chiefly to the fruitless issue of the Regulation at Alamance, which made most of them quit the Province, some heading west to the upper Yadkin-Watauga country, the rest went to South Carolina." [13]

Richard Braswell didn't take to the hills right after Alamance but he left Anson County when the Revolutionary War shifted South in 1780 after Lord Cornwallis invaded South Carolina.

A courthouse fire in 1868 destroyed most of Anson County's records but enough have survived along with North Carolina land grant records to place Richard with the remaining Baptist community on Little River until 1780. Richard Braswell was granted 200 acres on the east side of Little River by royal authorities on November 22, 1771[14] which he sold to Christopher Christian the following January 25th and witnessed by George Brasswell and Going Morgan, George's in-law. That was also the only surviving record ever signed by Obedience Braswell.[15]

An entry dated July 13, 1774, in the minutes of the Anson County Court of Pleas & Quarter Sessions: "Ordered that John Wilson be overseer of the road from Clark's Creek near his own house to Mark Allen's store on the Cross Creek Road near the ford of the Little River, and those hands Sias Billingsley. . . . George Braswell, John Cheek, Isaac Cooper. . . .work same." [16]

By 1777, the Revolutionary War was underway and conditions even more unsettled. George Braswell and his wife, Polly Morgan, in that year moved east into what is now Moore County. They were in the company of some other Morgan family members. George settled on Wolf Creek and the Morgan's on nearby Cabin Creek. A son was born to George and Polly about 1780. They named him "Morgan."[17]

Meanwhile, Richard Brassel, Junior (#36) and Richard Brassel(#37) signed the following petition:

"Petition of the inhabitants of Anson County. 1777: Because of the Pee Dee River dividing the County it is very inconvenient to many of the inhabitants; they ask for a d'vision of the county with the river as the dividing line....Court House now stands in ten or twelve miles of South Carolina and is extremely inconvenient."[18] In 1778, Montgomery County was formed from Anson County.

In 1835, the Montgomery County Courthouse burned with all records. A North Carolina record shows John Wilson patented Grant #211 for 150 acres " Beginning near the poplar branch then runs into Richland Creek on the North side against Richard Brasswells plantation" and dated November 16,1778.[19]

THE WHITE FAMILY

About a quarter of a million people lived in the North Carolina Back Country by 1776. Most of them came from Pennsylvania. The incoming waves of Scotch-Irish and German-speaking immigrants rolled through Pennsylvania, past Lancaster, up against the Appalachian barrier, then spilled off to the South. The 1750's saw them moving into the rich lands behind the pine barrens in North Carolina.

William White owned land on Savannah Creek near Pee Dee River in Anson County. His wife, Jemima White, submitted his estate inventory on April 1, 1767. It included a prayer book and psalter,[20] Presbyterian Scotch-Irish belongings. His widow, Jemima White, later married Thomas Cannon. Moses White, William's son, bought from Thomas Cannon a tract "on Savanna Creek So. W. of Pee Dee River" on October 21, 1771. The tract granted to Jemima White, *deceased*, on May 4, 1769, "and since became the property of said Thomas Cannon by marrying of her the said Jemima White and now convaid to Moses White as it appears."[21] Moses White was Jemima, Junior's older brother. He evidently moved later to the eastern part of Anson County where Jemima met Richard Brazil. Here the oldest legend in my Bracewell history began, "The courtship of Richard Brazil and Jemima White:"

According to my Aunt Laura Brazil, "Moses White was a tight-fisted Scotch-Irishman who didn't believe in giving away anything including his sister whose work he needed. Therefore, when young Richard asked him for her hand in marriage, he refused until Richard agreed to go to work for him free. Months later, after Richard had cleared a large tract of forestland for him, Moses White finally consented. Richard would later joke about the experience and compare himself to Jacob of the Bible (Genesis chapter twenty-nine) who had to labor fourteen years for Laban before Laban would consent to his marriage to daughter Rachel.

According to Richard Brazil's Bible, Jemima White was born December 25, 1764, and married Richard Brazil on May 15, 1780.[22]

WILKES COUNTY, NORTH CAROLINA: 1780-1786

Richard and Obedience's family moved from Anson County to Wilkes County, North Carolina, after Cornwallis' invasion. Wilkes County, a raw western frontier area, had a small settlement of Ex-Regulators, Baptists, Scotch-Irish, and other unruly groups. These "Over Mountain People" as they were called were mostly Scotch-Irish, but the mixing had already begun. Among the people who mixed were sizeable numbers of English-origin folks like Richard Braswell.

Some Over Mountain People lived in the extreme northeastern corner of what is now Tennessee, along the Watauga, Nolachucky, and Holston Rivers, where Tennessee, Virginia, and North Carolina meet. The British authorities considered them squatters on Cherokee land since government policy was meant to keep white settlers east of the mountains. To that end, the British drew the Proclamation Line of 1763 following the Appalachian Ridge but the Scotch-Irish ignored it.

A line on British maps didn't prevent sixteen families from North Carolina from crossing the mountains and stopping their wagons on the banks of the Watauga River at a spot called Sycamore Shoals, now Elizabethton, Tennessee. There they established the Watauga settlements and leased two large tracts of land from the Cherokee. Three years later the Watauga Association purchased their leased lands from the Indians, but other Cherokee, including young Chief Draggmg Canoe, strongly objected.

Dragging Canoe and several hundred warriors came back in 1776, this time in war paint. However the besieged settlements, outnumbered and on their own, held out and from the one fort the Over Mountain riflemen sallied forth and in a hard fight on the South Fork of the Holston, defeated the Cherokees. Scotch-Irishmen were used to constant fighting long before they came to America.

BACK COUNTRY MILITIA

When Cornwallis marched north in 1780 and invaded North Carolina, Richard Braswell joined a Wilkes County militia group to oppose them. One of these volunteers described a band of Southern Back Country militiamen as

. . . a set of men acting entirely on our own footing, without promise or expectation of any pay. There was nothing furnished us by the public; we furnished our own clothes, composed of coarse material, and all home spun; our over dress was a hunting shirt of what we called linsey Woolsey--coarse linen and wool, or cotton and wool, well-belted around us. We furnished our own horses, saddles, bridles, guns, swords, butcher knives, and our own spurs; we got our powder and lead as we could, and often had to apply to the women of the country, for their old pewter dishes and spoons, to supply the place of lead; and if we had lead sufficient to make balls, half lead and half pewter, we felt well supplied. . . .They made their caps of leather greased with tallow, with two steel straps crossed to reinforce it. . . .We carried no cooking utensils, nor any thing to encumber us; we depended on what chance or kind providence might cast in our way, and were always ready to decamp in a short time.

Most militiamen had families to worry about, unlike the American Continentals who were typically young and unmarried. Spring planting had to be done by a certain time or there would be no crops, and crops planted but unharvested crops helped no one. Cows had to be milked, hogs had to be slopped, butchering had to be done, fences had to be repaired. The women were often as tough as their men and women and children could do much but farming was a partnership. One person cannot do it all, and boys old enough to do the work of their fathers usually served with them in the militia.

British sympathizers were everywhere in the Back Country. Militia bands like Richard Braswell's unit were located in Wilkes and Surry Counties on the upper reaches of the Yadkin River under strong leaders like Colonel Benjamin Cleveland.

The Over Mountain Men were armed with tomahawks, and large knives for cutting, eating, fighting, and scalping. Across the pommels of their saddles rested their principal weapon for which they were famous on two continents, the American rifle. Long, slim, elegant, the American rifle at its best was a masterpiece of the gunsmith's craft. Deadly at 200 yards, in the hands of an expert marksman it was dangerous at 300 to 400 yards. .But the American rifle had serious drawbacks as a weapon of war. It was a hunter's weapon with a smaller caliber that enabled the rifleman to carry more ammunition on a long hunt. In contrast to the musket, it was more fragile and it couldn't be used as a club. There was no way to attach a socket bayonet to defend oneself when the rifle was empty. It took a minute to reload, and in one minute on open ground a charging English or Hessian soldier armed with a bayoneted musket could cover a lot of ground.

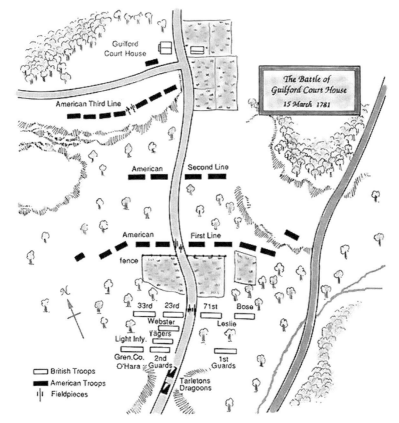

The Battle of Guilford Courthouse
(Courtesy of Wikipedia)

THE BATTLE OF GUILFORD COURTHOUSE

Richard Braswell fought at the Battle of Guilford Courthouse, an important turning point in the Revolutionary War. American General Greene, his regular army and the North Carolina militia engaged Cornwallis near the courthouse on March 15, 1781.   Nathanial Greene had about 4,440 troops. Of these some 1,762 were regular Continentals. He deployed them in three lines. In the first line were his least reliable troops, about 1,000 North Carolina militia.

William Richardson Davie who was at the battle recalled many years later that about half of the militia stood behind a fence, a "cover too insignificant to inspire confidence." The militia was on either side of the road, just before it disappeared into the tangled forest behind them. Nathaniel Greene rode down the split-rail fence to talk to the militiamen and rouse them into a fighting mood. He spoke of liberty and the cause and their honor and all he asked of them was to shoot twice then they could leave.

The North Carolina militia listened, stared at the spot where the British were coming on the New Garden Road from Hillsboro, and waited. About 1:30 PM, the head of the British column appeared on the road and marching to the beat of drums and sounds of fifes. Highland troops crossed the brook and spread in both directions on the cleared field.

Captain Anthony Singleton of the Continental artillery, another witness, said "the militia, contrary to custom, behaved well for militia." And British officers who courted death on that rain-soaked field had no doubt of the damage inflicted by the militia volleys. One British captain said "one half of the Highlanders dropt on the spot." On the American side of the fence, an American thought the British lines resembled "the scattering stalks of a wheat field when the harvest man passed over it with his cradle." But the British sergeants bawled their orders and dressed ranks and the officers shouted words of encouragement and the British and German mercenaries stepped over their dead, dying, and wounded men and kept coming.

Another witness, a British sergeant, said of the Americans "their whole line had their arms presented, and resting on a rail fence and taking aim with the nicest precision." That shook even the most disciplined Redcoats but they kept coming. But when the Americans saw all the bayonets coming at them, it was the end of the line for the North Carolina militia. It was bayonet time and not their way of fighting. They had more or less delivered their volleys and General Greene himself had said they could then retire. They headed for home.

When it appeared the British were losing their fight against the Continentals, Cornwallis ordered his cannons to fire on all of them with grapeshot, killing both British and Americans. American General Greene knew that he had to keep his army intact so he ordered a withdrawal.

Cornwallis lost more than a quarter of his men. Tactically, by a narrow margin, Lord Cornwallis had won the Battle of Guilford Courthouse. But now his force was reduced from 3,300 before the Battle of Cowpens to slightly over1,400 after Guilford Courthouse so they were no longer able to go after the Americans.

Strategically, by a wide margin, Nathaniel Greene had set up Cornwallis for an even worse disaster: Yorktown and American victory. Cornwallis said about Guilford Courthouse, "I never saw such fighting since God made me. The Americans fought like demons."[23]

Richard Braswell, along with 533 other North Carolina militiamen, were captured by Lord Cornwallis but later paroled. He was one of seven men captured from Wilkes Country.[24]

Unlike his brother-in-law, David Hall, Richard Braswell did not apply for his Revolutionary War pension. Here is David Hall's 1832 application:

. .he was born in Henry County, Virginia, on the 25th day of March 1760 as well as he is informed, where he continued to live until sometime about the commencement of the Revolutionary War, when he moved to Wilkes County North Carolina where he continued to reside during the whole of the Revolutionary War-that sometime in the spring of 1780. . .he thinks it was about the time of the battle of Guilford, he entered into the service of the United States as a volunteer—that he enrolled himself into a company of lighthorse commanded by Captain Wittherspoon. . .that he enrolled himself for an indefinite period of time but was to continue in service while ever it would be necessary to keep down the torries—that his company first rendezvoused at Wilkes courthouse, and marched up the river. . .and from there, down the mountain into Burke County and through many counties around, where ever it was understood there was a collection of tories—he recollects while marching near where the counties of Wilkes and Burke join each other, his company had separated with the understanding that if one division should hear the other firing upon the tories, that the other should immediately join them—that at the time spoken of the company had just separated, the division to which he did not belong fell in with a company of tories dispersed them and killed one man—that upon hearing the firing the party to which applicant belonged, immediately rode to where the firing was heard, but before they reached there, the tories had fled and applicant recollects distinctly of seeing the man who had been killed, whom they left to be buried by the women while the company proceeded on after the tories—applicant states that he continued in this kind of warfare scouring the country, sometimes under the command of the said Captain Wittherspoon and sometimes under the command of John Cleveland. . .for a period of three months....afterward he staid at his Fathers house, in Wilkes County, about one week, when he again marched with his company under the same different commanders, doeing the same sort of service, and suppressing the tories whenever they attempted to embody themselves—During this tour applicant states that Colonel Benjamin Cleveland commanded his company on a tour up into the mountains in Wilkes County, where they came upon a parcel of tories six of whom they took prisoners, and Colonel Cleveland ordered three of them to be well whipped, and released the whole of them—applicant thinks he was out in actual servce during this campaign three or four months—In all which time he was engaged in marching through the mountain counties of North Carolina to disperse the tories and keep the disaffected in awe—after this time the tories became less troublesome applicants company was disbanded and he returned home where he remained a few weeks, until he came over the mountain to what is now Washington County, Tennessee, in the Geecy cane on Chucky river to a place where the whites were forted, at a place called fort Sevier—where he volunteered as an Indian spie. . .and a party of whom were sent each day about twenty-five or thirty miles to look out for Indians and then to return again to the fort—if upon the return of any of the spies any trace of Indians had been discovered, the whole company marched out in search of them—In guarding this fort and the neighbouring frontier applicant states that he continued to serve as a spie and a guard in said company for two years, when his whole company marched under the command of Colonel John Sevier into the Cherokee nation, and burned their towns, nine in number, took some prisoners and killed some of their men—in this expedition applicant states he was about four weeks gone when applicant returned to the said fort where he remained three or four weeks, to be cured of small pox, and then returned to his fathers in Wilkes County N. Carolina. . . . he was married in Wilkes County N.C. and moved to Greenville District S. Carolina where he lived about ten or eleven years, when he moved to the same neighborhood in Anderson County Tennessee where he has continued to live ever since. . . . [25]

David Hall was the son of Samuel and Millien Webb Hall. They moved from Virginia to Stony Fork in Wilkes County, North Carolina, where on January 20, 1784, David married Richard's daughter, Obedience Braswell.[26]

After the war, the younger Richard Braswell moved to the Watauga Settlement in East Tennessee for a few years. Again, records left by him are scarce. But he was recorded in 1782 as a witness in a trial, State versus

Thomas Carder, in an "indictment for stealing a small peace of steel." Carder was found not guilty.[27] Richard's last record in Wilkes County before he left for South Carolina appeared on the county's 1785 tax roll with the notation that he owned 100 acres.[28]

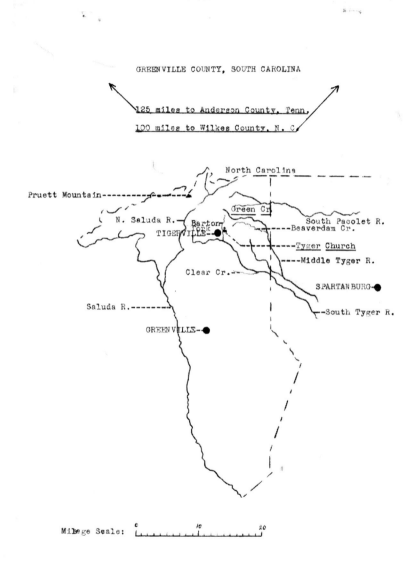

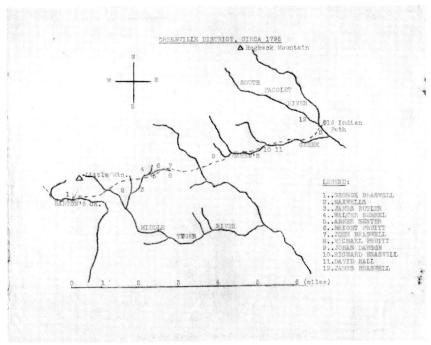

The Richard Braswell Settlement in Greenville District, South Carolina

GREENVILLE DISTRICT, SOUTH CAROLINA: 1786-1799

Richard Braswell's first appearance in the records of Greenville District occurred on October 28, 1786, when he was granted 165 acres on Clear Creek of the South Tyger River next to William Ussery.[29] Richard never settled on this grant. Thirty-four acres of it was awarded by an Arbitration Board to two other pioneers because the survey was done wrong. He sold the remaining 120 acres four months later on March 1, 1787, and bought his actual homestead on Green's Creek on the South Pacolet River next to his son, Richard Braswell, Junior, and David Hall. The deed called for fifty pounds sterling in return for fifty acres and dated December 1, 1789.[30]

About 1790, Richard, Senior's youngest son, John Braswell, married Rebecca Pruitt, daughter of Michael and Elizabeth Pruitt. In addition, around that same time, the first Federal Census taker counted the people in Greenville District:[31]

David Hall	1 male 16 & over, 3 under 16, 1 female
Seven other households, then---	
Richard Braswell	2 males 16 & over, 1 under 16, 5 females
four other households, then---	
James Brasall	1 male 16 & over, 1 under 16, 3 females
three other households, then---	
Valentine Braswell	1 male 16 & over, 2 females.
Thirty-six other households, then---	
Richard Braswell	1 male 16 & over, 3 under 16, 3 females {Richard, George, William, Richard III, Obedience, Margaret, Jemima)
Bright Pruitt	2 males 16 & over, 1 female
two other households then---	
John Braswell	1 male 16 & over, 1 female

According to Baptist historian Leah Townsend, "About 1791, the members of the Reedy River Church began fussing among themselves. This led to a split in the church, part going to the Bethel Association and the majority of the former Reedy River Church members under the leadership of Reverend Edmund Bearden constituted a new church with the name of Head of Tyger River Church." [32]

South Carolina gave generous land grants to these Out Back people, the largest of which was a 666-acre tract on Green's Creek of the South Pacolet River, including the village of Billewsfield, and a branch of Tyger River awarded to Richard Braswell, Junior, on June 24, 1793. [33]

In 1794, the Head of Tyger River Baptist Church had twenty-six members. Besides the pastor, Rev. Edmund Bearden, and Richard Braswell, Junior, the church officials this year included Richard Braswell, Senior, and David Hall. Messengers to the Association included James Butler in 1795-96 and in 1797, Richard Braswell and David Hall.

By October 1795, the first two men from Richard Braswell, Senior's family—James and Valentine Braswell—had crossed over the Appalachians and bought property in "the County of Knox, Territory South of the River Ohio," soon to become Anderson County, Tennessee.[34]

By 1800, all but John Braswell had sold their Greenville District holdings and moved over the mountains into Anderson County. Finally, John Braswell "of the state of Tennessee and white county" sold his last piece of land in Greenville District on February 8, 1809. It was the 65-acre tract George "Brasel" bought from David Hall in 1795 that John in turn bought from David Hall in 1800.[35] John appeared on the 1800 Federal Census in Greenville County as "John Brassel." He had one male child under ten and another, one male 26 to 44 with three females under ten and another, 16 to 25.[36]

Richard Braswell, Senior, died April 1, 1799.[37]

CHAPTER FIVE

RICHARD BRAZIL (1759-1842)

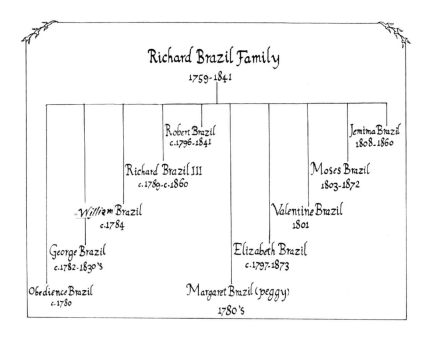

Richard Brazil Family
1759-1841

Robert Brazil
c.1796-1841

Jemima Brazil
1808-1860

Richard Brazil III
c.1789-c.1860

Moses Brazil
1803-1872

William Brazil
c.1784

Valentine Brazil
1801

George Brazil
c.1782-1830's

Elizabeth Brazil
c.1797-1873

Obedience Brazil
c.1780

Margaret Brazil (Peggy)
1780's

Richard Brazil's 1834 Bible

ACROSS THE APPALACHIANS

The first record of our family in Tennessee was dated October, 1795, in which James Brasel bought a 50-acre tract on Grassey Creek. 1 On October 20, 1795, Vawl "Brazeal" bought a 200-acre tract on the south side of Clinch River on Mayberry's Branch on the side of Piney Ridge. 2 This started the family's next community--on Clinch River in Anderson County.

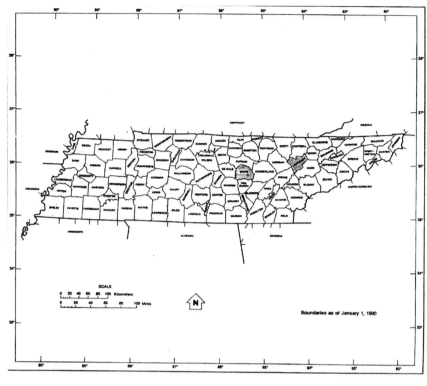

Tennessee

THE MURDER OF JAMES BRASWELL

Two brothers, Robert and James Braswell, were traveling in Roane County east of Anderson County. They were likely delegates en route to a Tennessee Baptist meeting on that awful day, July 29, 1799, when the Harps murdered James Braswell.

The Harps were Scotish Loyalists. During the Revolution, they wore British uniforms and fought with the British at Kings Mountain. After the fighting, "Big Harp" and "Little Harp'" were among the few who escaped the American rebels. They went to their old home in Mecklenburg County. In addition, thinking like Calvinistic Presbyterians, they decided the cause of the king was lost, that it was evidently "foreordained from the foundation of the world." They agreed that all their own tendencies were evil; and applying their logic of predestination to themselves, they decided they were evidently predestinated to be damned, and that there was no use fighting against fate. So they decided to abandon civilization, join the Cherokee Indians in Georgia, and lead lives of outlawry and warfare against the human race. In one of their first acts, they kidnapped Susan Wood and Maria Davidson and compelled them to live "as man and wife." The Harps then started a random killing spree that alarmed the whole region.

This notice appeared in the *Knoxville Gazette* on August 7, 1799:

On Monday, the 29th, James Brazel was found murdered on the road leading to Stogden's Valley, in Price's Settlement. This unfortunate man is supposed to also have fallen victum to the above named atrocious villains {the Harps}. Upwards of four hundred and fifty dollars have been subscribed by the citizens of Knoxville and its vicinity to any person or persons who will apprehend and commit to the jail of Knox County the above mentioned Harps; which, together with the reward offered by the Governor and citizens of Kentucky, amounts to upwards of two thousand dollars.

One writer gave this account: "It chanced that day in 1799 that they {the Harps} met James and Robert Brazel soon after committing another outrageous murder, on the trail in the forest, stopped and told them of the killing and said they were out looking for the killers. Then suddenly they accused the Brasel's of the crime. They ordered they boys off their horses. Robert broke for the underbrush and escaped, but James was shot and killed. Robert made his way to habitation and tried to rouse a posse to pursue the Harps, but people were too timid and nothing was done, to Robert's indignation."[3]

John W.M. Brazeale, a nineteenth century lawyer and Knoxville writer, wrote a longer account in 1842:[4]

"In the year 1797 or 1798, two men named Harp came into the county of Knox. Shortly after this, the Harps commenced the bloody work of inhuman and ruthless murder; which they prosecuted to an extent that alarmed and terrified the inhabitants of the whole country below Knoxville. These tragic deeds aroused the whole community. Every man carried his fire arms, his dirk of his butcher knife about him.

Companies were raised, scouts kept continually out, and rewards offered for the apprehension of these murderous and marauding wretches; in consequence of which they were compelled to seek shelter in a more wild and uninhabited region; and they, therefore, fled, taking their women with them, to the mountains along the line between Tennessee and Kentucky; occasionally breaking into the settlements, as well in Kentucky as in Tennessee, and committing the most awful, horrible and bloody murders.

They crossed Clinch river, at the Pawpaw ford, in the eastern end of Roane county. Thence they proceeded, along what was then called the Kentucky trace; ascending the Cumberland mountain, and crossing Emery's river about one mile above where the town of Montgomery, in the county of Morgan, is now situated. About a mile and a half or two miles beyond the river, they met two men, one by the name of Brasil, whom they murdered; the other, whose name I have not been able to ascertain, made his escape. Brasil had with him a rifle gun, which the Harps battered over the rocks, shattering the stock to pieces. He also had in his pockets a quarter of a dollar, which was left in his pocket, and found with his corpse. The place where he was murdered, being on a spur of the mountain, yet bears the name of Brasil's knob...."

In Henderson County, Kentucky, they killed a Mrs. Stegall and her child "then set fire to the house and fled. . . .Stegall, not being a great distance from home, was soon informed of the direful tragedy. Thomas Leiper, Stegall and Williams, with some others, made immediate pursuit; and overtook the blood-thirsty wretches the next day, about noon, quietly resting, in supposed security, in their rocky dwelling on the mountain. . . .The Harps were not apprised of danger until they were fired upon, and the big Harp (as Micajah was called) wounded. Upon being fired on, they flew to their horses, leaving their women to their fate. . . .They dashed off at full speed, in different directions.

Leiper was mounted on an animal, fleet of foot, and possessing great elasticity of bottom; and he, therefore, was soon out of sight of his comrades. The race continued for about eight miles, over hills, across ravines and through thickets. . . .Harp's mare finally began to fail and Leiper discovered he could soon overtake him. . . .He dashed suddenly upon him, fired, and broke his arm, the ball passing, also, through the side of the chest. Harp fell from the noble, but jaded animal, that bore him, rolled over, and crawling up by a log, that lay hard by, he seated himself with his back against it. Leiper. . . . did not approach him, until he reloaded his gun. Then, cocking his piece, and presenting it at Harp's breast, he advanced to him, telling him that, if he moved a hand, he would send the contents of his rifle through him.

Leiper, having satisfied himself that Harp had no arms about him but a butcher-knife and tomahawk, made him surrender these, and then entered into a conversation with him; with a view to ascertain, if possible, the reasons that prompted him and his brother to the commission of such savage and cruel deeds.

Harp said his brother and himself (for he declared Wiley Harp was his brother) had become disgusted with all mankind, and agreed with each other, to destroy as many persons as they could. He knew, at the time they commenced the perpetration of these bloody deeds, they he must die, some day, by the hands of man. . . . but he determined to risk the consequences, and slay as many as he could, before the sword of justice should overtake him. He said he never had committed but one murder for which he felt remorse; and that was the murder of his own child. It cried, and vexed him, and he killed it. He confessed that, his brother and himself had committed many murders, some of which related by him, had never before been heard of.

The object of Leiper was to extract from him a full account of all the bloody deeds perpetrated by him and his brother; but, the remainder of the company coming up, Stegall with them, who was burning with rage, on account of the cruel and inhuman slaughter of his wife and child, an end was put to the conversation, by Stegall cutting off the head of Harp. Stegall took Harp's own butcher-knife, which Leiper had compelled him to deliver up, and taking Harp by the hair of the head, drew the knife slowly across the back of his neck, cutting to the bone; Harp staring him full in the face, with a grim and fiendish countenance, and exclaiming, 'you are a G-d d---d rough butcher, but cut on and be d-----d.' Stegall then passed the knife around his neck, cutting to the bone; and then wrung off his head, in the same manner a butcher would that of a hog. . . . Some of the company happened to have with them a bag, into which they put Harp's head, and set off on their return march.

They carried Harp's head to the nearest justice of the peace, by the name of Newman, and, having made satisfactory affidavits, before Esquire Newman, that it was Harp's head, they then took it to the nearest cross roads, and put it upon the top of a lofty pole. . . .The spot is near the Highland Lick in Union county, and is still known by the name of Harp's Head."

Wiley Harp made his escape, and fled to the neighborhood of Natchez, Mississippi, but in 1804, he was recognized and hanged.

An eighty-year old woman in Morgan County, Tennessee, reported in 1971 to her distant cousin, Pal Brasel Spencer, that "James Brasel, her husband's great-grandfather, was slain and buried in the west end of Morgan County. She said times were so hard that a coffin couldn't be obtained so relatives skinned green bark from trees and wrapped his body for burial. Her husband's grandmother told her about this."[5]

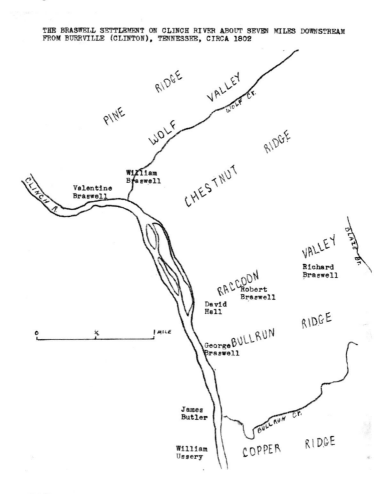

THE BRASWELL SETTLEMENT ON CLINCH RIVER ABOUT SEVEN MILES DOWNSTREAM FROM BURRVILLE (CLINTON), TENNESSEE, CIRCA 1802

ANDERSON COUNTY, TENNESSEE: 1799-1809

David and Nathan Hall and William, Richard, Valentine, George, Morgan, and Robert Braswell signed a petition addressed to the Tennessee Legislature in 1799, asking that body to create a new county from Knox.

"TO THE HONORABLE GENERAL ASSEMBLY OF THE STATE OF TENNESSEE

The petition of sundry Inhabitants of Knox County humbly sheweth that their local situation is such as renders it very inconvenient for them to attend the usual place of holding courts, general musters, elections, etc. some of us having at least 25 to 40 miles to travel, and generally very bad roads, having sundry large water courses, and ridges to cross, your Petitioners humbly conceive their grievance might be much alleviated by a division of KNOX COUNTY. . . ."

The Legislature created Anderson County out of part of western Knox County on November 6, 1801.

During this time, Valentine 'Brazeal', Richard Braswell Senior's youngest son, showed signs of his half-Scotch-Irish, militant nature. On September 29, 1800, he was commissioned an ensign in the Knox County militia.[6]

Also during this period, Richard Braswell's brother, George Brazle, sold his 100 acres in June 1803, and his family headed for Wilson County and later, Rutherford County, Tennessee. George and his growing family finally settled in Walker County, Alabama.

Life was hard and justice cruel in Anderson County. On September 14, 1803, William Brazle and David Hall were jurors in State versus James McMurry. The verdict: "the Defendant guilty whereupon it is considered by the court that James McMurry receive three lashes on his Bare Back at the public whipping post of Anderson County to be executed by the Sheriff thereof between the hours of two & four o'clock of this day. . . ." [8]

Life was also short. According to Isabelle Steele's Bible record, James Butler had already died by "Aug. ye 21st 1803."[9] Anderson County's records shows that Butler's brother-in-law, William Brazle, soon stepped forward to help: On September 12, 1803, "Ordered by the court that Elizabeth Butler, widow and relict of James Butler, have leave to administer the estate of the said James Butler, they having entered into bond with Augustin Hackworth and William Brazle in the sum of $800 and qualified as the law requires."

Two years later, Richard Braswell, Senior's widow, Obedience, died in Tennessee on October 28, 1805.[10]

A YEAR IN WHITE COUNTY, TENNESSEE: 1808-09

After their mother, Obedience, died, the Braswell brothers drifted apart. Valentine and Robert were the first to go. They left for the Cahokia District in St. Clair County, Illinois Territory, late in 1805.[11] On June 10, 1807, William sold his one hundred acres and Lot Number 39 in Burrville which "said lot was willed to William Brazle."[12]   David Hall, Nancy Hall Braswell, widow of James Braswell, and Moses White, brother of Jemima White Braswell, stayed on in Anderson County for a while longer. Tennessee was the jumping off place for pioneering the huge Mississippi valley region.

Richard Braswell moved to White County by November 16, 1808.[13] Eight days after, on November 24th, he was granted 100 acres on the north side of Calf Killer's Fork of Caney River in the Third District of White County.[14] Richard's youngest brother, John, from South Carolina, joined Richard's family for just a few months in 1809. Then Richard decided to head out for Illinois Territory.

On September 20, 1809, Richard Braswell "of the County of White and State of Tennessee, being about to remove to the Mssissippi Territory" appointed "my true and trusty friend Samuel Usrey of the County of White" his attorney to sell his 100-acre grant.[15] Samuel Ussrey sold the tract to William B. Ussery on May 4, 1811.[16]   White County in 1811 was still very much pioneer country. There were just 511 white polls in the whole county and only two retail stores.[17]

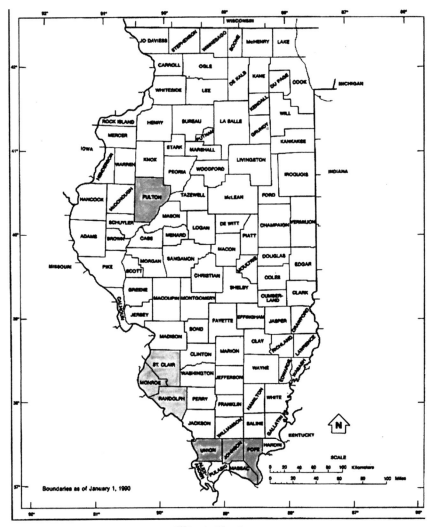

Illinois Territory

RANDOLPH COUNTY, ILLINOIS TERRITORY: 1809-15

One of the earliest records in Randolph County show that Richard Brazil married Mary Ann "Poly" Allen on March 13, 1810.[18] Later that year, Richard Braswell, Senior's clan appears on the Federal Census of 1810, Clear Creek area of Randolph County as:

R (ichard) Brassel   2 under 10 (Valentine and Moses), 1 10-15 (Robert), 1 16-26 (William)
females: one under 10 (Jemima) , 1 45   & over (Jemima, Sr.)

#887 D(ick) Brasel   1:16-26   (Richard) "D"—Dick (the newlywed son of Richard, Sr.)
females: one 16-26. (wife, Mary Ann "Polly" Allen)

#889 G(eorge) Brasel   2 under 10 (Robert, Jesse) 1:26-45 (George)[19]
females: 1 under 10, 1:16-26 (Mary)[20]

Johnson County was created from Randolph County in 1812. Robert Brazil (1796-1841) married Sarah Ann Terry by a peace justice in Johnson County in 1813.

At the same time, a mill located in the western part of the county was known as Brazel's Mill. Someone in the family, maybe William, had become a miller.

THE WAR OF 1812

The major battles in the War of 1812 affected the people of Illinois Territory only from a distance. They were too remote, living hundreds of miles west of Washington in the wilderness when the British attacked and burned the capital. Neither were they personally involved when the British invaded Louisiana. But British prompting of their northwestern Indian allies to raid Illinois white settlements did get their attention. Illinois volunteers were eager to fight the British Indian allies in "The War Against the Six Nations."

Military service records for the war at the National Archives show Privates Richard Brasel and his brother William Brasel enlisted in Captain Owen Evan's Company of Mounted Militia, Illinois Territory, on August 20, 1814, for service against the Indians. They mustered at Johnson Court House. Richard Braswell said he lived six miles from the place of rendezvous.[21]

Arkansas Territory

THE MISSOURI-ARKANSAS BORDER AND LAWRENCE COUNTY, ARKANSAS TERRITORY: 1816-25

The year Mount Tambora exploded in Indonesia and created for North America "the year without a summer" when crops failed, Richard Brazil senior's clan moved again. In 1815, Richard left Johnson County, Illinois Territory, for the headwaters of Fourche de Thomas Creek in Missouri Territory near the Arkansas border. They didn't stay long. These pioneers squatted on land they farmed because there was no Federal Land Office in which to stake their claim.[22] Grandpa Valentine had set the example.

Richard Braswell was by now semi-literate and settled upon his surname spelling. He chose *Brazil,* a name still worn by about ten percent of the Reverend Robert Bracewell's descendants. No one knows when or how the original "s" sound hardened to "z." Pronunciation of *Brazil* shifted to "sound like the South American country" in my branch about 1890.

RICHARD BRAZIL FOUNDED THE OLDEST BAPTIST CHURCH IN ARKANSAS

OLDEST SITE—The Rev. L. C. Tedford, left, North Little Rock, chairman of the Arkansas Baptist Historical Commission, and the Rev. H. W. Johnston, missionary of Current River Association, are shown standing at the site of the oldest Baptist Church constituted in 1818 when Arkansas was a territory. The site of Salem Baptist Church in Jarrett Community, Randolph county, is marked by a huge stone of Batesville marble weighing 3,000 pounds, which was set up by the commission recently. Mr. Tedford is pastor of Grace Baptist Church, North Little Rock.

Monument to Salem Baptist Church[23]

By late 1818, Richard Brazil senior co-founded Salem Baptist Church, on Fourche de Thomas Creek in Jarrett community, Lawrence County, Arkansas Territory. In Missouri's Bethel Association Minutes an entry for September 26, 1818, read "Letter from Salem Church on Thomas Creek in Lawrence County, constituted that year, was received which upon being found orthodox was received by the moderator giving their delegates the right hand of fellowship and their names ordered to be entered into the minutes." The minutes noted that Salem's delegates were Benjamin Clark, Jesse James and Richard Brazil. The church originally had only twelve members.

In the Minutes for 1819, Union Church was represented by Jesse James, Richard Brazil, and R. Brazil with fourteen members. In the Minutes for 1820, Union Church was represented by Richard Brazil and Willis Wilson with ten baptized, four received by letter, and twenty-seven members in total.[24]

Squire Allen tarried in Lawrence County long enough at least in 1820 for Richard's next-youngest son, Moses Brazil, about seventeen, to marry Squire's daughter, Matilda Allen, aged fifteen. {See *The Allen's*, Chapter 6}

The Brazil Community in Lawrence County was in Current River township about eight miles southeast of the church. Among other buildings in the community were the Brazil farms and William Brazil's mill.

As always on the frontier, road building continued non-stop. An early Lawrence County circuit court record dated June 5, 1821, noted :
It appearing from a petition of sundry inhabitants of Brazil Settlement that a road leading from William Brazil's Mill to Davidsonville to pass by John Shoemaker's mill will be of public utility. Ordered the same be established and that John Shumake, Richard Brazil and Moses Simpson be appointed to view and mark out said road.

Six months later, January 14, 1822, the court changed its mind:
It appearing to the satisfaction of the court that the road leading from Davidsonville to goforth's ferry on Current River will be of public utility, it is ordered that the same be established and that the road leading to Brazil's mill from Davidsonville be disannulled.

In another road-building issue, on May 13, 1822, a Lawrence County record said

Richard Brazil, a Justice of the Peace, is appointed to lay off the road on the north side of Current River into road districts or road divisions and apportion the hands that are to work on said divisions.

However, it wasn't always drudgery on the frontier. The settlers around Fourche de Thomas celebrated the forty-fifth anniversary of the signing of the Declaration of Independence on July 4, 1821, with a big barbecue. "A liberty pole, taller than the trees, was erected. The pole stood for many years and became a noted landmark. A military parade was staged. "[25]

And death was always close by. Rachael Price and Robert Brazil, bonded on July 13, 1822, and tasked to be administrators for Samuel Price, "deceased, late a citizen of Lawrence County and township of Current River, died without making any last will and testament." Preston Goforth and Richard Brazil also signed the document.

Yet another family death record, Basil Boren's, followed Richard Brazil's family into Arkansas. He was Richard's daughter, Peggy's late husband. The elder Basil Boren was born 1758 in Orange County, North Carolina, son of Charles and Mary Boren. The younger Basil was born in Robertson County, Tennessee, and died in 1812 in Johnson County, Illinois. Lawrence records mentioned a "Bazel A. Boran, deceased." The bond of Peggy Boran and Reuben Rice administrators, dated January 21, 1825, stated, "there are six children" born to this marriage. Valentine Brazel, constable, was allowed $2.00 from Boren's estate as was Daniel Boyles who received $1.00.[26]

The rest of Richard Brazil's family moved to Pulaski County during the 1820's. By the time of the 1830 federal census, only Richard Brazil, Junior remained in Lawrence County. His family:

Richard Brazil   males 2:5-9, 1:10-14, 1:15-19, 1:30-39
                 females 3 under 5, 2:10-14, 1:30-39

Richard Brazil, Jr., named peace justice in Lawrence County on November 5, 1831, stayed in office until he resigned on November 12, 1833. He then moved to Pulaski County to be with the rest of his extended family.[27]

PULASKI COUNTY, ARKANSAS: 1825-35

"In 1820, Robert Brazil, Valentine Brazil, and Samuel Williams settled about this year near present Benton, Arkansas. They were among the first dozen white families in Saline County. ". . .When the first settlers came to Saline. . . . the terrain was covered by pine and oak. Here in the cool green depths of the forest, the friendliest of all Southern Indian tribes, the Quapawa, were living. The woods abounded in whitetail deer, occasional bear, buffalo, lynx, and multitudes of small, fur-bearing game. Here, too, the wild turkey roamed in flocks and each fall and winter the waterfowl frequented the deeper pools of the river, and of course, the streams furnished an abundance of fish for a relief from the monotonous meat diet."[28]

The Richard Brazil, Senior family moved to Pulaski County about 1825. They took with them two small children, perhaps orphans of William Brazil.

Their church was named Union Church: "Union Church in Saline County was the second oldest in Saline—Kentucky Church was slightly older. Union Church was organized in 1830 by Elder Jesse Bland. He and Silas Dodd organized it at Bland's house with eight original members. In 1835, a log church house was erected." Moses Brazil was a delegate to the Arkansas Baptist associational meetings from Union Church during the 1840's.[29]

1830 Federal Census of Pulaski County, Arkansas[30]

Robert Brazil	Males 2 under 5, 1:5-9, 2:10-14, l:30-39
	2 under 5, l:5-9, 1:30-39 (p.236)
Peter Alby	Males 1:10-14, 1:30-39
	l under 5, l:10-14, 1:30-39
Richard Brazil	Males 1:10-14, 1:60-69
	1:5-9, l:50-59
Carlton Lindsey	Males 2 under 5, 1:30-39
	1:5-9, l:20-29
Valentine Brazil	Males l under 5, 1:20-29
	2 under 5, 1:5-9, 1:20-29 (p. 239)

Richard Brazil and Valentine Brazil were appointed magistrates of Pulaski County on November 5, 1831.[31]

In 1833, Pulaski County made an inventory of its citizens' real and personal property: [32]

That same year, Brazils and other pioneers petitioned Congress for 'Squatter's Rights" and won. Their plea:

A petition to Congress by Inhabitants of the Territory which was referred December 19, 1833, to the Committee on the Public Lands—

"Your petitioners respectfully request that your honorable body pass a GENERAL PRE-EMPTION LAW, granting the right of preemption to all persons who are now settled, or may hereafter settle, on any of the unappropriated public lands of the United States and that every person . . . . be authorized to file with the Register of the Land District . . . . that the person receive from the Register a certificate authorizing such location or settlement, and that the person, previous to the same being offered at public land, at the *minimum* price of the public lands, a quantity of land not exceeding one hundred and sixty acres . . . .

Your petitioners would farther represent, in their opinion, a law on the plan proposed by them would have a tendency to put down those pestilential speculators who have stalked over the Territory of Arkansas, carrying privation, vexation, and distress, to the laboring class of the community, for the last eighteen years, and who have uniformly taken protection under the tail of loose ended laws which merely invited the laboring class to a benefit, but really made them a tantalus in favor of speculation. Your petitioners consider those unfair speculators, in a moral sense, as mere drones in the hive of nature. They produce nothing. They neither assist in forming the hive, nor in collecting the honey. They merely live to devour, by arrogating undue advantage to themselves. . . .

Your petitioners would farther represent, that the public debt of the United States being already in effect extinguished and the revenue of the nation amply sufficient to meet the ordinary annual expenditures of the Government, and to furnish a surplus to be divided among the several States and Territories, they can see no reasonable objection to the passage of the law prayed for. . . .All they ask is, that their improvement may be certain of obtaining indisputable titles for them, by paying the purchase money into the Land-office whenever the contiguous lands shall be brought into market. This would relieve the inquietude of their minds, and stimulate them to make valuable and permanent improvements, and comfortable habitations for their families, which they are now deterred from doing in consequence of the uncertain nature by which they hold them under the present law. "

Section One of subscriber signatures included Richard, Robert, Moses, John, and Valentine Brazil.[33]

On June 19, 1836, Robert Brazil was named a Justice of the Peace in Pulaski County.[34]

RICHARD BRAZIL HELPED FOUND BENTON, ARKANSAS

Richard Brazil's family weren't shy about using their influence as pioneers of Saline County. The county records show that on December 28, 1835, results of the county election held this date electing one each from the three county districts were from Brazil Township in northern Saline County, Richard Brazil, Junior; from Saline Township, John L. Lockhart; and from Davis Township, Resin Davis were chosen. These three were named as a commission to locate the county seat. They became founders of Benton, Arkansas. Moses Brazil, Sr. helped survey the original town plat of Benton.[35]

Following that, in Saline County's first election, Thomas Huchingson was elected county judge, Samuel V. Caldwell clerk, Valentine Brazil sheriff, A. Carrick surveyor, and Caleb Lindsey coroner. [36]

In its issue of June 7, 1836, the *Arkansas Gazette* described the new town of Benton, pointing out that it lay twenty-five miles southwest of Little Rock and that "the great road leading from Missouri to the Red river passes directly through the center of town." It was called the Military Road that ran from Missouri through Little Rock to the Texas border.

CHEROKEE INDIAN TROUBLE

Trouble erupted between whites and Indians on the western Arkansas border and Indian Territory, now Oklahoma. On August 12, 1836, a mass meeting was held in Benton in response to a call from the Governor based on a proclamation by Andrew Jackson, President of the United States, asking for volunteers to go to the aid of beleaguered white settlers. After Charles A. Caldwell made an impassioned speech, forty-six Saline contains stepped up quickly and signed the enlistment roll. Within a few days, they had reached Washington, Arkansas, under the command of Captain Valentine Brazil of Saline County.[37]

After they quelled the Indians, on October 1, 1838, Richard Brazil, Jr., sold a stallion named "Spectator" and a chestnut sorrel about sixteen hands tall for eighty acres four miles from Benton. Richard wasn't the only racing fan. As early as 1838 Benton had a jockey club and a race track. The entry fees for horse races ranged from $20 to $50 each, depending upon the classifications set up by the club.[38]

THE DEATHS OF RICHARD AND JEMIMA BRAZIL

The 1840 Federal Census came around and Richard Brazil, Senior, appeared as:

> Richard Brazil, Sr.   males 1:10-14, 1:20-29, 1:80-89
> females 1:70-79

Jemima White Brazil died not long after the 1840 census. Richard, Sr. then married the widow Jane Biles Carpenter in Saline County on September 22, 1841.[39]   Not long after his marriage to Jane Carpenter, Richard Brazil died. His name no longer appeared on Saline County records after 1841.

CAPTAIN VALENTINE BRAZIL (1765-1848)

Valentine's daughter, Mary Ann "Polly" Brazil, married Andre St. Jean in St. Clair County, Illinois Territory, on January 9, 1806,[40] the first Braswell family record west of Tennessee. Andre was born near Rouen, France, in 1744. He arrived in New Orleans in 1760 and in 1765, was sent to St. Louis as an agent for a French fur company. He traded with many Indian tribes to the headwaters of the Missouri River and west to the Rockies.

Andre St. Jean married an Indian woman in 1775. With her, he fathered Robert and Joseph St. Jean. Andrew could speak seventeen Indian dialects. At the outbreak of the American Revolution, Andre became a scout and interpreter for the French. He was stationed at Fort Dearborn. He is said to have carried an important letter from Kaskaskia to the Governor in Quebec.

After the war, he married Polly Brazil when he was sixty-two and she was seventeen. He was naturalized an American in 1816. In 1826, Andre moved his family from Madison County to a place near Springfield. Ten years later, in 1836, he moved to Buckeye Township, Stephenson County, Illinois, where he died in 1849, aged 105 years. His wife, Polly Brazil St. John, moved to JoDaviess County to be near her late father, Valentine Braswell, where she died on February 22, 1851.[41] She barely outlived him.

Valentine applied for 320 acres on August 29, 1807, saying that he had occupied that land before March 3rd. The Land was on the east side of Silver Creek joining Looking Glass Prairie with Robert Brazil on the north and William Brazil on the south.

Besides being a military leader, like his brothers, Valentine was also a Baptist spiritual leader. For example, on October 9, 1807, Valentine and Robert were Messengers from Richland Church to the Illinois Association of Baptists. Then on June 17, 1809, Valentine with Robert and William Brazle were Messengers from their newly formed "Looking Glass Prairie Church."[42]

As long as he was able, Valentine Brazil led the local militia. On July 4, 1809, Valentine was a captain in the Second Regiment, St. Clair County militia. On February 7, 1812, Captain "Brazeal" signed a petition, "Resolutions of the Officers of St. Clair County," addressed to the governor and complained "that with pain we look back at the many depredations committed by Indians, on our frontier Inhabitants, by stealing horses to a very considerable amount, plundering of the property, and by the massacre of many of the inhabitants. . . .our frontier to continue {as usual} unprotected & as much exposed as ever to Indian violence. . . ." Thus began the "War Against the Six Nations."[43]

Valentine stayed active in Illinois Territory militia affairs after 1812. He, along with his son, Richard, and brothers William and Robert Braswell, served in William Jones' Company of Volunteer Infantry, Illinois Territory, in the War of 1812. Then in 1814, he joined Captain Jacob Short's company of United States Mounted Rangers against the Indians. He served a full year. [44]

In 1816, Valentine Brazil and Thomas Higgins purchased land and built a log house. It was the first house erected in Ramsey Township, Fayette County, Illinois Territory.[45]

In April 1824, Valentine Brazil married second the widow Nancy Journey.[46] His pious Baptist neighbors considered it scandalous that he lived with Nancy before marriage but Valentine didn't seem to care. Valentine ran for county commissioner in Fayette County in 1824 and 1826.[47] By 1830, Valentine was in Fulton County where he lived near his nephew, Moses Brazil, and his brother William. In 1837, he sold out in Fulton County. By 1839, Valentine was in JoDaviess County, Illinois, where he died intestate on May 9, 1848.[48]

REVEREND ROBERT BRAZIL (1773-1825)

Robert married Isabelle Lester in Greenville District, South Carolina, on January 31, 1797. Of his ten children, the fifth, born in 1805, he named Isabelle. We recognize her now because her Bible tells us much about on our family in early Illinois. Isabelle married William Steele in Madison County, Illinois, on August 19, 1822.[49]

The Harps in Tennessee murdered his brother James on that awful day in July 1799, when only Robert managed to escape the killers.

Unlike his brothers, Robert did not leave Madison County, Illinois. He was even more active than his brothers were in Baptist church affairs. For example, in 1807, he met with two others and wrote the constitution of the "Arm of the Baptist Church of Christ at New Design." A year later, the church now called "the Richland Church" and he and his brother, Valentine, were messengers for it to the Illinois Association of Baptists. Robert functioned as an ordained minister, the one sent to "Supply the different Churches" when they had no minister. Elder Robert Brazil was ordained to the ministry there in 1808. William Brazil was named a deacon at the same time.

By 1809, Robert and his brothers Valentine and William served as messengers from the newly formed Looking Glass Prairie Church to the Illinois Association of Baptists. Elder Robert Brazel gave the introductory sermon from Second Chronicles, 4th Chapter and part of the third, fourth, and part of fifth verses, "Brother Brazel Moderator proceeded to business and the Association divided asunder and the party desiring to support the General Union of United Baptists" with five churches and seventy-eight members carried on. "We believe it right not to commune with those that have left the General Union at large." [50] The Baptists continued to show their tendency to fragment into new denominations.

Like his brother Valentine, Robert also had his Scotch-Irish fighting side. From March 9 to May 9, 1813, Sergeant Robert Brazel served with his brother William in Captain William Jones' Company in the War of 1812. Then the next year, December 6, 1813, Robert was appointed justice of the peace in Madison County[51] He was appointed again as justice in March 1819.[52]

Robert "Brasele" appeared on the 1820 federal Census for Silver Creek, Madison County, with males—one under 10 (George), two 10-15 (Robert, William), one 16-25 {Actually, Robert—a census taker's mistake} and females—two under 10 (Charlie, Reney), one 10-15 (Isabelle), and one 36-45 (Isabelle Lister Brazle).

In March 1823, Isabelle, Robert's wife, died. Then on May 17, 1825, after an accidental burn, Reverend Robert Brazle also died.[53]

ELDER WILLIAM BRASWELL   (1766-c. 1856)⁵⁴

William Braswell was the true family gadabout. It's fitting that William is buried farther west than any of his brothers. He and his second wife, Elizabeth Medford, lie in a cemetery near Berryville, Carroll County, in far northwest Arkansas.

William married Katherine Lister in Wilkes County, North Carolina, in 1785. He then disappeared for fourteen years. He rejoined his family in 1799 in Knox County, Tennessee, where he signed the petition to have Knox divided to form Anderson County. He co-signed a bond in Anderson County to help his brother Robert Braswell administer their brother-in-law James Butler's estate.⁵⁵ Then four years later, in 1807, William sold his land on Clinch River and moved with his brothers Robert and Valentine to the frontier Goshen Settlement in St. Clair County, Illinois Territory.

William, Robert, and Valentine Brazil all applied for government land on Silver Creek on the same date, October 2, 1807. Along with his brothers, William was very active in the Richland Baptist Church, later renamed Looking Glass Prairie Church. In 1809, he was named an Elder at the same time his brother, Robert, was ordained.

William "walked his talk." In 1818, St. Clair County appointed William Overseer of the Poor. William helped paupers by farming them out to other landowners as paid labor. As late as 1821, he still held that job.

Again with his brothers, William signed up to serve in Captain William Jones' Company of the Volunteer Infantry, Illinois Territory, during the War of 1812.

William Brazel appeared on the 1820 federal Census for Chambers township, St. Clair County, as:

    2 males under 10 (Samuel b. 1811 and Robert b. 1815)
    l male 45 & up (William, b. 1766, 54 years old)
    2 females 10-15 (Isabelle b. 1811 and Nancy b. 1804)
    2 females 16-25 (Jane b. 1800 and Sarah b. 1800)
    1 female 26-45 (Katherine, b. 1775-1794)

William discovered in 1822 that speech from the pulpit isn't the same as speaking in front of neutral witnesses. In a minor court case against

Thomas Flannigan with Robert White as defense witness, William Braswell said publically about White "The damned old perjured rascal—damn him, he has committed perjury and I can prove it - - it is old Robin White."

Robert White then filed a libel suit against William who was tried and found guilty in 1823. William finally surrendered his rich St. Clair County homestead on July 14, 1828, when the sheriff sold the land to pay his fine. Sadly, of all William's healing words, only these remain.

William liked to travel. He went back East to visit his brother John Braswell and other kin in Jackson County, Tennessee. Joshua Chilton, William Braswell's son-in-law, stated that his wife, Nancy Brasel, William's daughter, and he were married in Jackson County on the "1ˢᵗ day of September 1825."[56]

William also stopped off in White County, Tennessee, where he visited his Ussery in-laws who remainder there after his brother, Richard, left in 1809 for Illinois. William's last reminder of his visit to White County, a letter he wrote with the endorsement, "Remaining in the post office at Sparta, Tennessee, on June 29, 1829, which if not taken out before the first day of October will be sent to the general post office as dead letters."

William's son, Samuel, probably met his future wife in White County. She was Phoebe Tabor, born in Tennessee about 1817, daughter of Solomon Tabor, whom Samuel later married on May 20, 1832, in Gasconade, Missouri.

Afterwards, William and another son-in-law, Oliver Brock, moved to Fulton County, Illinois, and settled near his nephew, Moses Brazil, son of his brother Richard Brazil. William bought an eighty-acre tract in 1829. After harvest in 1830, William Braswell and his nephew Moses Brazil left Fulton County.[57] William went southwest into Missouri Territory, where he stayed for a time in Gasconade County. There, on May 20, 1832, his son "Samuel Brasile" married "Feby Tabour."

Later in 1832, William Braswell along with Henry and Robert Tabor settled on War Eagle Creek in Benton County, Arkansas. He stayed there until about 1838 when he moved next door to Carroll County, Arkansas. There he lived out the rest of his long life, dying near age ninety about 1856.

Chapter SIX

MOSES BRAZIL (1803-1872)

Moses Brazil, c. 1860

Born in 1803 in Anderson County, Tennessee, in 1820l Moses Brazil, aged seventeen, married fifteen year-old Matilda Jane Allen, in Lawrence County, Arkansas Territory. They remained in Lawrence County for about five years. Then in 1825, they moved to Fulton County, Illinois.

Matilda Jane Allen (1803-1872), c. 1860

THE ALLENS

According to Lois Hubbard, "The first account of our Allen's, Anthony Allen, was born in Dorsetshire in southern England in 1577. He married Hester Squire and they had four children. "Their oldest son, Ephraim John Allen, was our first American Allen."[2]

Ephriam Allen was born in 1602, and married Deborah Hunt in Somerset, New Jersey, in 1621. He became a member of the New Reformed Dutch Church in Somerset. Ephriam next married Elizabeth and they had at least three children, the oldest being John Annanias Allen born in Somerset. His father, Ephraim John Allen, died in New Jersey in 1651.

John Ananias Allen, Ephriam's son, married Mary in 1664. Their only known child was Annanias, Junior. John Ananias Allen, Sr., died in Orange County, North Carolina.

John Ananias, Junior, was born May 6, 1699, in Somerset and married Hannah Hester in 1724. Their youngest child was Gersham Allan, who was born February 10, 1734, in Orange County, North Carolina. He married Patience Graham on May 12, 1755, in Orange County. Their third child was Squire Allen, born September 12, 1763.

Squire Allen married Matilda Snow in Wilkes County, North Carolina, on August 3, 1789. He was in Pendleton District, South Carolina, by 1790. In the 1800 census, his household included three males under ten and two males ages sixteen to twenty-six with two females under ten and one sixteen to twenty-six. From 1804-08, Squire lived onTrammels Creek in Warren County, Kentucky.

The 1810 federal census found Squire at Wilkersonville, Randolph County, Illinois Territory[3]:

#784 S. Allen's	3 under 10, 3:10-16, 2:26-45	(Jesse, Merril, Alfred, Eleazer, Squire)
	females: 3 under 10, 1:26-45	(Polly, Matilda, Martha T.)
#785 G. Allen	1:45 & up (Gershom Allen, father of Squire Allen), one female 1:45 & up.	

No records exist for Gersham Allen after 1811 in Randolph County.

Squire and Martha "Tilda" Snow Allen appeared on the tax list of Pulaski County in 1819. Then they showed up on the Harden township list for the 1830 census of Conway County, Arkansas as:

Squire Allen	males: 1:10-14, 1:15-19, 1:50-65
	1:50-59, 1 slave
Sarah Giles	males: 1 under 5, 1:5-9, 1:20-29
	1:5-9, 1:10-14, 1:30-39

Sarah later married Richard Brazil, Senior.

On the 1840 Federal Census of Saline County, Squire appeared as:

Esquire Allen	males: 1:70-79
	1: 70-79

One of Squire's sons, Eleazer Allen, sold a forty-acre tract in 1841 to Moses Brazil. Squire Allen, justice of the peace, witnessed the deed along with another of Squire's sons, Jesse Allen.

On November 5, 1842, Squire died intestate in Saline County. Wesley Allen was appointed administrator on November 26th. Later, Richard Brazil, husband to Polly Allen, took Wesley's place and was appointed administrator on January 2, 1843.[4] On April 1, 1844, Richard Brazil sold Moses Brazil three slaves out of the Allen estate appraised at $1,145.00.

Squire's widow, Martha "Tilda" Allen died intestate on October 9, 1843. Moses Brazil, Senior, her son-in-law, was appointed administrator on October 27th. Richard Brazil took over the job as administrator on October 25, 1844, upon giving a $400 bond.[5]

FULTON COUNTY, ILLINOIS: 1825-1830

Moses Brazil took Matilda Allen Brazil from Lawrence County, Arkansas, and with Preston Goforth, went to Fulton County, Illinois, early in 1825. His first record, an entry in the county book of marks and brands, called for " a swallow fork on each ear, an underbit on the right, and an under nick" to identify all his loose livestock.[6]

Moses Brazil was in Lawrence County for the Illinois state census of 1825:

Moses Brassel – one white male 25 & up, one white female.[7]

Moses' land deeds in Fulton County gradually increased his farm size. One parcel was including eighty acres bought from William and Elizabeth Medford. He also attracted other Braswells. Late in 1828, Oliver Brock, husband to Jane Brazle and son-in-law to William Braswell (1766-1856), moved next door to Moses. Moses sold him eighty acres.[8] In the spring of 1830, Moses' uncle, William Braswell, moved there and William sold Oliver Brock, a horse trader, yet another eighty acres.[9]

The Moses Brazil family, there for the 1830 federal census, somehow was missed on the final schedules. These family members did appear:

| Valentine Brazle | males: 1:5-9, 1:50-59 |
| | 1:5-9, 2:10-14, 1:40-49 |

Three other households, then...

William Brazle	males: 1:50-59
	1 under 5, 2:20-29
Oliver Brock	males: 2 under 5, 1:5-9, 1:30-39
	1:5-9, 1:30-39

Just as Moses Brazil led the way into Fulton County, he led the way out. After the 1830 harvest, on September 30, 1830, with Valentine Brasil as a witness, Moses Brassel sold his farm and headed south, back to Arkansas.[10]

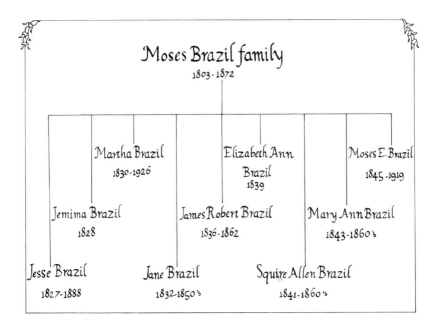

Moses Brazil family
1803-1872

- Jesse Brazil
  1827-1888
- Jemima Brazil
  1828
- Martha Brazil
  1830-1926
- Jane Brazil
  1832-1850's
- James Robert Brazil
  1836-1862
- Elizabeth Ann Brazil
  1839
- Squire Allen Brazil
  1841-1860's
- Mary Ann Brazil
  1843-1860's
- Moses E. Brazil
  1845-1919

SALINE COUNTY, ARKANSAS: 1830-1869

A cabin in abandoned Brazil, Arkansas, 1965

MOSES' BROTHERS BOUGHT LAND
UNDER THE PREEMPTION ACT

Moses' brothers Richard and Robert Brazil bought 160 acres from the federal government under the Preemption Act of 1834. Richard submitted the required statement to prove his eligibility for preemption rights. He said that he was the actual settler on this tract, that in 1833 he cultivated about twenty acres of cotton and corn on it, and that he hewed a dwelling house, kitchen, smoke house, corncrib and stables. He also planted about 300 fruit trees. He was in possession of the tract on June 19, 1834--the date of the Act and "still possesses and cultivates same." His family consists of a wife and seven children.

Richard also said Robert Brazel was an actual settler and occupant in the year 1829 on the northwest part of said tract, that in 1833 Robert had in cultivation about fifteen acres in cotton and corn, that he had two log dwelling houses, a kitchen, smoke house, corn crib, stable, and blacksmith's shop; that Robert was still in possession of same; that Robert " is a married man with a large family consisting of a wife and ten children" and that " he resides at this time on purchased land." Witnesses: near neighbors George James and George S. Terry."[11]

Valentine Brazil and George James bought federal land on April 22, 1836. Valentine signed this statement: "In 1831, he settled on the tract, cultivated same to 1833, when and where he cultivated about four acres of sand in corn and had about 200 peach trees, a good hewed log dwelling house, smoke house, kitchen, corn cribs, and stable; that he had the possession of same on the 19th of June 1834 and still continues to cultivate the same up to this date; that he is a married man, has a wife and a family of five children; that George James cultivated about eight acres of land on the north part of said quarter section in corn and cotton and had a log dwelling house, smoke house, in the year 1833 and in the year 1834 had a horse mill erected; that George James commenced his said improvement in the year 1831 and is still there; that James is a married man and has a family consisting of a wife and six children." Witnesses were "near neighbors," Robert Brazil and Andrew McAlister. No doubt, Moses Brazil developed his own new land in Saline County in the same way.[12]

McAlister, a much-abused Union sympathizer during the Civil War, later received compensation from the U.S. Commissioner for Civil War Claims for his losses during the war.

CHEROKEE INDIAN UNREST

President Andrew Jackson ordered remaining Cherokee Indians to leave the Southeastern United States and move to Oklahoma Territory. The Cherokee "Trail of Tears" passed through Arkansas. When some of the Indians raided pioneer white families in northwestern Arkansas, the Saline County militia was nationalized to help put down their raids.[13]

The company commander, Captain Robert Brazil of Company "B," Saline Volunteers and John Brazil lived in Owen Township, Saline County, west of Benton. His brother, Richard Brazil, and nephew Richard, Jr. lived in northern Brazil Township. The regiment served in eastern Oklahoma. None of the Brazils was injured in this military action.[14]

By the time of the Federal Census of 1840, Saline County was filling up with Brazils— Andrew Jackson, Robert, Moses, Jr., Aaron, Alfred, and Valentine Brazil—and Moses' family:

Moses Brazil	males: 1 under 5, 1:10-14. 1:30-39
	1 under 5, 2:5-9, 1:10-14, 1:30-30
	slaves: 1 male under 10, 1 female 10-24

In 1840, Richard Brazil, Junior, was elected to represent Saline County in the Arkansas Legislature. Interviewed by the *Arkansas Gazette*, he said he was fifty-two and gave his birthplace as Greenville District, South Carolina.[15] Richard's family were divided later over the Civil War, perhaps reflecting his own ambivalence about the war.

On February 7, 1844, Moses Brazil bought slaves from the estate of Squire Allen from Richard Brazil. The slaves were "one Negro woman named 'Meriah' and two Negro children, 'Jefferson' and 'Miner.' Three weeks later, on February 27, 1844, Moses Brazil sold Andrew Jackson Brazil the Negro woman named "Meriah,"about 24 years old, for the token price of five dollars:

For affection I have for the family of my brother, Richard Brazil, I hereby sell to Jackson Brazil, whose real name is Andrew Jackson Brazil, one Negro slave named Meriah. Said slave to be in the trust of Mary Brazil, wife of Richard Brazil, for her sole use and for the use of her children by her present husband, Richard Brazil.

Moses's brothers Valentine and Richard moved from Saline County to Ouachita County, Arkansas, by 1845. Richard, owner of a hotel in Benton, made some losing investments and on August 29, 1843, had to ask George S. Terry and Moses Brazil to pay off a loan to Arkansas Real Estate Bank for $204.82. Valentine, former owner of a grocery store in Benton, lived out the rest of his life in Ouachita County but Richard returned to Saline County and died there in 1860.[16]

Richard Brazil, aged "about 62," of Ouachita County, Arkansas, applied for a bounty land warrant in December 12, 1851, based on his service in the War of 1812 and in the "Indian Disturbance" of 1836. A report from the third Auditor of the U.S. Treasury Department stated that Richard Brasel served in Capt. Owen Evans' company of Illinois Militia from August 20, 1814, to October 19, 1814.   The company was discharged at Johnson County courthouse.

Richard referred to his unit as the "Johnson County Mounted Rangers" in Major General Harrison's Division in the "War Against the Six Nations." He said he served at Fort Masak and that " I would further state that it is very probable that my name was enrolled as Richard Brasil or Braswell as it is by some pronounced."[17]

Moses and Matilda Brazil's children married during this period. Jemima Brazil, Moses' daughter, married in Saline County on February 17, 1845. She died in Saline County during the 1850's.   On April 2, 1845, Jesse Brazil, Moses' son, married Martha Jane Huchingson. Jane Brazil, Moses' daughter, married Mark Miller on March 3, 1850.[18] Jane, like her sister Jemima, also died in the late 1850's. Jane gave Miller three daughters before she died. Squire Allen Brazil married Mary Jane Holland in Saline County on March 27, 1859. Moses Brazil allowed his ward, Jacob Prillaman, 18, to marry Eda Crow, 20, on May 19, 1859.

The census of 1850 expanded the information recorded to include the names of every free person, their age and sex, whether in school if under aged, how employed if over fifteen and how much their property, real and personal, were worth, and their state of birth.[19]

Brazil,	Moses	47 M	Farmer $2500		Tennessee (owned a ten-year old slave boy)
	Matilda	45 F	(married 1820)		Kentucky
	James R.	14 M			Arkansas
	Elizabeth A.	11 F	"		
	Squire A.	9 M	"		
	Mary	7 F	"		
	Moses	5 M	"		
Miller,	Jesse	18 M	Laborer		Georgia
Brazil,	Jesse	23 M	Farmer $300		Illinois
	Martha	20 F	married 1845		Alabama
	Matilda J.	4 F	Arkansas		
	William	3 M	"		
	Mary Frances	1 F	"		
Brazil,	A. Jackson	33 M	Farmer		Missouri
	Nancy A.	30 F	(married 1850)		Arkansas
	William	11 M	(in school)		"
	Richard	9 M			"
	Mary	8 F			"
	Nancy	4 F			"
	Elizabeth	1 F			"
Brazil,	Richard	24 M	Farmer		Illinois (son of Jesse Brasel, Moses' nephew from Union County, Illinois)
	Elizabeth	22 F			Alabama

On August 20, 1853, the Post Office Department appointed Moses Brazil as the first official postmaster at Brazil, Arkansas.[20]

Moses Brazil's store account for Horner James, 1857

The 1860 federal census for Brazil Post Office, Saline County, listed sixty-two families. Of these, fifty-eight were headed by a farmer or farm laborer.

The other four heads were a wagon maker, mechanic, blacksmith, and a physician. Besides the four Moses Brazil families listed below, counted also were Bettis, Richard, and George Washington Brazil, another Brazil cousin from Union County, Illinois:

Brazil Post Office, July 9, 1860

Brazil,	Moses	57 M	Farmer $1200-$4000	Tennessee[21]
	Matilda	55 F		Kentucky
	Moses, Jr.	14 M		Arkansas
	Elizabeth Miller	20 F	{widow of Jasper Miller}	"
	Jesse F. Miller	10/12 m.		"
Brazil,	James B.	23 M	Farmer $200	Arkansas
	Martha	18 F		"
	Thomas (twin)	2 M		"
	Jesse	2M		"
	Moses	4/12 M		"
Bolt,	Thomas	36 M	Farmer $250	Arkansas
	Jemima	31 F		Illinois
	Aaron	13 M		Arkansas
	Moses	12 M		"
	Matilda	10 F		"
	Martha J.	9 F		"
	Mary A.	7 F		"
	Frances M.	5 F		"
	James M.	2 M		"

THE CIVIL WAR, 1861-1865

Like most Southern families, the Moses Brazil family suffered terribly in the Civil War. Moses was too old to bear arms himself but his sons and sons-in-law were the right age. This is a summary of their Civil War service records, beginning with Lieutenant William Brazil, husband of Mary Ann Brazil, daughter of Moses Brazil:

According to his Texas niece, Ida Brazil Bolton, "Wild Bill" Brazil was a Confederate hothead. As the war broke out, he cut off the head of a Union sympathizer. Before the body could be buried, a wild Arkansas razorback ran off with the head. William Brazil enlisted on July 27, 1861, at Benton as a Private in Company "B," 11th Arkansas Infantry commanded by his former brother-in-law, Lt. Colonel Mark Miller. Captured at the surrender of Island Number 10 on April 8, 1862, William was released with the rest of his regiment near Vicksburg, Mississippi, on September 20, 1862. Advanced to the grade of "Senior 2nd Lieutenant" in the new Company "A" by December 2, 1862, William drew his last pay on February 13, 1863.[22]

Lieutenant Brazil drowned in quicksand after he rode out to show his men a river crossing was safe. "Both horse and rider went down with William waving his sword as he sank." His widow, Mary Ann, also died in the war. Their daughter, Matilda, was taken in by her grandparents Moses and Matilda Brazil who brought her to Texas. There she later married Thomas W. Gage. Altogether, said Cousin Ida, Moses and Matilda "reared four sets of Civil War orphans."

Moses' son, James Brazil, enlisted in Company "H" of the 1st Monroe's Arkansas Cavalry at Benton on June 19, 1962. He died December 12, 1862, at the Confederate Hospital at Van Buren, Arkansas.

Moses' daughter Martha Brazil married Thomas Colbert on February 3, 1848. Colbert enlisted in Company "B," 1st (Crawford's) Arkansas Cavalry on August 15, 1863. The only notation in his service record said Thomas "Deserted on retreat from Little Rock, September 14, 1863."[23] Just how he died in the war isn't known. After the war, Martha married Yankee colonel, William Hepple, a German, in Arkansas on January 14, 1866. They lived for many years in Brenham, Texas, among other German-Americans. She died in Dallas, Texas, December 3, 1926.

Benjamin L. Chastain, husband to Elizabeth Ann Brazil and Moses and Matilda's son-in-law, enlisted in Company "B," 25th Arkansas Infantry Regiment, on March 1, 1862, at Little Rock. On April 1, 1862, he was appointed regimental teamster to haul supplies for the regiment. He remained a teamster until he "Deserted about the 15th of July, 1864."

Jacob Prillaman, Jr., a brother to Jane Brazil, wife of Jesse, enlisted as a private in Company "E," 1st (Colquitt's) Arkansas Infantry at Benton on February 20, 1862. The company muster roll for June 30-August 31, 1863, recorded Jake was sent to the hospital at Holly Springs, Mississippi, on May 5, 1862, and "Has not been heard from, supposed to be dead."

It is said that Jacob, like Squire Allen Brazil, died of measles while in Confederate service. According to the late Ida Brazil Bolton, his niece, "Squire died of measles he contracted as a Confederate soldier. He died shortly after returning to his home."

Jesse Brazil's service will be described in the next chapter.[24]

Moses and Matilda Brazil's daughter, Jane Brazil, married Mark S. Miller on March 3, 1850. They had three daughters— Sarah M., born 1850; Oregon C., 1854; and Mary Ann, born 1856. After Jane died late in the 1850's, Mark Miller then married Mariah E. Janes, aged 22, in 1860. Mariah's account of her experiences during the War, including her three stepdaughters-grandchildren of Moses and Matilda Brazil-appears below.

In June 1861, Mark Miller organized a company of state forces at Benton and the troops elected him colonel. Lieutenant William Brazil joined Miller's outfit. Here's Mariah's war story:[25]

At the time the war broke out, I resided in Benton on what was then called the Old Military Road. I resided in a cozy little cottage situated on the Main street of our village. . . .Just the time of the election {for Secession}, I was united in the holy bonds of matrimony to Mark S. Miller who was at that time sheriff of Saline County, afterward Colonel of the Eleventh Arkansas Regiment. He was a widower with three little girls.

The excitement waxed warmer and warmer until in April, the first company of soldiers left our village to go to the field. Then and there did our sufferings commence, to last until the bloody strife was ended..

. . . On the 20th of January, 1862, Colonel Miller returned to his regiment which was then stationed at Island No. 10 on the Mississippi River. On the 8th of March he was captured by Yankee Soldiers and there I received news of his death. I thought I had trouble before but that had not even commenced. Now they broke upon me in such a deluge, it seemed more than I could bear.

My supplies were almost exhausted, and no money with which to replenish them, but Confederate bonds. In July, 1862, I resolved to take boarders and succeeded very well but still there were no clothes nor money to buy them with. Cold weather was forth coming and I had to go to work and make cloth, as well as to provide food. Medicine could hardly be bought at any price. Just imagine paying $12.00 an ounce for quinine and morphine and $5.00 for coffee by the pound. I continued keeping boarders until September. . .I bought two horses and a wagon and rented ten acres of land three miles from town and commenced farming. I had it sown in wheat, and with the assistance of two negro boys, my farm proved quite a success.

The first of October I received a telegram stating that my husband was on his way home. . .and on the 8th of October he arrived home. Just to think of seeing him again whom I had long mourned as dead. It seemed still more like the dead coming to life for he had been quite ill and looked like a walking skeleton. He was very sick on account of which he resigned his office and remained at home until February, 1863. He was again called back. On leaving me he encouraged my farming and I still continued at it by going back and forth twice a week to give my negroes the necessary instructions concerning the crops. In February I commenced making cloth and from the first of the month until the first of September I made 150 yards of cloth and had it made into wearing apparel, which at that time was very valuable. In June my husband was ordered to the north part of the State and again I received word that he was dead, this, however, was soon corrected. The woods were now full of "Bushwhackers" and no one was safe at any time.

On the 4th of July, 1863, a battle was fought at Helena. We heard the cannons like peals of thunder in the distance. . . .the enemy continued to press onward and in September a rumor was sent abroad that Little Rock would either fight for its freedom or fall into the hands of the enemy. About the 10th my husband sent me word to come to him immediately. On receiving the news I mounted my horse (a very fine pacer which had been a present from him in the summer) and started from home at sunrise the next morning accompanied by a negro boy. At half past eleven o'clock I arrived in Little Rock, a distance of twenty-five miles. I met my husband and was with him until three o'clock and the conversation of this interval was like that of a dying man to his wife, advising and instructing me concerning my future way of gaining support for myself and children.

I arrived home at sunset. A series of skirmishes ensued, lasting for three or four days, and at length the Northern Army being too strong for the Southern the latter was forced to retreat. The 12th of September, the retreating army passed through our village and from early morning until about dark my husband's three girls stood at the well all day, giving the poor thirsty soldiers water until the well was entirely dry. My husband and all the Confederate Officers spent the day at my house. About dark, a courier came in great haste to inform them that the Yankees were coming. They carried with them every man in the village save four old gray-haired men who were not able to walk without assistance of their cane. Not a man in town! So the women and children were left to the mercy of the Northern men. I entreated him to take me with him but he said it was too late. He called his mother and sisters to come and stay with me. His mother and sisters came and stayed with me. We were afraid to go to sleep or have a light for fear of attracting the attention of passers-by. We barred the windows and doors and pulled down the curtains to hide the light. We tried to talk but failed for every heart was too full of its own trouble to utter one word. We could not read so we betook ourselves to prayer. But never my tongue refused to move as it did that dreadful night.

Mother said "Hark! What was that?" and as we listened, the heavy trap of feet and the clash of arms broke the silence of the night. My house was surrounded. The next thing we heard was a loud rap at the door and repeated orders to "Open the door or it will be burst in!" I asked mother and sister to go, but it was useless for they both sank back in a dead faint. I went and opened the door, expecting every moment to be shot on the spot. The Federal soldiers rushed in but there are no soldiers in my house and to come in and search if they were in the least bit of doubt. They did not come in, however, any further than the door but asked me a great many questions about the Southern army.

On the fourth morning afterward at the breakfast table, we were speaking of the war and the children and their papa when lo! The door opened and who walked in but that personage himself. He sat down and ate breakfast with us and said he would be home for dinner. After the morning meal was finished he went down to his store on business, and I like all other good housewives do, busied myself with getting a nice dinner. Then about 11 o'clock, my second little girl came running in from the back door, screaming "Oh! Mama, Mama, I see a man riding so fast!" She had not finished this sentence when the oldest daughter came in, almost breathless, saying "Oh! Mama, I see so many men coming with blue coats on!" In less time than it takes to write it, the bullets were flying thick and fast past my door. All the noise of battle was made more hideous by the cries of my children saying "Oh! My papa – don't kill my papa. Don't kill my papa!" My husband mounted his horse in haste and got away. The Federals followed him and his little squad of men two miles until they reached the river. The soldiers came to the bank of the river and seeing that there were only seven men, they turned round and came back to our village and pitched their tents to all parts of my house.

They pulled the pickets off my fence to build fires, killed my chickens, went into my garden and stripped it of vegetables, and no less than twenty-four hours I did not have a vegetable out of the whole garden, nor a chicken out of a hundred except one old hen and two little chickens which stayed under my kitchen. I fed them through the cracks in the floor for three months. They killed my hogs and dressed them right before my eyes, and then asked me if I would not like a piece of fresh pork but this kind offer I declined. Last but not least, they carried their ridicule so far as to plant the Federal flag over my house, and I am a Confederate Colonel's wife. They took possession of my barn, turned out my cow out, and used everything just as they liked.

I bore it patiently as long as possible and then, following out the advice of my husband, I went to see the commanding officer, and telling him that I was a Mason's wife, I asked his protection and he asked me if I wanted guards? I replied that I did. When the guards came, they looked like savages indeed. I gave them seats scarcely knowing what to do or say. Pretty soon one of my little girls came in and they said "Sissy, what is your name?" The poor child was frightened so badly she could not speak, for she had a mortal dread of the blue coats. They sat in silence a few moments, then asked if they could go to their camps and their supper and feed their horses. It must have taken quite a while to do this, for in the whole stay of three months that the troops made their stay here I never say my guards any more, but I was never bothered by the soldiers any more.

Things passed on just the same for about a week when there arose quite an excitement in the camps of the soldiers. We learned they were expecting an attack from the Confederates. One evening we were sitting around our fireside when we heard heavy feet without and found it to be reinforcement of several thousand men. Thus the blue coats became more numerous than ever. The officers were going to take my residence for a hospital when an unknown friend stepped out from an oak tree and said "Take your sick down to the other end of town to the Church, which is now used as a hospital, and if you desire better quarters for your men, take them to the hotel. No sick shall be taken in that house. It is a private residence." The next day he came to my house and mad himself known: he proved to be a cousin that had been in Benton ever since the first soldiers arrived.

The soldiers commenced foraging and taking everything in their reach for miles and miles around, and I could see all the fruits of my farm labors melt like snow in the sun. Starvation seemed to be staring me in the face. I had raised about fifteen bushels of corn which they confiscated for their own use. I went to the officer in command and entreated him "for mercy sake" to let me have two loads of corn. He was very kind and had two very large wagon loads of corn hauled and thrown into one of my bedrooms.

When the fresh troops arrived, I had about fifty bushels of corn and five hundred bales of fodder in my barn to feed my stock on through the winter. They used all of this for their own purposes. I went to the Colonel again and asked him to pay me something for what the men had used. He gave me an order for thirty dollars, payable at the headquarters of the troops in Little Rock. But I had no horse nor any other way of getting there, so I asked him for some means of conveyance which he granted.

I arrived in Little Rock, went and drew my money and spent the night with an aunt. The next morning I did my trading and as soon as possible, got a permit to pass the picket lines and started for home.

Things went on very smooth until about the last of October (1863) when my provisions were again decreasing and I did not know what to do. So I resolved to do what my husband had advised me to do, take some of the officers to board. But the greatest obstacle to overcome was to get them.

So one evening a sick man came and wanted to know if he could get board for a little while. He proved to be Captain Cherry of the Missouri regiment. He stayed two weeks and recovered his health entirely then left. He recommended me so highly that in a few days I had from twelve to fifteen boarders of the best class, and from that time henceforward, I had boarders and had no more trouble about provisions.

Colonel Caldwell, the new local commander, was now joined to my number of boarders. When they would go out on a scouting expedition he would say, "We will bring Colonel Miller in with us and you can put him in a cage, and keep him in the house like a bird." Or "Oh we will make the Rebs nip the dust" meaning he would kill them. I was always tormented in this manner but bore it as patiently as possible. Then the (Southern) deserters commenced to join the northern army, and were sworn in and enlisted in their number. After they were sworn and enlisted they would go to the clothing store and get their blue uniforms, then strut up the street as exalted in their estimation as General Grant. There would be twenty to fifty join every day. The hillsides were covered with people who had not so much as a tent or a change of clothes in their possession. They distress and sufferings were indescribable. . . .

On the evening of the 20th (December, 1863) there was a terrible excitement and they commenced moving out in the direction of Little Rock. The infantry all left the cavalry and claimed that the latter were going to remain. About midnight the cavalry set fire to all their ammunition for fear the Confederate soldiers would reap some benefit from it. The roar of the cannon balls and the explosions of the cartridges one after the other fairly made the earth shake. By three o'clock in the morning all the soldiers had dispersed save a few stragglers who remained bent on mischief. They tried to set the town on fire in places. I woke my little children up, dressed them, and put them one at each corner of my house and stood at the other corner myself to prevent them from setting it on fire. It was attempted twice between three o'clock and daylight. We stood guard until it became light, then all the vagabonds had mysteriously disappeared. After they all went away, the women and children of the town went to their camps and found everything but money—kraut, meat, crackers, coffee, sugar and all kinds of cooking utensils and dishes. These things were highly appreciated by everyone. There was a man who had thirteen bales of cotton which the soldiers took to make their beds of. The women and children took as much as they wanted and still there was a great deal left.

The weather was very disagreeable when on the 29th of December on Sunday morning, we were all very much frightened by the arrival of a posse of men in blue uniforms. We did not know whether they were Rebels or Yankees, but come to find out they were bushwhackers. About 12 o'clock they went around and set fire to the deserted winter quarters. We were surrounded by flames that looked like they reached the skies. The cries for water were terrible. Women were filling every little vessel with water. It looked like the Almighty hand of God was our only aid in this hour of trouble, for it was perfectly calm and the flames wound themselves heavenward until they disappeared in space. It there had been the slightest breeze there would not have been a vestige of this town left and it would have been difficult to save our lives exclusive of anything else for the whole town was encircled in flames. The flames burnt for two days until a rain put them out.

Time passed quietly and gloomily on until the tenth of January, 1864, when a courier arrived with a letter from my husband, stating that he was very ill and if I ever wanted to see him alive again to come at once. He was at that time in Camden, Arkansas, about 125 miles from where I was. I had a lady friend whose husband was in the same place as mine so I went to her house and fortunate for both of us both, she had a little mule which was so small the soldiers would not have it and I succeeded in finding a little pony equally as small. So the third morning we were ready to start. We had a little boy to drive us and we both took our little girls which at that time were about two years old. I reached Camden. On the 24th of January, he was taken sick with a chill. I sent for a doctor and on his arrival he pronounced it to be congestion chill. He never recovered from this attack, notwithstanding all the tender care and good medical aid that could be procured. After lingering for three days he died on the 27th of January, 1864.

Texas

BASTROP COUNTY, TEXAS: 1869

Moses and Matilda Brazil's family suffered other frightful losses in the war: the loss of much of their property through the conversion of their money to worthless Confederate notes; their Brazil Store plundered; two of their four sons and one son-in-law killed; their eldest son permanently crippled; and a revolution in their old society that toppled them from their former social position, putting others in control. Everything changed.

The Brazil Post Office was closed June 22, 1866, and reopened September 26,1876, with Wiley B. Fowler as postmaster. Fowler served until June 5, 1895. The post office was permanently closed on August31, 1924.[26]

Elizabeth Brazil Fowler, daughter of Richard and Jemima, finally moved from Ripley County, Missouri, to Saline County. In 1840, Elizabeth moved to Perry County where she lived up to her death in 1873. Their son, Wylie B. Fowler, was born in Ripley County on February 3, 1818. He became the second postmaster of Brazil, Arkansas.[27]

On February 15, 1864, George Washington Brazil enlisted in the 4th Arkansas Federal Infantry. When he enlisted, he gave his age as forty-five and said he was born in Johnson County, Illinois. He wasn't alone. Many other Arkansas men including other Brazils enlisted in Federal regiments after 1863. George and wife Keziah "of Marion County, Illinois" who worked for Moses Brazil before the war and owned a small cotton farm, now sold his sixty-three acres in Saline County on April 29, 1867, and went back to Illinois.

Moses Brazil filed claim #21516 with the U.S. Commissioner of Civil War Claims for $1385 for "commissary and quartermaster stores" stolen from him during the war. The Commissioner denied the claim because Moses clearly backed the Confederacy. National Archives personnel could not find his original claim.

After deciding to move to Texas, starting on October 29, 1869, the Brazils began liquidating their Saline County holdings. Moses and Matilda Brazil sold William Dyer the 80-acre tract that included their homestead. According to a local historian, "Their home was erected in 1830 by Mr Brazil and most of the work was done by slaves who occupied the second story. It was a two-story log house in Holland Township."[28] Moses and Matilda Brazil also sold their Brazil Store to William Dyer.

They sold another property to their daughter, Elizabeth Ann Chastain, wife of Benjamin Chastain. Jesse Brazil " of Bastrop County, Texas," sold William Grummett his last tract containing forty acres. Five days later, on November 7, 1869, Moses and Matilda Brazil sold J.N. Chastain their last piece of land.

The rest of Moses Brazil's "Gone to Texas" caravan included Jesse Brazil's four oldest children by his late first wife, Martha Jane Huchingson; Jesse's wife, Eliza Brazil; their eight year-old daughter, Martha and four year-old son, Jesse Calvin Brazil; the four sets of orphans from the Civil War; and a freed slave, Rose, Jane's former maid servant, who wanted to stay with the family and try her luck in Texas.

Moses Brazil, Jr. was in charge of driving the family hogs from Arkansas to Texas. Once he came upon a water pool full of water moccasins. His sisters screamed but the fearless hogs dove in. The sows grabbed each end of the snakes and pulled them apart, devouring them.[29]

The Brazil caravan arrived in Texas in time for the 1870 census. The census taker counted the people on Barton's Creek in Bastrop County on August 6, 1870.[30]

Jesse Brazil	44 M	Farmer	Illinois
Jane	35 F	Keeping house	Tennessee
M.F.	20 F		Arkansas
Elizabeth	19 F		"
Jesse	10 M		Texas
Martha	7 F		"
Laura Ida	1 F		"
George Townsend	23 M		Arkansas
Moses Brazil	67 M	At Home	Kentucky
Matilda	67 F	Keep. House	Kentucky
Cordelia	16 F		Arkansas
M.E.	13 F		"
Jesse	12 M		"
H.T.	10 F		"
R.P.	8 M		"
Moses Brazil	24 M.	Farmer $200	Arkansas
William C.	21 M		"

On August 9, 1870, Jesse and Moses Brazil bought a one hundred-acre tract "situated partly in Fayette and Bastrop counties about fifteen miles west of the town of La Grange" or about five miles southwest of Smithville on Barton's Creek. The seller, Nancy Jane Sawyer, and the price, $1500.[31]

SAWYER CEMETERY, 1872

After having gone out one cold night to take care of a farrowing sow, Matilda caught a cold which progressed to pneumonia. She died on February 4, 1872. Only two months later, on April 3, 1872, Moses Brazil, Senior, died of influenza "and grief" according to his grandchildren.[32]

Moses and Matilda Brazil lie buried in the Sawyer Cemetery overlooking Barton Creek, part of their original one hundred-acre Texas farm. Their grandson Richard Allen Brazil insisted they had headstones. The stones aren't visible anymore in this abandoned cemetery but could be covered with tree litter or perhaps taken later by others for farm use. Several graves have no stones. Five marked Sawyer gravestones can still be read: the oldest, patriarch Robert Sawyer (1816-1894) and wife. The markers of the Smiths--Nancy (1832-1901) and George (1848-1895) and "Baby Turner" are the only ones still marked.

The cemetery is located on the R & R Ranch, three miles down Zapalac Road, about five miles south of Smithville, Texas, on Texas Highway 95. The owner in 1970 was Vince Rawl of 11800 Silkwood Cove, Austin, Texas.

The closeness of Sawyers to the Brazils is suggested by the 1880 Bastrop census which show Robert Sawyer living next door to his son Dan whose Arkansas-born wife, Oregon, was the orphan of Sarah Brazil Miller of Brazil, Arkansas. Oregon Sawyer knew how to midwife and in 1896, helped Sarah Gage Brazil give birth to Etheridge Brazil, my father.

PROBATE PAPERS

Since Moses Brazil died intestate, Jesse Brazil, as eldest son, became administrator of his father's estate on December 7, 1872. On May 6, 1873, the appraisal of Moses Brazil, deceased's estate took place:

Fifty acres of land at $15 per acre $750
One bay horse, fifteen years old $75
One dun horse, ten years old $60
One sorrel colt, two years old $50

Seven head of stock $35
Seven head of hogs $21
Household and kitchen furniture $100
for a total of $1091

Moses Brazil, Jr. was later bonded as administrator. On February 9, 1874, Moses Brazil, Junior, sold Jesse Brazil his half interest in the 100 acres above mentioned for $400 in gold.[32]

TWO OF MOSES BRAZIL'S CHILDREN:

Martha Brazil Hepple (1830-1926)

MARTHA BRAZIL HEPPEL
(April 29, 1830-December 3, 1926)

Etheridge Brazil knew her in old age : "She always had her face powdered, her hair combed. She was very stylish and aristocratic in her bearing. She was good humored. In her old age, she drank sienna tea for some malady."[33]

Moses Brazil, Jr. with wife, Martha Gage, c.1905

MOSES BRAZIL, JUNIOR
(December 28, 1845- January 28, 1919)

Etheridge Brazil described Moses as "six feet tall, ruddy complexion, red hair. He was hit by a baseball in youth, which caused Moses a permanent stooped posture. However, it did give him exemption from the Confederate draft." Moses Brazil's probate papers, Case #522, are filed in San Saba County and dated February 10, 1919.[34]

MARTHA ELLEN "Marty" GAGE BRAZIL

"Marty had brown hair, grey eyes, fair complexion, and a small build. She was a kind, loving, and supportive woman, a beautiful, giving person. Always in good humor, Marty loved all her kin.

Marty was a constant Baptist churchgoer, first at the High Valley Baptist Church then at the church in San Saba. She even attended church the Sunday before she died. Marty had a strong intellect and was a good expositor of the Bible. Very practical and level-headed, Marty helped anyone in need."

Moses Brazil left Chappel around 1903 and bought a small farm on the San Saba River near San Saba town. He then sold it and bought a livery stable, a business he had learned in Brazil, Arkansas. His livery stable provided fresh horses for travelers.[35]

Chapter SEVEN
JESSE BRAZIL (1827-1888)

Jesse Brazil in a tuxedo later painted over his Confederate uniform, c. 1863

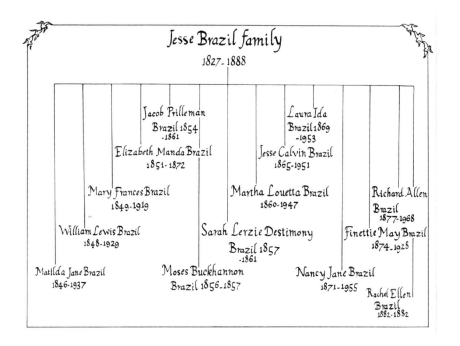

Jesse Brazil family
1827-1888

Jacob Prilleman Brazil 1854 -1861

Elizabeth Manda Brazil 1851-1872

Laura Ida Brazil 1869 -1953

Jesse Calvin Brazil 1865-1951

Mary Frances Brazil 1849-1919

Martha Louetta Brazil 1860-1947

Richard Allen Brazil 1877-1968

William Lewis Brazil 1848-1929

Sarah Lerzie Destimony Brazil 1857 -1861

Finettie May Brazil 1874-1928

Matilda Jane Brazil 1846-1937

Moses Buckhannon Brazil 1856-1857

Nancy Jane Brazil 1871-1955

Rachel Ellen Brazil 1882-1882

Jesse Brazil was born April 5, 1827, in Fulton County, Illinois. When he was three, his parents, Moses and Matilda Brazil, moved him to northern Saline County, Arkansas. There, three days before his eighteenth birthday, on April 2, 1845, he married Martha Jane Huchingson.1

THE HUCHINGSONS

Martha Jane, born August 25, 1828, in St. Clair County, Alabama, the daughter of John Grover Huchingson, born in Georgia about 1800 and married her mother, Jane, in Alabama in 1823. Jane Huchingson was born in North Carolina about 1802 and died in Saline County on July 25, 1860. Her father, John G. Huchingson, died between 1854 and 1860.

The Hutchinson's were wealthy, influential cotton planters. Martha's grandfather, Joseph J. Huchingson (1768-1855) was elected Saline County's first county judge in 1835?. He already owned ten slaves by 1830. Judge Huchingson married Mary Story (1771-1854) in Georgia in 1790.

Jesse Brazil's first daughter, Matilda Jane Brazil, was born on March 28, 1846. Matilda was followed by William Lewis Brazil on June 22, 1848, and Mary Frances Brazil on October 9, 1849. The family appeared on the 1850 Federal Census of Saline County, Arkansas, as:

Jesse Brazil	23 M	Farmer $300	Illinois
Martha	20 F	(married 1845)	Alabama
Matilda J.	4 F		Arkansas
William	3 M		"
Mary Frances	1 F		"

Jesse's third daughter, Elizabeth Manda, arrived on January 22, 1851. She married Ellis Massey in Fayette County, Texas, on November 30, 1871, and died there the following January 20, 1872, of measles, complicated by pregnancy.

On March 18, 1852, Jesse Brazil's first wife, Martha, died in childbed with their fifth child, a stillborn, in Saline County.3

JESSE BRAZIL MARRIED ELIZA JANE PRILLAMAN

Two years after Martha Huchingson Brazil's death, Jesse Brazil married eighteen-year old Eliza Jane Prillaman in Saline County on February 5, 1854.4 Their first child, Jacob Prillaman Brazil, arrived on December 15, 1854. According to Laura Brazil, Jacob died after falling from a tree on Big Sandy River in Texas on August 15, 1861, as they looked for a safe haven away from the growing threat of civil war.

Jesse and Jane's next child, Moses Buchanan Brazil, came October 15, 1856. He died in infancy on February 10, 1857. Jesse decided to move to Perry County not long before Moses Buchanan died. On January 1, 1857, he and his wife, Jane, sold John Barron twenty-one acres on the Saline River in Saline County for $800. Sarah Lerzie Desdemona Brazil, was born in Perry County on December 19, 1857. She died of a childhood disease on Big Sandy River, Texas, on August 6, 1861, the week before Jacob Brazil fell from his tree. Jane Brazil thus lost two children within one week. Jesse Brazil "of the county of Perry" decided to return to Maumelle Creek in Pulaski County. He bought an 120-acre tract from Susan Patterson of Pulaski County on August 30, 1858.5

Beginning October 21, 1859, Jesse stood in for his wife, Jane, in Cause #41 in the Saline County Chancery Court. The "Complainants" were Jacob Prillaman, Junior, and his sister, Eliza Jane Prillaman Brazil. Robinson Prillaman (1824-1863), Jane's half-brother, defended himself on the equitable settlement of the estate of Jacob Prillaman, Senior, namely the disputed ownership of slaves "Luke and Mary," two properties of the estate.

Robinson as executor had sold the slaves at auction to himself for $600 each. Chancellor Clendinen found for the complainants and ordered that the $1200 should be deducted from the estate and added to the complainants' 1/8 portion of the estate residue, that is, 1/8 of $7171.22 plus $600 each or $1496.46. Since Jane had already received $1,005.15 from the estate, she was awarded, through her husband, $491.31. Jacob Prillaman, Junior's full share was awarded to his guardian, Moses Brazil, until he turned twenty-one. Robinson Prillaman was obliged to pay all attorney and court costs. [6]

Meanwhile, Jesse continued to add more land to his farm. He bought 120 acres from D.P. Rainwaters in Maumelle on March 10, 1860.[7] Then on March 4, 1861, Jesse bought thirty acres from the estate of E.H. Patterson, and part of a tract of 400 acres that was "was purchased by Susan Patterson by her paying the residue of a certain Mortgage to Jesse Brazil which was on said lands." He purchased another fifty acres for $400 on January 7, 1862, from his brother-in-law, Jacob Prillaman, in Saline County.[8]

When the 1860 census taker came arrived, Jesse and his brother Squire Allen Brazil still lived in Maumelle Township, Pulaski County:

Squire Allen Brazil	19 M	Farmer	Arkansas
Mary Jane	16 F		Mississippi
Jesse Brazil	32 M	Farmer	Illinois
Jane	25 F		Arkansas
Matilda	13 F	(in school)	"

William	12 M	"
Francis	10 F	"
Elizabeth	9 F	"
Jacob	6 M	"
Sarah	3 F	"

Contrary to today's notion, fewer than five percent of Southerners could afford to own a slave. The 1860 Slave Schedule indicated that Jesse owned a fifteen-year old female mullato, Jane's wedding present from her brother. Her name was "Rose" and she went with the Brazils to Texas after the Civil War. Later, Rose married another ex-slave in Smithville, Texas.

The last of Jesse's children to be born on Maumelle Creek, Martha Luretta Brazil, arrived on October 19, 1860. She married William B. Wall at Bend, San Saba County, Texas and died at the home of her daughter Ella in Calvert, Texas, on December 7, 1947. Both are buried in the Powers Chapel Cemetery near Rosebud. Texas.

Confederate Dead

THE CIVIL WAR

In September 1862, the Confederate Congress extended the draft age from eighteen to forty-five making eligible for the draft thirty-five year old Jesse Brazil.

In 1863, Federal troops gained their principal objective in the West, the control of the Mississippi River. Grant besieged Vicksburg, the last Confederate stronghold on the river in May. On July 4, 1863, in a final desperate attempt to divert part of Grant's troops away from Vicksburg, Southern regiments launched a costly attack on Helena, Arkansas. They were driven off and Vicksburg surrendered on the same day. The Federal army in Helena began a drive toward Little Rock in August. Outnumbering and outflanking the Southern defenders under General Sterling Price, the Federals took the capital on September 10, 1863.

In 1863, the Confederate state government of Arkansas moved southwest to Washington, Arkansas. Early in 1864, pro-Union delegates from twenty-three counties met at Little Rock and drew up a Unionist constitution. There were thus two civil governments in Arkansas during the later years of the war. The dividing line roughly followed the Arkansas River.[9] Even as early as April 2, 1863, well before the capital fell, one could already hear the skirmishes between Union and Confederate forces in Pulaski County on the road between Little Rock and Benton.[10] It was high time for Jesse Brazil to move his family to Texas, away from the fighting.

Jesse chose a safe place north of Dallas at Prairie Point in Collin County, Texas. In addition, faced with being drafted as a foot soldier, Jesse chose to enlist in Company "I," Stone's, later Chisum's 2nd Partisan Rangers,[11] a cavalry regiment recruited from the Dallas area. He enlisted as "J. Braziel," the name on his tombstone. No record shows when he enlisted but it was probably in Spring, 1863.

Horses and leather were scarce in the South by the second year of the war. "Eliza Jane cut her hair to make a halter rope for Jesse's horse as he went off to war." Someone stole the horse but according to his daughters, Laura and Jane Brazil,[12] authorities recovered it later and returned the horse to Jesse because it was easy to identify it from the hair rope. Latter in the war, Bushwhackers tried to take Jane's horse while she was outside doing the laundry. She pulled up a sheet out of the boiling pot and drove them off with a hot sheet on a broomstick.

Jane, brought up a planter's daughter, never did field hand labor before the war yet she had to farm to keep herself and her children from starving. Nevertheless, Jane did have a good knowledge of herbal medicine so she traded her information on home remedies for help from other women with her farm chores.13

Special Orders #67 came down from Confederate headquarters on April 24, 1863, ordering
"The officer in command of Stone's regiment Partisan Rangers will immediately take up his line of march for Louisiana, via Crockett, Nacogdoches, and San Augustine. On approaching the Sabine River he will send forward to Alexandria couriers to report to Lieut. Gen. Kirby Smith for orders." [14]

Private Brazil took part in the march. He also caught malaria in Louisiana. He was given sick leave to return to Texas and while on leave, Eliza Jane conceived her first Texas-born child, Jesse Calvin Brazil, born on January 3, 1865. The two major battles in the Red River Campaign, the fights at Mansfield and Pleasant Hill, took place on April 8th and 9th, 1864. That was about the time Jesse Calvin was conceived so we don't know whether Private Brazil took part in those battles. Nearly ninety years later, Jesse's son, Richard, remembered only that he was wounded fighting federal gunboats and that he repaired shoes for comrades who were still left to fight.

Louisiana was obviously an unhealthy place in those days. On August 8, 1863, Alex Crain, Jesse's comrade in Stone's regiment, wrote his wife from western Louisiana on August 8, 1863:

. . . .I still keep well but there is a great deal of sickness in Camp & a great many Deaths   the Yankies have all left the country and I am glad of it for I want to leave this sickly country and get out where it is healthy. . . .I would be glad to get a Letter from home   never wanted to here from home so bad in my life   if this war would Stop I would be the hapist man in the wourld and so would a great many more   our regment is all tore to peaces. . . .a Soldier may fight ever day and he will not get any thanks for it   we are treated verry bad   nothing to eat half our time..[15]

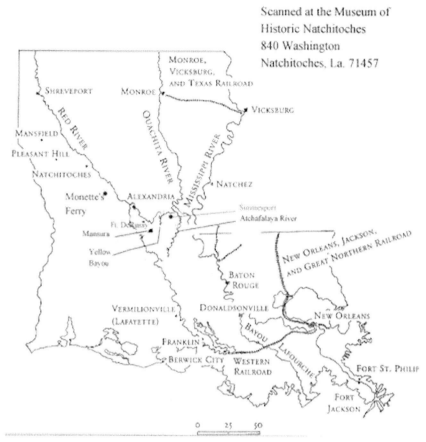

The Red River Campaign, 1864

OPERATIONS AGAINST BANKS' RED RIVER CAMPAIGN, MAY 1, 4-5, 1864: THE FIGHT AT DAVID'S FERRY

After federal General Banks' defeat at the Battle of Mansfield and his near-disaster at Pleasant Hill, he ordered his army to Grand Encore on the Red River, there to board ship and escape the Confederates.

The engagement at David's Ferry, upstream from Yellow Bayou, was the only recorded contact between Admiral Porter's gunboats and Jesse's regiment. General Major filed this report on the action at David's Ferry and Grand Encore:

On May 1, the brigade was ordered to Wilson's Landing, on Red River. On arriving I learned that the enemy were constantly passing in transports and gun-boats. Before we could get the artillery in position a transport came by. She was captured after an exciting chase of 2 miles by Chisum's regiment and the Arizona scouts. Her captain and crew were sent to the rear and the boat (the Emma) burned.

On May 3, the City Belle was captured and a portion of the One Hundred and twentieth Ohio Regiment on board was captured. Colonel Hardeman was present with a portion of his brigade. They did all the firing with small-arms. I cannot speak too highly of the splendid practice of West's battery, under Lieutenant Yoist. The second shot from the Parrott rifle entered the boiler, when the enemy began jumping overboard.

On May 4, Colonel Hardeman's brigade was placed to support Lieutenant Yoist's section, Chisum's regiment remaining also. On May 5, the enemy were reported coming down with 2 gun-boats and a transport. Colonel Hardeman being absent sick the brigadier-general commanding left me in command of the forces on the river. The enemy passed the upper section after being roughly handled by the artillery and small arms. The transport came ahead and received the first shot from Lieutenant Lyne's section, which disabled her. The gun-boats then opened fire, and being armed with two 30-pounder Parrott guns, the two 12-pounder Dahlgren guns, four 24-pounder howitzers on one (the Signal, No. 8), and the armament of the other being nearly the same, some idea may be gathered of the hot fire our one Parrott gun had to undergo and of the accuracy of her gunner who brought them both to a standstill.

Getting behind the bend they began a furious cannonade of our guns. I ordered Colonel Madison, who was on the extreme left, to move up opposite the gun-boats and open fire with his Enfields. The order was promptly and gallantly obeyed, thus drawing a portion of the fire. I sent an order to Lieutenant-Colonel Hampton that if his left was secure and no other gun-boats in sight to send down Lieutenant Yoist with the Parrott gun and we would capture the boats.

I soon had the pleasure of hearing the gun open above us on the enemy, who had to take shelter from the gun below. Lieut. W.H. Lyne asked permission to move his piece up and open on the transport that was sheltered by a bend on the left bank of the river. She surrendered after a few shots.

The enemy finding that they were assaulted from above and below anchored the Signal No. 8 so as to present her broadside to the section below, and the Covington moved up {and} engaged Lieutenant Yoist, who was keeping up a steady, unerring fire. A courier from the pickets below brought word of the approach of another gun-boat, and the booming of her guns announced her near approach. It was evident that we must work fast. I ordered Major Saufley, commanding Lane's regiment, to move up opposite the gun-boats and close their port-holes, if possible.

A portion of Chisum's regiment arrived about this time, having run on foot from the upper section and joined in the hour. I had the pleasure of seeing the smoke issuing from the Covington, and she was soon wrapped in flames, her crew escaping to the opposite side of the river under a hot fire from our Enfields. The Signal No. 8, still continued the contest, no doubt relying on the assistance from the boat below. Lieutenant Lyne soon sent the advancing boat down the river badly crippled.

The Signal still continued the fight. The fire having reached the guns and shells of the Covington, they kept up a continuous roar. This deceived the enemy below, who again came up to the attack and was a second time driven back. All of our forces now attacked the Signal. The men moved up to the bank of the river and closed her port-holes, when she surrendered. None of the crew of the Covington were captured and only a portion of the armament of the Signal, a quantity of ammunition and some of her stores.[16]

Including the *Emma* and the *City Belle*, General Banks and Admiral Porter had lost in five days three transports, two gunboats, and some 600 soldiers and seamen, "all at little cost to the Confederates."[17] Maybe at little cost to the Confederates but it was a big sacrifice for Private Brazil, seriously wounded by the shrapnel.

General Sherman's march to the sea campaign happened at the same time as the Red River Campaign and captured the attention of historians as well as Civil War buffs. Yet Banks' Red River disaster prolonged the war at least several more months because it diverted federal resources away from the East.

After more engagements in Louisiana and Arkansas, the 2nd Texas Rangers regiment returned to Texas. Because of his injuries, Private Jesse Brazil was reassigned to the Confederate Shoe Shop at Taylor where he repaired shoes for his regiment. A note dated April 7, 1865, in the Federal Archives states that "J. Braziel" was listed on a brigade report for "I" Company, with the notation, "absent enlisted men accounted for--Shoe Shop at Taylor Standing Order No 52"[18]

Two months later, on June 2, 1865, all Confederate troops in Texas surrendered at Galveston. Jesse was tempted to join other ex-Confederates and move his family to South America to avoid Union rule.[19]

GONE TO TEXAS

On March 10, 1866, Jesse sold his fifty-acre farm on Pilot Grove Creek in Collin County, Texas, and went back to Saline County. [20] He hoped to resume his life in Arkansas after the war but conditions in that state and his damaged health caused him to seek a drier climate: Texas. Three years later, in 1869, Jesse, his father, Moses Brazil, and all their whole caravan of Civil War orphans and refugees left Arkansas for Bastrop County, Texas.[21]

Laura Ida Brazil arrived in Bastrop County, Texas, on January 6, 1869. Laura's first appearance on the census schedules:

The Federal Census of August 6, 1870, for Bastrop County, Texas--

Jesse Brazil	44 M	Farmer	Illinois
Jane	35 F	Keeping house	Tennessee
M.F.	20 F		Arkansas
Elizabeth	19 F		"
Jesse	10 M		"
Martha	7 F		"
Laura Ida	1 F		Texas
George Townsend	23 M	Laborer	Arkansas

Jesse returned to Arkansas to take hot bath treatments at Hot Springs to relieve his rheumatism but without permanent relief.

Nancy Jane Brazil was born in Bastrop County on May 11, 1871. She died in Hamilton County on August 12, 1955. Nancy's younger sister, Finettie May Brazil, arrived at Chappel, San Saba County, on December 12, 1874. Finettie's was Jesse and Eliza Jane's only birth recorded by the Texas Reconstruction government.[22] The first syllable of Nancy's birth name dropped off through children's usage. Later they just called her "Nettie." She died in San Antonio on December 13, 1928.

Jesse moved his family from Bastrop County to San Saba County to be with his younger brother, Moses Brazil, and to get away from certain kinfolks, Blacks, and Catholic "foreigners." He also wanted cheaper land. Jesse Brazil bought his first farm in San Saba County, 113 acres on Cherokee Creek, on January 13, 1875. Witness: his friend, W.W. Millican.

JESSE BRAZIL RODE THE CHISUM TRAIL

Jesse took part in at least one cattle drive up the Chisum Trail. Chisum preferred ex-Confederate cavalrymen because they were already experienced horsemen and used to danger. On one drive, Jesse and his crew met up with a band of starving Indians in Oklahoma Territory. The Indians begged for food and threatened violence if they didn't get it. The cowboys cut out an old cow who looked like she wouldn't make it to Kansas anyway and gave it to them. The starving Indians fell on the poor beast with their hunting knives and devoured her, insides and all. One squaw was happy to have the cow's raw liver which she sprinkled with gall. Another cracked its bones to get the marrow.

Uncle Richard Brazil told of another incident in which Jesse got the best of a traveling con man. The con man's game: ask for overnight lodging for a dollar. Next morning, he would produce a $100 bill which most farmers couldn't cash. He visited Jesse's home and tried the same trick on him. Much to his surprise, after rummaging around in his hiding places, Jesse came up with the change and kept the $100 bill!

JESSE BRAZIL HELPED FOUND HIGH VALLEY CHURCH

Pastor J.R. Miller, Deacon Moses Brazil, and Deacon Jesse and wife, Eliza Jane Brazil, were among the nine founding members on October 29, 1876, who started the Cherokee Baptist Church. Chapel, Texas, was a Methodist community with no Baptist church. Jesse saved money for seven years to buy lumber for a new plank house but he gave the money to build the new church instead. When the original church was rebuilt in 1907, most of the same lumber was reused.

High Valley Baptist Church

From a simple beginning with only nine souls in 1876, the church grew to a membership of more than one hundred by 1885 and remained a sizeable rural church until World War I. After the war, its membership dwindled, mirroring the population shift from rural to urban areas that characterized the twentieth century. The name of the church changed from Cherokee to High Valley Baptist Church in 1890 because Baptists in Cherokee, Texas, now needed the name.

J.R. Miller held the pastorate from 1876 until 1887. Following that year, there followed a procession of pastors, none of whom stayed no more than a year or so because of the meager salary the church offered. Rev. Jesse Calvin Brazil held the pastorate from 1908 to 1910.[23]

The year after they started the church, on February 19, 1877, Jesse's son Richard Allen Brazil was born at Chappel. He married Zera Beatrice Sullivan at San Saba on July 16, 1910. She died at Temple, Texas, on November 11, 1957.   Richard also died there in the care of his nurse daughters on April 8, 1968.

Richard Allen Brazil (1877-1968)

The John Wesley Sullivan family
(bottom row—John, Sarah Frances, "Pick" Sullivan; top row—Mary
Etta, Zelma Elizabeth, Zera Beatrice, Gertrude, and Louella Sullivan)

The census of 1880, San Saba County, Texas, listed [24]

Brazil,	Jesse	53 M	Farmer	Il.-Ky.-Mo.
	Eliza	44 F	Blind[25]	Tn.-Va.-Tn.
	Jesse	15 M		Tx.-Il.-Tn.
	Laura	11 F	Blind	"
	Jane	9 F		"
	Nettie J.	5 F		'
	Richard	3 M		'
Brazil,	Moses	34 M	Farmer	Ar.-Tn.-Mo.
	Martha	24 F		Tx.-Ar.-Ar.
	Ida L.	3 F		Tx.-Ar.-Tx.
	Willie	4 1/2 (mo)F		"

Eliza Jane and Jesse Brazil, c. 1880, San Saba County, Texas

The enamel paint on this picture cracked with time

Rachael Ellen Brazil, Jesse's eleventh and last child, was born in Chappel on September 25, 1882, but died four days later, on September 29.

Appointed to a committee at High Valley Baptist Church in 1885, Jesse Brazil was asked to investigate charges against a member for "falsehood and intoxication." A family story said Jesse himself also was called down by the church for helping Abe Walden cut his grain one summer Sunday to save it from an approaching storm. Jesse didn't apologize but got angry and swore that he would do the same thing again if called on "When a man's ox is in the ditch," quoting from the Bible.[26]

On October 17, 1885, church officials brought up expulsion charges against William Wall. After some discussion, they upheld his dismissal. Then "Sister M. L. Wall requested a letter of dismissal for herself." The following month, she read this note before the church: "I renounce Christian fellowship with Seth Moore {the man who had brought the charges against her husband}, J.R. Miller, the Elders, and the Brazils." It was signed by Martha L. Wall. Later the Walls moved to Hearne, Texas. According to Joanne Aman, who is married to a Wall descendant, "William Wall fatally shot his brother-in-law for continuing to abuse Wall's sister even after several warnings." She also stated that " Lou {Martha Brazil Wall} went blind before her children were grown and needed help from the eldest in rearing the younger ones".[27]

Appointed a committee on February 19, 1888, Brothers J.T. Teague and S.M. Moore were to visit Brother Jesse Brazil " to learn if the church could do anything for him in the way of breaking land for a crop. . . ." His final illness had begun. Jesse was confined to his bed for nine months before his death. "His joints were swollen terrible and he got awful thin and was helpless."[28]

While Jesse lay dying, one of his daughters, Laura, went up on the hill, known locally as "Brazil Mountain," and prayed for his recovery. When she came down, he scolded her for wishing to prolong his suffering and said that he only wished to die. On July 18, 1888, he got his wish. Jesse Brazil died "of rheumatoid arthritis caused by his Civil War malaria."[29]

Ida Brazil Bolton who was eleven years old at the time of his death said of Jesse, "Uncle Jesse was a fine, good man. He loved his home and he taught his children to love God. He suffered a long time with rheumatism but he was so patient. . . .as well as I can remember he was about Dick's {Richard Allen Brazil} size, had a long red beard, auburn hair, and blue eyes."[30]

Eliza Jane and Laura Brazil, c. 1890

On August 1, 1892, before a lawyer, Eliza Jane Brazil stated that her late husband died intestate on July 18, 1888, and listed his living children:

Martha Wall	age 32	wife of William Wall
Jesse C. Brazil	age 27	married
Laura Brazil	age 23	single
Jane Brazil	age 21	single
Nettie Brazil	age 17	single
Richard Brazil	age 15	single

The deceased's "children by another marriage":

Matilda J. Stafford	age 45
William L. Brazil	age 44
Mary Frances Millican	age 43

Eliza Jane was appointed administrator.
The appraisers' report:[31]

481 acres on the Colorado River	$1000.00
Three horses	100.00
16 Head of cattle	80.00
4 hogs	6.00

	$1186.00

Jesse died at his Colorado River place but asked to be buried beside his infant daughter Rachel in the plot that was only a few yards away from his first homestead in San Saba County. According to Etheridge Brazil, they removed the caskets of Jesse Brazil and Rachel Ellen Brazil in 1907 and reburied them in High Valley Baptist Cemetery alongside his wife's remains.

JESSE'S CHILDREN BY MARTHA JANE HUCHINGSON

The Family of widow Matilda Brazil Stafford (1846-1937)

The tallest boy may be Valentine Stafford

MATILDA BRAZIL STAFFORD

Matilda was a brunette in youth. She was widowed young. Blind in later life, "she was not a pleasant person" according to Etheridge Brazil. For instance, she criticized Evelyn Price Brazil's 1920's makeup, saying about her lipstick, "Your mouth is painted up just like an Indian!" All the Huchingson children could be caustic. "Tildy" was not popular. She was cold and quick to anger.

Tilda's children were Valentine Stafford or "Vol; "   Carl, "who just disappeared;" Earl or "Bud," his mother's favorite; and Ella, who married William Gage, Etheridge's spiritual mentor.

However, "Tildy" was a practicing Christian. For example, she bought the first carbide house lights for High Valley Baptist Church.[32]

William Lewis Brazil (1848-1929)

WILLIAM "Billy" BRAZIL

Etheridge Brazil described his Uncle Billy as "A very active, quick-witted, small, wiry man of average intelligence. He married Catholic Rachel Tiffany. Billy had a good sense of humor. For example, he gently teased pregnant Abby about 'how short her apron was gettin' to be."

Billy frequently visited the Calvin Brazils. He preferred Calvin to his own sisters. He had two children, James "Jimmy" and Elizabeth "Lizzy."

Rachel died first, her will leaving the bulk of her property to Jimmy and his children. William died eight years later, leaving his estate to Lizzy and her children. Someone contested his will but the Bastrop County Probate Court rejected it.1

Like the other Huchingson Brazils, Billy was quick to express his opinions. He loved kids, was always supportive of them and very generous. Billy had the reputation of a hard worker but not very religious, perhaps his way of getting along with his ex-Catholic wife.

Mary Frances Millican (1849-1919) with children and grandchildren

MARY FRANCES MILLICAN

"She was very motherly" according to Etheridge Brazil. They lived about 500 yards from the Methodist camp meeting grounds, which was across the creek from Jesse Brazil's first place on Cherokee Creek.   For a child wanting to see her, she had dogs and vicious biting geese that made visiting her like running a gauntlet.

Etheridge described Mary Frances as "a sparse-built woman, she was stooped in old age and Bill {William Millican} walked with a cane. Fanny stood only about five feet tall, had dark hair but was fairer complexioned than Billy. She converted to Methodism, her husband's religion. A person of average intelligence, she was soft-spoken and happy to defer to her husband. She was very devoted to him and their children."

CHAPTER EIGHT
THE PRILLAMANS

Unlike Jesse's first wife, a respected Huchingson, the Prillaman's were new to Saline County. Nonetheless, they were acceptable to the Brazils because they were Baptist and had money. Jacob Prillaman and Moses Brazil owned land near each other. Prillaman Springs fed a small creek that flowed through Moses Brazil's hamlet, Brazil, Arkansas. Jacob Prillaman, Senior, married Sarah Terry Brazil, widow of Captain Robert Brazil, in 1852. In 1854, twenty-six year old Jesse Brazil courted and married Eliza Jane Prillaman, eighteen.

THE IMMIGRANT

Jacob Bruellmann, the Prillaman immigrant ancestor and Eliza's great-grandfather, was christened at Evangelisch Kirche Amriswil, Canton Thurgau, Switzerland, on February 4, 1720.1 In 1747, Jacob Bruellman immigrated from Lohn, Schaffhauser, Switzerland, to Philadelphia. His entry on the ship's log read "Lohn: Brullmann, Jacob. Mit W. und K., nach Pennsykvanien."2 Hans Jacob Brulman arrived on the ship *Lydia* on September 24, 1747, bound from London to Philadelphia.3 Jacob settled in Maryland.

Jacob Prillaman sold his hundred acres in Conegocheague, Frederick County, Maryland by March 5, 1763, and three months later on June 13th sold another one hundred fifteen acres, in preparation for moving to Virginia. He paid L2 and L2.6.0 respectively in "Alien fines." 4 Jacob's first land transaction in what became Franklin County, Virginia, happened on May 28, 1772. " Jacob Brilliman" (his German *B* pronounced as *P*) bought 160 acres on Mill Run of Blackwater River.5 Jacob Prillaman, Senior, and sons, Jacob, Junior, and John continued to work hard and pay their taxes.6

The will of Jacob, Senior, signed July 19, 1796, was probated the following September in Franklin County, Virginia. In it he disposed of over 1,000 acres in Franklin and Montgomery counties:

*"...to my daughter Anne Sowder also to my son John Prillaman I give a survey of 160 acres which lieth on daniels run below my son Jacob Prillamans line...also 50 acres adjoining....Lands to my said {son} John Prillaman. . .on his paying thirty Pounds good trade equal to money to my Daughter Barbara Martin two years after my decease and also to furnish my sd. wife with a good warm dwelling house also plenty of good Suitable Diet Clothing washing and firewood and all other necessary attendance During her natural life. . . ."*7

JOHN PRILLAMAN, SON OF JACOB AND WALBURGA PRILLAMAN

John Prillaman, born about 1754, came to Virginia with his father Jacob. In 1782, John paid taxes in Henry County along with his father and brother. He appeared on the first tax list for newly created Franklin County in 1785. He was assessed on three head of cattle and eleven stud horses. A prosperous farmer, John added to his livestock holdings every year.

No one knows the name of John's first wife. He probably married her after the family came to Virginia for their first child wasn't born until about 1781. After the death of his first wife, John Prillaman married Lucy Wilson whom he married in Franklin County, about July 30, 1810, the date of their marriage bond. Lucy was born about June 1768, in Nelson County, Virginia, and died December 1, 1853, "aged 85 years 6 months." She may have been a widow when she married John Prillaman for Minor Wilks married a Lucy Walker in Franklin County on June 23, 1797, likely the same woman.

John Prillaman wrote his will October 18, 1838:

In the name of God Amen, I John Prillaman of the County of Franklin, being far advanced in years, and knowing that by course of nature I am not to remain long in this life, do make and ordain this to be my last Will and testament. In the first place to my Daughter Catharine who intermarried with John Dennis, and to my Daughter Anny who intermarried with Henry Hickman, I give them severally, nothing but what they have already received; to my son Jacob I give the sum of Sixty Seven Dollars, to be paid to him in money by my son Abraham which will make with what he has hitherfore received, the sum of about five hundred dollars and no more. To my Daughter Elizabeth who intermarried with Moses Fuller, I give the sum of four hundred dollars to be paid to her by my son Abraham, and no more. To my son Isaac I give all my land on the South side of the Long hollow Ridge, the Summit of the ridge to be the dividing line between him and the land herein after devised to my son Abraham and my daughter Susannah, to my said son Isaac and his heirs forever. To my son, Abraham & to my Daughter Susannah jointly I give the Tract of Land on which I now live, and if my said Daughter Susannah should marry or die before my son Abraham, then the entire tract to become the sole property of my son Abraham and his heirs forever, my said son Abraham to see my said Daughter Susannah supported and maintained during her life. To my present wife Lucy, I give one negro boy named Nelson, to be absolute property, and to be disposed of as she may think proper. I also give to my said wife Lucy another negro boy named Dick, during her life, and after her death I give the said negro Dick to my son Abraham. To my daughter Susannah I also give my negro boys Peter and Andrew, and my negro girl named Phebe, and the future increase of the said Phebe, during the life of my said Daughter Susannah, and after her death I give the said negro boys Peter and Andrew, and the said negro girl Phebe and her future increase to my son Abraham. I likewise give all my stock and perishable property to my wife Lucy and my son Abraham and my Daughter Susannah for their support.

I appoint my son Abraham Prillaman, sole Executor of this my last will and Testament. In Witness whereof I have hereunto set my hand and seal this nineteenth day of October in the year of Christ 1838. 8

John (X) Prillaman

"A gravestone in the Prillaman Cemetery at Callaway, Virginia, where old Jacob is buried is marked 'J. P. – 1842' and may mark his grave." 9

JACOB PRILLAMAN

Jacob Prillaman, son of John Prillaman by his first wife, was born in 1783 in Franklin County, Virginia. Family records owned by W.A. Prillaman show he left Virginia in the 1820's and went to Tennessee then later to Arkansas. About 1825, Jacob Prillaman settled in Rhea County, Tennessee, where he appeared on the 1830 census. His sister Barbara and her husband Henry Hickman had moved to Rhea County also and were living near Jacob on that census.

Jacob's first wife was Elizabeth Grayson whom he married about 1806 in Virginia. She was the daughter of William and Rachel (Cooley) Grayson of Montgomery County, Virginia. In 1801, William Grayson mentioned her in his will as unmarried. Rachel Grayson cited Elizabeth in her 1842 will as "the heir of my deceased daughter Elizabeth Prillman." On August 24, 1824, Jacob Prillaman and Elizabeth his wife of Franklin County, Virginia, were parties to an agreement dividing the estate of Reuben Grayson.

As shown by census and court records, Elizabeth and Jacob Prillaman had ten children. Jacob's first eight or nine children were born in Virginia, probably in Patrick or Floyd counties. The tenth child was born in 1829 in Rhea County, Tennessee. In 1830, his first wife died there.

Jacob Prillaman bought a tract in the Hiwassee District of Rhea County, Tennessee, on August 15, 1826, for $3,000. Then on August 1, 1829, Jacob donated three acres ". . .for the use and benefit of the old Unighted Baptist Church of Christ and for the purpose of building a meeting house thereon to be known by the name of Good Hope Meetinghouse...."10

1830 Federal Census of Rhea County, Tennessee, counted:

Jacob Priliman   owned 4 slaves

Henry Hickman   male 20-29   {husband to Barbara Prillaman}
                                      female 20-29

J.W. Germen   males: 2: 5-9.   1:40-49;
                                      1: 5-9, 1:10-14, 1:30-39[11]

After J.W. Gorman died, Jacob married next Gorman's widow, Desdemona Gorman. Their marriage license was issued on September 23, 1833.[12] Desdemona Gorman, born January 2, 1803, in Newport, Tennessee, was the daughter of John Gorman (1783-1847) and Mary Sandusky (1785-1842).[14] By his second wife Jacob had two children, one born in 1835 in Tennessee and the other born in 1839 in Arkansas.

In the summer of 1835, Jacob left for Arkansas. On the journey, riding a flatboat down the Cumberland River near Nashville, their first child, Eliza Jane Prillaman, was born. In Arkansas that fall, the family settled in Hot Springs County, Arkansas. Desdemona died there in 1840, aged 36.

Jacob moved from Hot Springs to neighboring Saline County in 1842 and settled near the Brazil community. He purchased property which included many good fields as well as a "mountain" or hillock which to this day is still called "Prillaman Mountain" even though no Prillaman has lived in Saline County for more than eighty years. From the base of this mountain flows a cold mountain spring. Around this spring the village of Brazil, Arkansas, was built before 1850. The remains of the village are located about three miles southwest of Paron but are now covered by a pond that dams Prillaman Springs.

Federal Census of 1840, Hot Spring County, Arkansas:

Jacob Prilleman   males: 1 under 5, 1 10-14, 1 15-19, 1 50-59
                    1 5-9, 1 10-14, 1 15-19, 6 slaves

After Jacob Prillaman moved to Saline County, on October 29, 1842, he married his third wife, Sarah Brazil. She was the widow of Captain Robert Brazil, one of the first settlers of Saline County. Sarah, born in 1799 in Kentucky, came with two children, Stephen and Robert Brazil. Jacob and Sarah had no children of their own.

Prillaman Springs near Paron, Arkansas, 1965

Federal Census of 1850, Saline County, Arkansas, revealed:

Prilleman,	Jacob	67 M		Virginia
	Sarah	51 F	married 1842	Kentucky
	Eliza J.	16 F		Tennessee
	Jacob	11 M		Alabama
Brazil,	Stephen	16 M		Arkansas
	Robert	13 M		"

Nine slaves: one each of females aged 48, 26, 7, and 2; males, 35, 28 (mullato), 25, 8 (mullato), and 4.¹⁵

Jacob, Senior, lived in Saline County for the next ten years. He died intestate on November 20, 1852, aged about 70. The Saline Probate

Court divided his estate equally among his children in Arkansas. He had previously given one of his house slaves meant for Eliza Jane Prillaman, his daughter, as a wedding gift. Jacob owned nearly a dozen slaves when he went to Saline County. His widow, Sarah Ann, later remarried to a Mr. Giles. She died on November 18, 1855.

Eliza Prillaman Brazil kept up with her Prillaman relatives after she moved to Texas. One of her children, Richard Allen Brazil, said "Sterling Bolen, Elizabeth Prillaman's husband, was killed in the Civil War. His widow never remarried. She came to visit Eliza Jane Brazil, her sister, in San Saba County, during the 1880's or 90's. Elizabeth lived out her life in Falls County, Texas, with her son, Jacob."[16]

Jacob Prillaman, Jr. in Confederate vest, c.1862

Eliza Prillaman Brazil's favorite among her Prillaman relatives was her younger brother, Jacob, Jr.   Jacob J. Prillaman's Confederate service record said he enlisted as a Private in Company "E," First (Colquitt's) Arkansas Infantry, at Benton on February 20, 1862, for two years' service.   Marked "absent sick" on the rolls for August 31 to October 31, 1862, on the roll for June 30 to August 31, 1863, the record noted "Dropped from Roll by order Col. Colquitt. Sent to Hospital 5 May 62. Has not been heard from, supposed to be dead."[15]

CHAPTER NINE
REVEREND JESSE CALVIN BRAZIL (1865-1951)

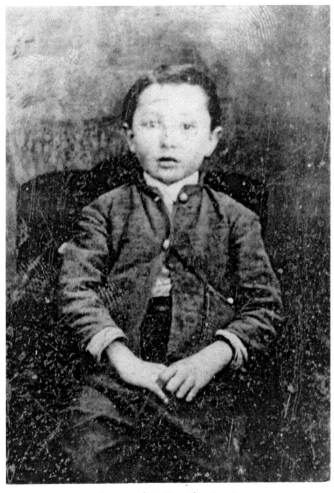

Jesse Calvin Brazil, c.1870

TOUGH TIMES IN RECONSTRUCTION TEXAS

Born on January 3, 1865, at Prairie Point, Collin County, Texas, Jesse Calvin Brazil was nicknamed "Old Furlough" by his step-siblings because he was conceived when his father was on leave from Confederate service. Cal had no name until his father came home and named him.[1]

Cal received only a fourth-grade education at the local subscription school, in session four to six months a year between cotton and pecan harvesting and spring plowing. The school was held on split log seats in a small house downhill from High Valley Baptist Church. Only teachers owned books. They were barely qualified to teach. The children had to write on slate and memorize from *Guffy's Reader* and spelling books. Math meant "doing sums" on their slate tablets.[2] There weren't any public schools in Reconstruction Texas.

In October 1879, Reverend J.R. Miller "saved" thirteen-year old Jesse Brazil. He was converted and baptized in Cherokee Creek after which he joined the Cherokee Baptist Church. [3]

Cal courted "Abby"Abigail Gage at her mother's home on Lynch's Creek, Lampasas County. "They had first met at her sister Martha Gage's place in San Saba."[4] After their courtship, Cal eagerly announced to Abby's widowed mother, Sarah Gage that he and Abby were planning to get married. She replied sarcastically, "Ye air, air ye? Then why air you a-tellin' me about it?" Cal was already used to having his own way. On February 23, 1886, Cal married Sarah Abigail Gage.

On May 27, 1887, their first child, Zeddie Calvin Brazil, was born. But on April 14, 1888, Zeddie died of scrofula, a form of tuberculosis. Abby said Zeddie was "one of her prettiest." Jesse and Jane Brazil, her in-laws, admonished her for idolizing that poor child and hinted that might have been why he was taken away.

On October 22, 1888, following a debate held at Bend School on the 16th, the Cherokee Baptist Church record proudly announced, "Resolved that we the Baptist Church at Cherokee endorse the able manner that our Pastor Elder James Elder vindicated the scripturalness of the Baptist cause in the recent debate between himself and W.R. Alexander the Cambellite Preacher and that we are perfectly satisfied with Brother Elder as a defender of the scriptures as understood by Baptists."

To show how important was their belief in religious conformity, church records noted on January 18, 1890, "Brothers W.H. Gage and Moses Brazil are appointed as a committee to investigate the charge against Brother Thomas Smith for using profane language." Smith was excluded from the church on February 15th.[5]

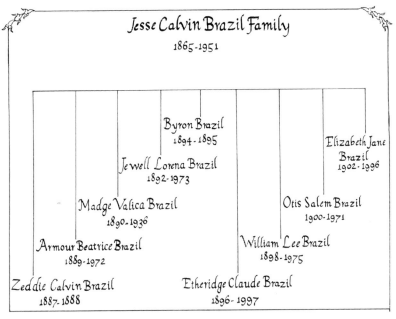

Jesse Calvin Brazil Family
1865-1951

Byron Brazil
1894-1895

Jewell Lorena Brazil
1892-1973

Madge Valica Brazil
1890-1936

Armour Beatrice Brazil
1889-1972

Zeddie Calvin Brazil
1887-1888

Etheridge Claude Brazil
1896-1997

William Lee Brazil
1898-1975

Otis Salem Brazil
1900-1971

Elizabeth Jane Brazil
1902-1996

The Calvin Brazil Family, 1902

(L to R: Madge, Etheridge, Abby, Armour, Lee, Cal, Otis and Jewell)

Cal and Abby's first surviving child, Armour, was born on January 23, 1889. As first-born, Armour was a natural leader. For example, once Cal's helper, Ed Combs saw Armour riding astride with her bare legs showing while in company with some cattle buyers. Almost as "bad," he saw her roll and smoke a Bull Durham cigarette. Ed told Cal who grabbed his quirt and took Armour to the shed. Clever Armour talked him out of whipping her by pointing out that riding astride was far safer than riding side-saddle.

Their next child, Madge was born on August 24, 1890, then on March 6, 1892, Jewell arrived. Madge and Jewell in contrast to Armour were easy-going and passive. Byron Brazil came on December 8, 1894, and named for Abby's uncle, "By" Nettles, a respected law officer. Byron died the next summer of malaria and buried in the Fondren family cemetery. The loss of her first two sons, Zeddie and Byron, was Abby's greatest sorrow in life. All her life she missed Zeddie, who was named for Biblical Zedekiah, her "beautiful, perfect child," who was "dark-eyed like the Prillamans."

Cal ran a cotton plantation near Bay City, Texas, in the summer of 1895 for a Mr. Bolen. Bolen was killed by some of his Negro laborers. Cal took his body to Bay City for burial. By autumn, Cal and family lived on R. F. Stafford's farm in San Saba county, helping him gather his crops. Then spring into fall of 1896, Cal lived on his Uncle Billy Brazil's farm near Smithville, Texas, on the old Moses Brazil farm.

Etheridge Brazil was born on Moses' farm on April 27, 1896. He was Abby's first son to survive and so much like her, he became Abby's favorite.

His older sisters called him "Ma's old pet." Etheridge's namesake, Reverend N.S. Etheridge, preached at Cherokee Baptist Church in June 1886, the year Cal and Abby married.

In those days, High Valley Church had no doubt understanding right from wrong. A church entry dated February 20, 1897, announced: "On motion the church decided that sociables partaking of the nature of revelry to be inconsistent with the requirements of the Gospel, and that members visiting or taking part in such sociables and plays shall be subject to the discipline of the church the same as for visiting the ballroom and partaking in dancing." This judgment followed a long debate about whether serving lemonade at church meetings was sinful.[6]

From 1896 until 1898, Cal lived at the Morris farm across the Colorado River from his mother. William Lee Brazil, born at his mother's rent house at Morris farm on January 8, 1898, was named for Abby's beloved brother, William Gage. "He was self-assertive like Armour and a very loud child" joked Etheridge.

Cal bought and farmed the 640-acre R.W. Self Farm on Cherokee Creek at Chappel in 1898, the first land he owned. On March 8, 1900, Otis Salem Brazil was born on the Self Place and named for Doctor Otis Mathis who delivered him. On October 29, 1900, Cal sold the remaining 320 acres to Edgar Sawyer for $1500, having already sold the rest to M.A. Millican.7

Cal and his Uncle Moses Brazil bought the 272-acre Rhoda Evans farm, part of the sandy R.D. McAnelly Survey in Lampasas County later in 1900. Cal only stayed long enough to plant and harvest one crop. Elizabeth Jane Brazil, born on the Evans farm on November 1, 1902, was named for both her grandmothers, Elizabeth Nettles and Jane Prillaman. "Patsy" was loved by everyone including both her parents whom she took care of during their last years.

The name "Patsy," short for Martha, honored her Aunt Martha Hepple.
Cal allowed Abby to name all of her children save the last, Elizabeth Jane, whose name was changed to "Patsy" by Cal. Patsy said of her name, "When Daddy saw me, he said 'That's too long a name for such a small baby. I'll just call her Patsy." 8

THE PERSONAL JESSE CALVIN BRAZIL

Like most of his peers, Cal demanded and received unquestioned obedience from his family. He could be a strict disciplinarian, handy with the razor-strap. But overall Cal was an affectionate and loving father. He showed it more by his attitude and actions than words, such as bringing them presents from town.

Harvesting Hay, c.1890

(L to R: Dave Matsler, William Millican, Cal Brazil with whip, William Gage)

Cal bought a reed organ for the family from a traveling salesman.   He also bought Abby a Singer treadle sewing machine.   He bought a Spaulding hack with springs to improve their travel comfort and to equal his Uncle Moses' new hack.   Cal's first car, a Marion-Handley, was usually broken down.   He next owned a Fordson farm truck.

Travel for anything other than business was almost unheard of for Cal but he did visit Henry Wall in Calvert at the end of World War I. The family knew that Henry Wall went through Hell in France. Everyone marveled that the Marion-Handley made it to Calvert and back without a single breakdown.

Like the Arkansas aristocrats who raised him, Cal found no one in the county quite good enough for his children to marry. An over-protective father, he kept his kids too busy to think much about courtship. He almost never approved of a suitor: Madge had to elope to marry Lewis Faulkner. Neither did he approve at first of Evelyn Price for Etheridge or Ina Mae Seals for Otis. Only Lee's choice suited him since the Ellis's were well-to-do land owners. Cal, now just an ordinary Texas Hill Country farmer-rancher and preacher, still thought like a Saline County aristocrat.

Cal loved all of his kids but he favored Armour and Lee the most. He loved Armour because of her hard work and management skills and dedication to his goals. The "old maid aunties" in his father Jesse's world, Laura, Nettie, and Jane, set the model for such "selfless dedication" like Armour's dedication to him. Lee he favored for entertainment. Cal gave Lee more than the others--two different farms--but he loved all his children. "A starter farm or college," was his offer to them all.

Very intelligent, calm, and even-tempered, Cal never swore or even used slang. Slow of speech, carefully measuring his words, Cal bored his audience when preaching. He typically wore a black Stetson broad-brimmed hat, black tailored suit, a conservative string tie, white shirt, and well-shined black shoes.

Calvin had a traditional, conservative personality. A very independent soul, he always owned his own house as soon as he was able. He never rented. Fearless, Cal would take his dogs and capture dangerous wild boars. The only time his son Etheridge ever saw him show fear was the time he took the wheel of his first Model T Ford and ran it into a pile of rocks. He made Otis take over and never tried to drive again.

Cal hated crooks and slackers. He was especially suspicious of Yankee traveling salesmen like the itinerant photographer or "artist" who tried to sell Cal a badly done family portrait. As Etheridge explained, "Mr. Enlarger Man brought from out of one of the buggies 'the Brazil group' and after pulling off its cover and displayed it with great pomp. I don't think he'd ever seen it before any more than we had. He was not the artist but was just distributing the works of artists somewhere up Northeast. Off came the veil and wide-open went nine mouths in sheer surprise and chagrin as the show proceeded. 'What do you think of this, Mr. Brazil?' the man ventured.

But that person was too flabbergasted to reply right then. All at once we all let out a concert of expressions--some good, some in disgust, even anger. Pa was overcome with mixed emotions. He was tickled at the absurd moustache that suddenly appeared under his nose in the picture. Said he, 'That's not me. You've got the wrong pig by the ear!' Then Armour spoke up, protesting the additions the 'artist' put on her. And Ma showed up with a collar and broach pin she never owned. In sum, the one who touched up the Brazil family group picture over did the job.

Pa refused to take the picture. The agents tried all his tricks to persuade him to take it, even a threat to tell the law. Nevertheless, Pa coolly met his threat with 'Well, now, mister, the sheriff you refer to, Edgar T. Neal of San Saba, is a personal friend of mine. Bring him on if you choose!' which put an end to the matter."

Etheridge wrote about a similar incident: "Widow Anne Alexander came back to Texas from New Mexico and settled on part of the Old Mag Alexander Place in a new plank house adjoining our Waldron Place. While at our house at cotton-picking time one summer day there came by a couple of city slickers who hustled the 'river people' in the Bend community. They didn't want to pick cotton for Pa but they did stay for noonday dinner.

The spokesman of this pair had a chart showing the different parts of the human brain. He told how each one of these areas controlled the different traits in good and bad behavior in people. Furthermore he could feel of a person's head and tell their fortunes. He called this 'phrenology' and charged half a dollar for each head he felt of. After doing one for his dinner, he proceeded to start one for pretty Anne, widow of Silas. But he made the mistake of touching her scalp without her permission as she sat at the dinner table. Her face red as a beet, Anne sprang to her feet, slapped his jaws, and ordered him to 'Keep your paws to yourself and get away from me, you rogue!'"

Ever careful with his hard-earned money, Cal often found himself fending off other salesmen who would try to sell something to Abby while he was away from the house. This included traveling salesmen of all sorts including lightning rods, vinegar powders, and eyeglasses. One salesman, posing as a doctor of ophthalmology, convinced Abby she had "myophobia" and desperately needed his twenty-five dollar glasses to save her eyesight. Cal told him he "wasn't satisfied with his diagnosis" and later bought her a much cheaper pair of reading glasses in Lampasas.

But Cal could be taken in. A salesman for "Stroud Motor Company" talked him and Bill Millican into buying stock in the company. It turned out to be worthless. Ever after, they would tease each other about "How good is you Stroud stock doin'? "

Calvin Brazil had an ego to match his ambitions. He would only accept the best of what was available, like Burpee Brand Seeds for his garden. His attitude to the world: "If you're not a producer on the farm or ranch, you're just a social leech, not a respectable citizen." Cal's major fault was not to be aware of any in himself. He almost never admitted his mistakes.

Cal had a healthy appetite, an omnivore, who would eat almost anything. Very regular in his eating habits, he always started the day with a good breakfast of oatmeal, biscuits, bacon and eggs, and honey or syrup or preserves for dessert. His favorite meal was chicken and dumplings topped off with a cobbler pie. Called to lunch with a Texas Longhorn dinner horn, the children sat on benches, girls on one side, boys on the other.

Part of the secret of Cal's longevity was his insistence of getting plenty of rest. "Give me the fore part of the night and you can have the rest," his slogan. Like his contemporaries, Cal only bathed when necessary: in the creek after a hot summer day in the field, or with heated water in the wash tub before church on Sunday.

Again like his peers, Cal chewed tobacco, his favorite was Drummond's Natural Leaf which he would typically chew after supper. Besides recreational use, chewing tobacco he considered good for insect bites, cuts, and a home remedy for worms in sheep.

Ever at home in nature, Cal could expertly read her signs such as an approaching "Norther." When it arrived in late spring, he would order the potato vines stripped away with a grubbing stick to prevent the potatoes from freezing. He never hunted except for meat like killing wild hogs or to get rid of predators like bobcats, wolves or bears.

An extremely hard worker, Cal and was good at "planning his work and working his plan." He was also a good negotiator. Whenever Cal put on his necktie, the family knew he was in a bargaining mood. Domestic chores like building chicken coops or digging flower beds bored him so these were usually left to his sons.

Cal always focused on whatever made him money. He never missed an opportunity to turn a profit. Once, when a flood on the Colorado caused the Cherokee Creek to back up with stunned, oxygen-deprived fish floating in it, Cal and Ed Combs put a net across the creek and captured hundreds of pounds of fresh fish which they sold everywhere.

Frank Moore, son of ex-Confederate and High Valley Church founder Seth Moore, was jealous of Cal. He admitted as much at a confessional meeting in a summer revival. He said to Cal and all gathered there, "I couldn't stand to see you prosper when I worked hard for so little gain." Life on the Texas post-frontier was hard and it took someone with good sense, shrewdness, and hard work to prosper. Farming and ranching in Texas hasn't changed much since.

Cal had a good reputation in the community for his kindness and consideration of others. Everyone called him "Mr. Cal." Cal served more than once as election judge at Bend and as a school board trustee. A Mr. Jackson on the San Saba road had some issue with Cal and confronted him at Jackson's front gate, holding a hammer in his hand. The matter was submitted to public arbitration in San Saba that Cal won, partly for keeping his cool "in a calm, Christian manner." That's how public disputes were often handled in those days, reminiscent of earlier days and open public trials.

Cal mirrored many of his fellow Baptists by condemning America's "declining morals" after World War I. But he did enjoy the technological advances that came such as mechanical reapers, tractors, radios, and if someone else would drive, the automobile. Cal regularly read the Bible as well as *Matthew Henry's Commentary* and *The Baptist Standard* magazine. For news he read *The San Saba News* and *The Farmer Stockman* and listened to the radio. He died before television.

Cal owned the Walden farm on the San Saba side of the Colorado for just two years, 1902-03. He built a two-story house but sold it and the acreage in 1903.[9] At Walden farm, Cal bought a McCormick grain reaper. Abby warmed Cal about a setting hen in the field but the farmers ignored her. Then everyone laughed when an angry hen with her tail feathers clipped off came running out from behind the busy reaper.

THE TOM BOYETT FARM, 1903-1927

Cal finally settled on the Tom Boyett Farm where he lived with only a short break from 1903 to 1927.[10] He became an ordained Baptist minister during this period. The High Valley church minutes record the date: "July 23, 1904: Brother J.C. Brazil, who had been elected deacon to be ordained during the meeting, stated to the church that he felt called to another work and asked to be released from the duty of deacon and bye motion he was released. By motion Brother J.C. Brazil was liberated to exercise his gift as a minister of the Gospel." [11]

After his farm work was well underway, Calvin decided to attend Baylor University for his ministry. He took a room at 919 Speight Street, Waco, Texas, and enrolled at Baylor on October 3, 1904. His first semester, he took *Arithmetic I, Grammar I, U.S. History,* and *Spelling.* He failed everything except spelling because he wasn't there for the final exams. In the spring semester of 1905, he returned and repeated those courses and another in *Geography.* After dropping arithmetic and history, he made a 'B' in spelling and geography and a 'C' in grammar. Later, he took a correspondence course in *Psychology* in the summer session of 1920. It was the end of his college career.[12]

During this time, his daughters Armour, Jewell and Madge attended Mary Hardin Baylor College in Belton, Texas. While in college, his Uncle Moses Brazil and family moved to the town of San Saba.

Cal was ill-prepared for college. But such education was in line with his twin ambitions of becoming both a successful farmer and a respected country preacher. At Baylor he studied "elocution" and his son remembered his practicing, *"Splendor falls on castle walls....ah...ah....ah"* which secretly tickled his kids.

Elected Pastor of High Valley Baptist Church on September 24, 1910, Cal also preached at other San Saba County rural churches. He preached for free. He read a Bible reading which he selected and mulled over, followed by an expository speech, the traditional Baptist sermon. Cal could quote Scripture at length. He was a "good, earnest preacher" and above all, he practiced what he preached.

After the drop in cotton prices to eight cents a pound in 1907, Cal switched to livestock. Cal leased seven sections of grazing land seventy miles north of Del Rio, Texas, which included three sets of windmills, corrals, and a five-room house. They ran a herd of about 750 head of sheep. Cal hired Julian Secavo as ranch foreman after Cal fired the first foreman for gambling and letting fifty-two head of sheep stray away.

Sheep-snatchers were a problem. "People who got away kept one to roast and several to sell for pesos." As time went on, the head count came up short again. Cal was suspicious of his overseer and sent eleven-year-old Etheridge to stay out at their camp to keep an eye on him and his crew. Cal lost his Edwards County lease through foreclosure, thanks to the Drought of 1907-08. But he never expressed grudges or regrets over this or any other loss.

Cal next turned to onion production. With the help of Richard Brazil and the Stafford's, Cal set up an irrigation system from the Colorado River and began large-scale production of onions and sweet potatoes. It required more farmland which required more tree and brush clearing.

As told by Etheridge, "When Cal Brazil's family got back from sheep-ranching in Edwards County, everybody was glad. The old Brazil Place, bought from the Boyett's, fronted the river between Jesse Brazil's place up stream and that of Elbert McCoury and Drury Beasley on the other. One hundred acres were in cultivation on the riverfront. It was good sandy loam. Then came sixty acres of black loamy soil enclosed as a horse and calf pasture. It was Bee Cave Creek valley, land suitable for growing bumper crops but it was grown up in trees, brush, and prickly pears. Clearing land for cultivation is expensive in time, money, and human effort."

Calvin Brazil got the elms, mesquites, chaparral, and cactus off his additional farm acres at a minimum cost by using his shrewd knack for trading. "Those traded with were 'wet back' hombres fresh from Coahuila, Mexico, who walked to the Colorado Valley behind a pair of slow-poke burros. They had not been used to American advantages so they'd work, heave and sweat the live-long day without as much as a gripe about anything or anybody.

Mr. Brazil sensed the hombres' yen for buggy-and-horse rigs and set out to buy some second-hand buggies. Since he had several old plugs of horses left over from the Edwards County experience, he could outfit the customers in waiting. And what an assortment of horses! They were clergy-kneed, wind-broken and bony. They were too old for the plow and too slow for the saddle. But they were gentle and gaited just right for pulling the light vehicles.

I knew each horse front and rear since I'd wrangled the dozen or more of them from the Rocksprings ranch to our Colorado River home. The 1907

Panic and Drought had busted us and this parcel of horses and a couple of spans pulling the wagons and hack were all we salvaged out of our 'Western tour.' We had no need of saddle horses now and we had plow teams so the nags went rolling merrily away with buggy loads of smiling Mexicans."

Cal gave sanctuary to the Marcos Tavadis' family, refugees from the Mexican Revolution, whom he hired as farm laborers. The Tavadas' were middle class landowners persecuted by Poncho Villa's rebels. Tavadis' brother-in-law was murdered by Villa's troops, his insides stuffed with his own wheat. Tavadis arrived from Nueva Rosita, Coahuila, with wife, Rosa, sons Marcos, Junior and Martin, daughter Maggie, and a widowed daughter.

The Tavadis' were the first of eight different Mexican families, up to thirty-two individual's altogether, to live and work on Cal's farm with Marcos as "jefe" or boss. The Mexicans cleared an additional seventy-five acres for cultivation to go with Cal's existing one hundred acres.

When Marcos' son, Martin, drowned in the Colorado River, a Catholic priest was brought in to bury Martin in High Valley Baptist Church Cemetery beside the large oak tree. The locals were scandalized, not least for a Catholic priest in a Baptist cemetery as for Marcos' jumping into the grave to tamp down the soil, violating a great taboo among Anglo-Americans.

The Mexicans were used for clearing brush, onion production, and sheep herding. When Cal switched to hog production, the Mexicans left, much to the relief of local whites who had not seen a Mexican before.

After the onion collapse, Cal went into hog production and made a good deal of money at it. His hogs, bought from farms all around the area, were a half-wild mixture of Chinas, razorbacks, and Reds. "They were turned into his corn field just passed the milk stage. They wallowed in the Colorado mud banks which kept them from getting screw worms. When fattened and ready, Cal shipped the hogs from Lometa by rail to markets in Fort Worth."

Etheridge described farming at the Boyett Place. "Corn was gathered into the big corncribs for man and beast. Cornbread and hominy was first choice, then came horse feed. Last was feed for laying hens and for fattening hogs. This insured most of the farming people's diet of eggs, poultry, breadstuff, lard, bacon, sausages, and ham. From a peach and pear orchard and blackberry patch came the canned fruits, jellies and preserves. Numerous beehives along the orchard fencerow yielded enough honey for everyone's sweet tooth, but coffee and sugar had to come from town.

We boys took care of the larger stock such as horses and pigs. We fed the horses ears of corn at the end of the working day and let them out to pasture at night. Pigs were fed corn and table scraps. The girls milked the cows twice daily, morning and night. They also did the laundry, boiling the clothes in large kettles with homemade soap. They also did the ironing with flatirons heated on the kitchen stove. During the long summers, both sexes were expected to hoe weeds from the fields."

Cal's cash crops were pecans, cotton, beef, and hogs. For Cal and family, he grew corn, pigs, geese for feather bedding, and wheat which went to the mill at Rough Creek for grinding. Cal took his cash crops to the railroad at Lometa for marketing. At market he would trade his produce for barrels of molasses, brown sugar, and coffee, indigo bluing for laundry, and medicines such as calomel, bolt cloth and thread. All of the children's clothes were homemade.

SAN ANGELO, CARRIZO SPRINGS, AND THE GREAT DEPRESSION: 1927-1933

"With very little forethought, Cal sold his Boyett farm to Otis Brazil and bought the Bismark Dairy Farm, 1,280 acres of former school land on the Concho River outside San Angelo. Cal drew irrigation water from the Concho River, mainly to grow corn and pecans.[13]

Cal never lost on a deal in San Saba and never won one outside his home county. In San Angelo he was talked out of his land on Concho River by a developer who convinced him to buy a truck-farming place at Carrizo Springs in South Texas," said Etheridge. All of Cal's sons had married by this time. Only Etheridge and Patsy were away at Howard Payne College in Brownwood. Armour was the last girl left at home with her parents.

The Carrizo Springs Chamber of Commerce still makes their area sound inviting: "A dam on the Nueces River allows for year-round irrigation.

The unusual 300-day growing season allows farmers to raise almost any kind of produce including citrus, carrots, broccoli, onions, cantaloupes, watermelon, Brussels sprouts, lettuce, spinich, peppers, eggplant, squash, beans, turnips, corn, tomatoes, and several other varieties. Cotton and feed crops are also grown extensively."

At the start in 1928, Cal had $70,000 in the Frost National Bank in San Antonio. Then he plunged everything into buying up to 750 acres at Carrizo Springs at an overpriced $312 an acre, a new house, and other farm supplies. His farm, a "show farm" for other buyers, was a beautiful spread complete with date palms.

Cal grew irrigated tomatoes, onions, and carrots but made no money because they were too far from American markets. Cal had to sign lien notes on the show place because it was overpriced. Richard Brazil, his uncle, sold the San Saba River place to buy in at Carrizo Springs. All together they had about 125 acres in cultivation, including some citrus trees that didn't have time to mature before everything was lost. Calvin Brazil, Richard Brazil, Marvin Thompson, Lewis Faulkner, and Lee Brazil all lost everything they owned at Carrizo Springs. Only Otis Brazil kept his farm in San Saba County. [14]

Elizabeth Jane "Patsy" Brazil, c.1920

The Great Depression began in October 1929 and everything was lost. Penniless and hounded by creditors, Cal moved into his daughter Patsy's apartment in Paint Rock, Texas. Thereafter, from the summer of 1933 until his death, Cal lived on the eastern half of the original Jesse Brazil place at Chappel which he bought from Otis Brazil.

During the Depression, Patsy, a public school teacher, was able to send her mother a little money to supplement her parent's earnings at picking cotton. She received his letter from Cal:

Chapel 10 mo and 10 Da 1937

PATSY Dear old Daughter:

Was glad to get your letter. Your mother sure appresisated the Dollar. I gave her another but she still wants to Pick more because she wants more money so you see there is nothing to do but let her Pick. I guess it is pretty good employment. We have picked 2500 lbs and am feeling fine over it so you see it is not hurtin us. Well we looked for you and Armour but saw a good rain and Br. Sparkman came in stead. So you see we wer not quit Disapointed so by by. We Love You. Your old Dad and mother\5

ABBY AND CAL'S FUNERAL

As Abby lay dying, she kept looking toward the door for her favorite son, asking "Is Etheridge here yet?" She died of stroke on February 4, 1945. Armour insisted she be buried the next day. The reason given was "to get everybody out of Daddy's house and take the pressure off of him." Etheridge raced back from military service in Florida with his family for the funeral but arrived at six o'clock. The funeral was at three.

Cal was basically healthy and happy all of his life until Abby died, after which his health began to fail. He felt he had no place in the world that was truly his.   His relationship with daughter Patsy Lackey's husband Ausley was hostile but he had nowhere else to live. Lonely in his last few years, he once remarked to his son, "Etheridge, I have more on the other side than on this side."

He developed chronic colitis and went to see a doctor in San Angelo. After returning home from a doctor's trip, Cal died of a heart attack on January 26, 1951,[16]

Buried in High Valley Cemetery on a very cold day in January 1951, Reverend Lancaster of the First Baptist Church, San Saba, preached his funeral sermon. Etheridge remarked that for the first time, he heard Cal's daughters "wail in helplessness like lost children."

His obituary appeared in *The San Saba News:*

"Mr. J.C. Brazil, 'Uncle Cal' to those who knew him, passed away Friday, Jan. 28, 1951, at his home in the Chappel community at the age of 86 years and 23 days. He had been in failing health for the past few weeks, but had not been confined to his bed. Death came as the result of a heart attack.

Jesse Calvin Brazil was born in Collin County near McKinney Jan. 3, 1865, and came to this county at the age of 8 years and settled in the Chappel community. He was converted when he was a small boy and united with a Baptist church. He has been an active Christian even up to the day of his passing. He was an ordained minister, pastoring churches after he attended Baylor University in 1905. He had committed large passages of the Bible to memory and could quote many whole chapters from memory. He could read without the aid of glasses. His father, Jessie Brazil, hauled the lumber from Round Rock and gave it to build the first Baptist church at High Valley. . . . A host of relatives and friends are left to mourn his passing."

His funeral announcement was posted in an earlier edition of the *San Saba News--*

"Funeral services for J.C. (Cal) Brazil, 86, retired stock farmer, were conducted at 3 p.m., Sunday from High Valley Baptist Church, with Rev. C.E. Lancaster officiating. Burial was in High Valley Cemetery. Brazil, who had lived in the county for about 78 years, died at 4 p.m. Friday following an illness of several months.

Surviving are six children, E.C. Brazil of San Saba, Mrs. Patsy Lackey and Otis Brazil of Star Rt., San Saba, Mrs. Armour Long of Big Spring, Mrs. Jewell Thompson of Mexia and Lee Brazil of Lometa; a brother, Richard

Brazil of Shive, Hamilton County; two sisters, Misses Laura and Jane Brazil of Shive; thirteen grandchildren and eight great-grandchildren."

His daughter, Patsy, was moved to write this poem in memory of her father:

"He's gone away and left them now,
His garden fork, his rake, his plow.
The soil he once did so carefully prepare
Stands untended now, forlornly bare.

No more will the jubilant call of spring
His bright and delicious strawberries bring.
Huge sweet onions, thriving with such lust
Have wilted, withered, returned to dust.

Blackberry and grape vines only remain
His masterful culture to proclaim.
And the old home seems so complacent,
For Father's chair is left ever vacant.

His beloved Bible is thumb-marked with use;
Because so constantly he pondered its Truths.
Last week his Maker invited him to come,
So Daddy went away to his beautiful, beautiful home."[17]

Cal is still a strong influence today.

CHAPTER TEN

SARAH ABIGAIL GAGE (1864-1945)

It likely wasn't Calvin Brazil's motive for marrying Abby Gage but when he did marry her, he gave himself and his offspring outstanding Texas credentials. Through her double Burleson connection, the source of Abigail's given name, Cal identified himself and his descendants with one of the most famous names in Texas, the Burleson's.

THE BURLESONS

Aaron Burleson I, born about 1690 and christened in Caerleau, Manmouth, Wales, immigrated to Baltimore, Maryland in 1726. There he married a woman named Sarah and moved to Lunenburg County, Virginia, in 1748. [14] Aaron died in 1763 in Rutherford County, North Carolina.

Aaron Burleson I had fourteen children, among them Aaron Burleson II, born in Baltimore and married Rachel Hendricks in 1748. At Watauga, now eastern Tennessee, he went out to hunt deer and was killed by Indians on November 16, 1781.[15] Whether this was the start of Burleson's' fight with the Indians or more likely, just part of their fighting heritage from Wales, it began the Burleson's' frontier conflict with Native Americans.

Aaron II was an ancestor of such remarkable Burleson offspring as the founder of Baylor University and the Postmaster-General in President Wilson's Cabinet.

THE GAGES

I only knew Abby as a child. She loved me wholeheartedly so I loved her too. I used to steal flowers and take them to her. Later, as an adult and genealogist, I began to see the aggressiveness of Abby's early Burleson and Gage ancestors as the key to their success. The Burleson's, Gages, Shipman's, and other allied families from North Carolina to Texas were the most closely-knit group of families I ever studied. Moreover, the Burleson's connection with minor gentry back in Wales suggested to me how a fighting spirit and fame seem to go together.

Aaron Burleson's murder by Indians in the Watauga Settlement in 1781 may not have been a cause of their aggressiveness but only a symptom. Wherever the Burleson's lived, they always fought with Native Americans. From North Carolina through Kentucky, Tennessee, Alabama, and Texas, Burleson's and their allies battled the Indians. Wherever the family branch of Southern Burleson's lived, they were ready for a fight. To me, their original fearlessness was nature, not nurture. In 1835, for example, the first shot in Texas' War for Independence, a cannon fired at Gonzales, Texas, at Santa Anna's troops, was lighted by a Burleson.

The Gages were also Welch. Nicholas Gage, Sarah's ancestor, was born before 1683 in Wales. He married Mary and had David Gage, born in Wales in 1701. His son, David Gage, Jr., was born in 1734 in New Jersey and died there in 1805. One of David's children was Reuben Gage, born February 10, 1770, in New York.

Reuben Gage married Abigail Burleson in September 1790 in North Carolina. Abigail was the daughter of Aaron Burleson II and Rachael Hendricks, born August 24, 1774, in Rutherford County, North Carolina. Abigail died in Texas on November 4, 1865. Sarah Abigail Gage's middle name, *Abigail*, was chosen to honor her double Burleson ancestress, Abigail Burleson.

Reuben Gage's children were recorded in his Bible:

MARRIAGES

Reuben Gage and Abigail Burleson were Married Sept. 1790

BIRTHS

Michel, the daughter of Reuben & Abigail Gage was born January 21st 1792

Moses the son of Reuben & Abigail Gage was born July 13th 1796

Joseph the son of Reuben & Abigail Gage was born January 25th 1799

David, the son of Reuben & Abigail Gage was born August 2nd 1801

Burleson the son of Reuben & Abigail Gage was born February 27, 1805

Jonas the son of Reuben & Abigail Gage was born October 27, 1807

Sally the daughter of Reuben & Abigail Gage was born October 8th 1810

Vany the daughter of Reuben & Abigail Gage was born February 24th 1813

Calvin the son of Reuben & Abigail Gage was born May 1st, 1817[1]

In the late 1790's, a group of related families left Rutherford County, North Carolina, and settled in Warren County, Kentucky. The families were Gage, McFadden, Shipman, and Burleson and others. All were related to the Burleson family by marriage.[2]

Reuben Gage and his brother, Moses Gage, applied for a state grant of 200 acres each on Sinking Creek, Warren County, Kentucky in August 1799.[3] Twenty years later, Reuben Gage lived in Howard County, Missouri, where his relatives, the Shipman's, tried to talk him into going to Texas.

Wrote a Shipman, "About this time, a father and an old friend, by the name of Reuben Gage, took a notion to move to the state of Arkansas. They sold out, and on the 5th of June 1821, they started from Howard County, Missouri; after about 25 miles, we crossed the Missouri River at Boonville, Copper County. Father broke a wagon wheel, he and old cousin Reuben Gage managed to have it mended, so that we got to a large creek called 'Mori'; by this time, the weather had become very warm and horse-flies so very numerous, that it was almost impossible to travel.

While there, his father heard tales of land on the Red and Sabine rivers and of the generous offers made by the Spanish Government to American settlers. His father was interested but 'it did not appear to take so well with our friend Gage.'

Our friend Gage agreed to meet us at Mr. Harrel's (the informant on the free lands in Texas) where we all were to meet and hold a general consultation. The result was that Mr. Gage and his family was to go to Gasconade, Missouri; Mr. Harrell, family, father, and our family went to Arkansas. So in two or three days, we all made a general start on the 23rd of October, 1821."[4]

REUBEN GAGE FAMILY REUNITED WITH THE BURLESONS IN TEXAS

In 1834, while Texas was still a part of Mexico, Reuben Gage moved his family to Texas and renewed his close relationship with his Burleson in-laws. Before Texas, the Burleson's had been in Alabama where they farmed and fought the Indians.

The Mexican government granted Sarah Gage Brazil's great-grandfather, Reuben Gage, a league of land—4,428.80 acres—in the Milam Grant on May 25, 1835. This made him an original Anglo-American Texan. In his grant application, he gave his age as sixty-five and his place of birth as New York.

On November 25, 1836, Reuben received a voucher for $120 from the Republic of Texas, payment for the loan of his wagon and team to General Edward Burleson, his brother-in-law, who commanded the center division at the Battle of San Jacinto. Texas won her independence from Mexico in that battle and became the Republic of Texas.

COMANCHE TROUBLE

The year after Texas joined the Union in 1845, two Burleson girls were captured and scalped by Comanche's. The girls survived but the Burleson and Gage men went on the warpath against the Comanches. David A. Gage may have paid the price for their lack of forgiveness. David A. Gage (1801-1846), Abby's grandfather, died in Bastrop County under mysterious circumstances. His death was never fully explained in his probate papers. He died in 1846 without a will. His probate papers only say that he died "in the month of April last." His body wasn't found for some time after he died.5 The Republic of Texas and the state's early years afforded little protection for its citizens. Everyone was on their own. Evidently, Burleson's and Gages' may have been singled out by the Comanches, the tribe everyone white or red hated and feared.

David's father, Reuben, and his brother, Burleson Gage, George Washington Gage, and Jonas Gage all went back east to Arkansas, away from Texas. The Gages settled in Saline County, Arkansas, on the Military Highway to Texas. Reuben bought 123 acres on September 8, 1840, from Abijah Davis, an old Saline County pioneer. He also bought fifty acres from John Lindsey, a Brazil relative.6 Reuben Gage died in Saline County on Halloween, October 31, 1844. The Brazils and Gages churched together but had no idea they would become relatives in Texas.

David Gage's estate inventory, dated August 24, 1847 included:

"In County of Bastrop: 11 cattle, all bought last spring; 3 cows without calves, 5 cows and spring calves; 1 yoke of work oxen, yoke, bows, ring & style; 1 mare and colt; 1 bridle, & gun, 2 bells; 1 foot adze, 1 log chain, 1 oven & lid, 3 pots; 1 skillet, 1 pr. pot hooks, 1 sack & contents; 1 wheel without a bench, Beds & Bed clothing. In Fayette County, David had irons of hubs of wagon wheels, and a 1 three year old steer, born last spring.

In Gonzales County, David had one cow & calf, 2 plain bitts, in possession of Zachariah Nettles of Gonzales County; 4 axes, 2 chissels, 1 auger and about 30 head of hogs in possession of Mr. Mullen of Gonzales County; 1 Paint mare, 1 gun, in saddle, & bridle in possession of Henry S. Gage.

"There is in possession of A.H. Wood, admr. a bond executed by one W.W. Ashby of this State for the sum of $400, dated May 1st. 1844, to David Gage."[6]

David A. Gage, born August 2, 1801, married about 1821 to a woman even whose first name was lost. David's third child by her was Henry Salem Gage (1829-1857), Sarah Gage Brazil's father.

HENRY GAGE

David Gage's probate papers, dated August 29, 1848, described Henry Gage as "a minor and heir of said deceased {David} who has in his possession a Sorrell and a paint Mare belonging to said estate."[7] A dispute had arisen over ownership of the paint mare. On September 1st, Henry Gage appeared in court, and upon motion of attorney the court appointed Moses Gage, his guardian in the interest of said minor. "It is further ordered that John Burleson, Senr and Joshua V. Stewart, citizens of the County of Gonzales bee summoned to appear at said term of court and give evidence in the case at the insistence of said Henry." On October 20,1848, the probate court "Ordered that Henry Gage, one of the Heirs of said David Gage decd return and hold the Sorrell Mare and become chargeable to said Henry at the price of seventy dollars."[8]

David Gage's second wife, Denisa, whom he married before coming to Texas, came up in David's probate proceedings dated July 26, 1847.[9] They only had one child before David died in 1847, Mary Abigail Gage, born about 1845. On February 16, 1849, the Probate Court ordered "....the property set aside at a previous term of this court for the benefit of the widow and children to wit 25 head of cattle; 1 Set of ----lings, 1 Log chain, Household furniture and one Bridle valued in the Inventory at $134.70 be divided equally and one half delivered to the widow and the other half divided between the Three Minors. . . ."[9]

The Probate Court in Fayette County on August 27, 1849, ordered Levi McClure to be appointed Guardian of the minor, Mary Abigail Gage, whom he represents as about three years old and he submitted the petition at the request of "the surviving parent." In January 1851, McClure was summoned by the court to give an account of his guardianship which he ignored. He was arrested and John S. Black "went his bond" for his next appearance.

In his final account, Levi declared that his ward has no property and that he "has had the care and keeping of said ward since being appointed guardian."10 Mary Abigail Gage relieved Levi of his responsibility by marrying, on June 21, 1860, at age fifteen, James M. Dancer.11

Henry Gage's report to the Bastrop County Probation Office, dated April 6, 1852, concerned his two minor siblings. He paid $7 for school and tuition for Hiram Gage, and stated: "Some increase in cattle but very small. The minors is doing well, are going to school, and have so far been able to maintain themselves with their own labors, and my assistance, without disposing of any of their estate."13

Henry Salem Gage, born 1829 in Tennessee, married first on February 5, 1852 to Rebecca Jane Nettles in Fayette County, Texas, the daughter of Shadrack and Anna Nettles. Shadrack's wife, Anna Burleson Nettles, whom he married in Crawford County, Missouri, on June 23, 1831, was the daughter of Aaron Burleson II. Sarah Gage Brazil was thus a double descendant of Aaron and his wife, Abigail.

Rebecca Jane Nettles was born 1833 in Missouri and died in Fayette County in 1856. Henry and Rebecca were married by Henry's uncle, Reverend Jonathan Burleson, the first regular Baptist preacher in Texas. Burleson baptized Sam Houston, the hero of San Jacinto and President of the Republic of Texas. When Burleson told Houston that his baptism would take away all his sins, Houston said, "Well, that's going to be some very dirty water."

Henry and Rebecca had two children:

> Thomas Washington Gage, born May 18, 1854, in Fayette County. He married Matilda Jane Brazil, daughter of Lieutenant William Brazil on June 20, 1878. Thomas Gage died at Chappel, Texas, on September 20, 1919. Matilda "Tildy" died at Chappel in 1925.

> Martha Ellen Gage, born in Fayette County on May 4, 1856, married there on October 18, 1875, to Moses Brazil, Jr. She died in San Saba, Texas on February 3, 1940.

After much convincing on the groom's part, Henry married second, on May 14, 1857, his late wife's sister, Sarah Elizabeth Nettles. Sarah was born February 10, 1840, at Morgouria, Missouri, on the White River. After Henry died, she married Felix W. West in Fayette County, Texas, on December 9, 1869. Felix died in December 1882. Sarah Elizabeth Gage West died in San Saba County on March 29, 1903. Henry and Sarah had three children:

> Betty Ann Gage, born 1858 in Fayette County and married December 11, 1872, to William Bogard, Junior. He deserted her and all his family. She married second, Andrew Hooten. She died in 1898.

> Sarah Abigail Gage, born April 25, 1864, in Cistern, Fayette County, and married Jesse Calvin Brazil in Chappel, Texas, on February 25, 1886. She died in Chappel on February 4, 1945.

> William Henry Gage, born June 25, 1866, in Fayette County, married Ella Stafford on March 5, 1893. Ella was born January 4, 1873, and died May 31, 1965. William died in San Saba, Texas, on August 20, 1944.

Abigail and William Gage, c. 1870

BUCKNER CREEK COMMUNITY

By the 1850's, kinfolks began to gather along the Bastrop-Fayette county line at Buckner's Creek. They stayed there until after the Civil War. When the census enumerator for Bastrop County came around on September 5, 1850, he counted Jonas and Jane Gage with seven children of their own and David Gage's three sons listed as farm hands. They were Henry Gage, born 1829 in Tennessee; Hiram Gage, born 1832 in Arkansas; and Thomas Gage, born 1835 in Tennessee.

By the time of the war, several related families lived on Buckner's Creek: Shadrack Nettles bought 450 acres on the creek on May 5, 1853. Joseph Gage, Reuben's third son, bought two tracts on July 10, 1852. Jonas Gage, Reuben's sixth son, also bought two tracts on Buckner's Creek on May 11, 1854. In the last year of the war, Henry Gage bought 100 acres on June 21, 1864.

But by the time of the federal Census of 1880, most families had left. The only one remaining, Robert Sawyer:

Household 317-320

Robert Sawyer	60 W	Farmer	Arkansas-N.C.-N.C. (birthplace of self and parents)

Four member of Sawyer's family, then. . . .

Albert J. Hill	47 M	Teacher	Mississippi-Ga.-La.
William Gage	14 M	Student	Texas-Tex.-Tex.

Now living in San Saba County in 1880 were:

Felix G. West	46 M	Farmer	Tennessee-S.C.-Tn.
Elizabeth	39 F	Wife	Missouri-?-? (empty blanks)
James	9 M	Son	Texas-Tn.-Mo.
Polly A. West	8 F	Daughter	"
Sarah A. Gage	16 F	Step-dau.	Texas-Ar.-Mo.
William	13 S	Step-son	"
Betty A. Bogard	22 F	Step-dau.	"
John	4 M	Grandson	Texas-Tx.-Tx.

REVEREND ETHERIDGE
BRAZIL'S IMPRESSIONS:

Sarah Nettles Gage West, c. 1890

SARAH NETTLES GAGE WEST

"Abby Brazil's aunt and step-mother, Sarah, had a small build and gray eyes. She was well-respected in the Chappel community where she lived out her years with her son, William Gage. She could be caustic and sarcastic. Sarah was famous for her quilt-making and her expertise at spinning and weaving wool." Sarah Nettles was slow to marry Henry Gage but for any woman to marry then it usually meant many children and the health risks that went with childbirth.

THOMAS GAGE

Henry's son by Rebecca Nettles and Abby's half-brother, everyone knew Tommy Gage the outdoorsman. He married Matilda Brazil, orphaned daughter of Civil War leader, "Wild Bill" William Brazil, on September 20, 1878.[16]

"Tommy loved to hunt, fish, trap, or do anything else outdoors including treasure-hunting. He was an expert trapper of foxes, wildcats, and other game and was a superb deer hunter and fisherman. He used a hollowed out Longhorn steer horn to call up his hounds. A dreamer with many children and hunting dogs, Tommy was rarely a landowner and moved about frequently when young. His half-sister Abby disparaged his vagabond lifestyle and would say of someone with no roots that 'they just pull around like Tildy and Tommy.'

For part of his adult life, Tommy worked as a ranch hand in the northwestern Hill Country. In 1907, Tommy herded sheep and kept a store and post office at Hext, Texas. He lived on some pecan bottom land on the Llano River. When Cal decided to go into the sheep business in Edwards County, weather-wise Tommy warned him about a possible drought. Cal ignored his warning and got wiped out by the Drought of 1907-08. In later life Tommy returned to Richland Springs where he bought a small place. He lived out the rest of his life there.

Tommy was no loner. He loved the company of others and was an excellent storyteller. He just didn't want to be tied down to anything or any place. Tommy lived a pioneer hunter-gatherer lifestyle. A dreamer and perennial treasure hunter, he was always looking to strike it rich. He is said to have once found a cache of gold but he talked too much about it and someone else made off with it before he could return to the cache site."

MATILDA BRAZIL GAGE

Wife of Thomas Gage, born February 12, 1860, in Perry County, Arkansas, the oldest daughter of William Brazil and his wife and second cousin, Mary Ann Brazil, daughter of Moses and Matilda Brazil. She died in 1925 in San Saba County.

" 'Tildy' had dark brown, curly hair, dark complexion, and a hefty build. A morose personality, this orphan of "Wild Bill" Brazil was raised by her grandparents, Moses and Matilda Brazil. Tildy seemingly had no ambitions and stuck by her husband Tommy through all his wanderings, bearing him seven children along the way.

Tildy was close to another Brazil orphan, Obedience 'Beady' Brazil Barker, who was a daughter of Andrew Jackson Brazil, a nephew and friend of Moses Brazil, Senior. Beady is said to have worked as a maid in Arkansas, been seduced by her employer who left the country after she became pregnant. Beady's baby died. She then married "Old man Nate' Nathan Barker and lived out most of her life with him at Nix in Lampasas County. Beady was a small, timid woman who dipped her snuff with a toothbrush. Nate Barker was remembered for his old fashioned expressions. For example, once when asked the next morning how well he slept, he said, 'That blessed old cow! She lowed and she lowed all night long!' Nate and Beady eventually returned to Arkansas."

Ella Stafford Gage and William Henry Gage

WILLIAM HENRY GAGE

"Abby's brother, William, was greatly devoted to his mother. When she died young, William took her death very hard. William was an ideal citizen, always useful to his community."

William related to Etheridge that "Uncle Jesse Brazil, at an 1880's brush arbor meeting, placed his hand on William's head and gave his benediction, "Oh God, please bless this orphan boy!" Jesse's belief in him was one reason William tried to be his best self. Jesse was like a surrogate father to him. William had a charming personality, very loving. Always in a good humor, he was chivalrous and courteous."

William came up the hard way. He never knew his real father and when his stepfather Felix West died in 1882 when William was only fifteen, he had to become the man of the family and take over the Gage farm on Lynch's Creek in Lampasas County. "He had to reach up for the plow handles when he was barely tall enough to touch them."

As a young man, William courted Mag Boyett, daughter of Zeke Boyett. She was away attending high school in San Saba so their relationship continued through the mail. The Millican boys wrote a fake "Dear John" rejection letter from Mag and gave it to William. William was taken in. He was devastated and went into the barn to cry. The Millican boys hid out and listened, snickering at William's pain. William cried aloud to himself, "Well, she has chirped too late!" Post-frontier Texas humor was as rough as the lifestyle they led.

"William already had his eye on Ella Stafford and he married her soon afterwards. William and Ella were a devoted couple to the end of their lives. A hard-working farmer, William had a well-mulched orchard and apiary, a row of bee gums. He had a full cellar of shortening, preserves, demi-johns of honey, beans and peas. He ran sheep and had provisions of all kinds. A good provider, at one time he loaned Cal Brazil seed corn. He raised turkeys, chickens, oats for the horses and mules, corn tops for fodder and garden vegetables. His sizeable pecan bottom fattened many hogs on leftover nuts. He was a High Valley Baptist Church deacon. His main readings were the Bible, *The Baptist Standard*, and the *Farm & Ranch* magazine.

William always wore his 'tall hat' or else his 'bee-keeper hat.' He had black hair, blue eyes, and a moustache. In later years he developed pleurisy, digestive system problems, and died of cancer in 1944. William was a true-practicing Christian, humble and never egotistical. He was an excellent bee-keeper, favoring the three-banded Italian species."

William and his sister Abby were the main influences in guiding Etheridge into the ministry. Among William's closest friends were Charlie Harris, Tom Matsler, and Cal Brazil. Joe Wild and his wife, Virgie Gage, William's daughter, took care of him in his last days.

Despite wartime shortages and absences, his funeral was attended by a huge crowd because William was known and loved by everyone "from Dan to Beersheba."

Genealogist and author Clyde V. Gage said of William Gage "He was a successful farmer and rancher. His home was noted for its warm hospitality and was the meeting place for his wide circle of friends. Mr. Gage was an exemplary influence on the religious life of the Chappel Community, studying and living his Bible with deep conviction and sincerity. The following expression from his pastor, the Rev. Ben H. Welmaker, is typical of the high regard in which he was held:

'. . . . I have known no other man with such an outstanding Christian character. . . . His life touched all in the community and without fail, it always had an uplifting effect on those he contacted. Mr Gage's judgment was always accepted. He was sought for an advisor in the community. He was a Deacon in the Chappel Baptist Church.' "[17]

Sarah West family, c.1883
(L to R: Abigail Gage, Sarah West, Elizabeth Nettles West, Annie West)

SARAH ABIGAIL "ABBY" GAGE BRAZIL

"As a young woman, Sarah Abigail 'Abby' Gage Brazil was pretty, fine-featured, weighed about 125 pounds with waist-length, thick, dark hair and greenish-gray eyes and a clear complexion. For church, she always had her special Sunday clothes that usually included a breast pin broach and a dickey 'vest.' She was a typical Gage: optimistic, social, and always happy" said Etheridge.

Cal was certainly not her only suitor. She had several, including a preacher named Elder. Her courtship with Cal was not always smooth sailing either. One moonlight night Cal and Abby were out buggy riding when distracted Cal didn't see a white cow that was sleeping on the road. He hit the cow and almost overturned the buggy. Abby swore she had never had such a jolt! Cal and Abby were married by Reverend Jim Elder. An *in fare supper,* a reception with a meal, followed the ceremony.

Abby loved life and all it had to offer including good food. "She loved a leisurely meal. Her favorite foods were cobbler, egg custard, with chicken and dumplings. She insisted on always having a 'Christian mealtime,' a pleasant, positive conversation around a table that usually held a vase of fresh flowers. Abby's tendency to overeat led to later health problems."

Abby was uneducated by today's standards and had many superstitions. For example, she believed that the static on early radios when she was trying to listen to some sermon was actually the work of the Devil. She was also superstitious of Fridays (the day of the Crucifixion) and would never start anything important on that day. She also believed that one should always fill in a grave before dark. She put great store by observing the moon's phase in planting and in making lye soap, believing that strong moonlight yielded light-colored soap.

Abby had other superstitions. If a rooster crows before dawn, someone would die within three days. She was also a great believer in the meaning of dreams, including the thought that if you tell a dream before breakfast, the dream will come true. Practically illiterate, Abby never wrote anything but her name and could only read the Bible and a few simple periodicals.

Besides her lack of education, poverty in her fatherless childhood caused Abby to have very frugal spending habits. "When traveling she would pack half a flour sack full of sweet breads she called 'tea cakes.' Once at a wagon yard she was seen holding the sack behind her back when uninvited guests showed up at their wagon."

She loved church music and singing. "She had a reed organ at first, then later a Jacob Dahl upright piano. She insisted her girls have music lessons. Among her favorite hymns were *'Must Jesus Bear the Cross Alone?,'* *'On Jordan's Stormy Banks I Stand,'* *'Whiter than Snow',* and *'My Home Over There."*

Abby was too compliant with whatever Cal wanted. She also worried too much about people she knew and loved, the weather, her kids, anything. When angry, Abby would first shout, then cry. She was very sensitive to criticism and felt inadequate for her lack of sophistication. Above all she was put off by "know- it- all's" who lorded their better knowledge over her. Abby never saw a doctor unless another baby was due. Instead, she favored such home remedies as *"Wine Accordia, Black Draught, Baby Percy,* and that most hated purgative, *Calomel."*

Cal and Abby never fought but quietly worked out their problems in private. Abby was thoroughly devoted to making Cal's life as pleasant as possible. At mealtime, for instance, she always set aside his favorite pieces of chicken. She and the children then took what was left. She vowed many times that "She wouldn't barter her man for gold and she wouldn't give a copper cent for another in his place. "

CHAPTER ELEVEN

REV. ETHERIDGE CLAUDE BRAZIL
(1896-1997)

CHILDHOOD, 1896-1908[1]

Etheridge's relatives told him about his birth: "1896 was a time of panic and drought. It dried the peaches on the seed and corn stalk leaves were sucked up by dry whirlwinds and dropped on the mud-cracked Colorado River. It was pokeweed-picking time and just before a rainstorm pushed into the Colorado Valley, things happened. Pressures within and without brought on a midnight alarm for ol' Miss Sawyers, the midwife. Jesse Calvin lit out leading a saddle horse into the lightening-lighted night. The stork ran the two riders {Cal and Mrs. Sawyers} a close second race. Along the horse-high front porch Calvin literally rolled the 250-pound Sawyers woman onto the porch. But once inside the fat lady turned into a competent woman doctor." [2]

Etheridge described himself as a bashful, timid child, overshadowed by his older sisters. In school, where he was called "Calvin" because he was slender and awkward like his dad, Etheridge was picked on by older boys who visited various indignities upon him. His father had taught him to "turn the other cheek" as Christ commanded, his motto being "I'd rather be called a coward than to always be fighting."

EDUCATION

He started reading at five, a skill he learned by rote. He had some harsh, insensitive teachers who failed to make allowances that he was always behind his peers in San Saba town because he was still picking cotton and pecans while the others were already long at school. Etheridge, like his contemporaries, loved Horatio Alger's rags-to-riches success stories. He also had a flair for poetry and performing in school plays.

Mr. Powell, a Bend school teacher, spoke with a deep Southern drawl. Etheridge made the mistake of correcting him once when he said *cah won* for *care worn* for which Etheridge got kept after school. No one loves a critic.

He went to Bend School for grades one through four, then in 1906 to San Saba city school, 1907 to Rock Springs school and 1908-09 to Harkeyville School. His teachers were a ragtag collection. The best was Dora Brown in San Saba and Miss Willie Bannister at Harkeyville. Miss Willie owned a small watch on a chain, which was accidentally jerked off by the flailing arm of a boy as she whipped him.

Etheridge loved the humanities--history, geography, and the like but not math. He loved to be called on for speech exercises and even looked forward to Friday spelling bees. He was also famous for being a good swimmer--in the Colorado River, Cherokee Creek--anywhere. He once pulled Elmer Mooney out of the river and saved him from drowning. Other favorite Sunday activities included swinging on vines, riding heifers, swimming, and races.

As a kid he loved to explore the rough country along the Colorado River. He especially loved to find and rob a bee tree. This was done by having one boy stand on the river bank where bees came down for water, another boy standing at an angle so as to be able to triangulate the direction the bees took after drinking, yielding the direction to their hive. Bees always made a "bee line" straight home. They robbed the hive at the end of summer when it was full. The boys used an axe, smoker, and tub to rob their hive.

Etheridge enjoyed music all his life. In childhood he and his peers played ring games where boys choose girls as partners. This was played to funny songs like *Hog Drovers,* an old Southern tune:

"Hog drovers, hog drovers, hog drovers we air,
a-courtin' yer daughter so young and so fair,

We'd like to have lodging here, oh here,
we'd like to have lodging here. . . ."

If the boy playing "Pa" didn't like the other boy facing a girl in the ring
when the singing stopped, the "drovers" responded,

"We care nothing for your daughter, much less for yourself!
We'll go a house farther and better ourselves.
We don't want lodging here, oh here,
We don't want lodging here."

At such gatherings, Etheridge often played the Jews harp with its one-sound twang.

ADOLESCENCE, 1908-1917

Brush arbor meetings remained the main match-making events, held twice
yearly after winter after crops were laid by and in summer after seedlings
were cultivated for the next crop. Baptists came from all around--Bend,
Chappel, Rough Creek, and The Colony.

Etheridge and Armour were converted and baptized in Cherokee Creek
during a summer revival in August 1907. After his conversion experience,
Etheridge went to his mother who said, "Son, you don't have to tell me
what happened to you. I can see it." Etheridge's parents recognized his
spiritual nature and knew early on that he might become a minister.

Elected Superintendent of Sunday School in High Valley Baptist Church at
only seventeen, Etheridge acted as a lay minister, opening Sunday School
services with scripture, prayer, and song.   His inaugural speech, on the
virtues of Alexander the Great, went on so long that his father interrupted
him and asked him to please "'speak of your other experiences."

Etheridge called himself a plodder in school. His motto: "The heights that
great men reached and kept were not attained by sudden flight but while
their companions slept were toiling upward in the night." His favorite
subjects were the social sciences, debating, and public speaking. He loved

adventure stories such as Livingston and Stanley in Africa and longed to travel himself.

LOMETA DAYS, 1911-1912

Etheridge went to eighth and ninth grades in Lometa, Texas. There he got his first paid job, a "Red Cap" or porter for the Burton Hotel next door to the Santa Fe railroad station. He met the trains, out-competed the other red caps from Page Hotel and the Jackson House for guests, then hauled guests and baggage to the hotel. But his last school year in Lometa was cut short in February because of his out-of-district residence status. He had to return to Bend. Yet the experience of meeting people from all walks of life opened his eyes for the first time to the possibilities of urban life. His teachers also helped liberate him from 'the sticks.' Seeing everyday people engaged in good railroad jobs--station manager, freight handlers, telegraph operators--showed him what could be done through education.

Regular movie attendance also opened Etheridge's eyes to the greater world. Every evening a "town crier" would announce, "At the Opera House tonight you'll see 10,000 feet of motion pictures." Etheridge saw Hoot Gibson, Mary Pickford and other Hollywood stars. He considered it twenty-five cents well spent.

Etheridge rode the Shoulton Brothers narrow gage railroad back and forth from the Bend. The English Shoultons exploited the huge stands of native cedars that grew at the Colorado-Cherokee confluence. The logs were too big to be hauled by wagon, some of them more than thirty feet tall with diameters greater than a wagon wheel.

The county road from Lampasas to Bend was crossed by east-west community roads whose intersection was at Nix, Texas. Nix wasn't a big place--only a post office store, blacksmith shop, and cotton gin. Said Etheridge: "Free lounging was also offered on wooden benches to one and all who'd care to spend the time of day. The young fry had one old timer in Nix whom they could bet on as a real standby friend, Uncle Nathan 'Nate' Barker. He was shaggy headed, bearded, but always out front in good humor, spinning yarns for all who'd listen to his bygone tales of Arkansas and pioneer Texas. He used antique expressions and words that tickled the young rowdies. He and his little pipsqueak wife, 'Beady,' had no kids so these youths compensated for that lack. The couple dwelt in a plank lean-to house only a stone's throw from the Nix crossroads gathering place. Like a woodpecker whose head is always poked out of the hole, Nathan saw and heard everything and everybody that passed by."

Nathan's wife, Obedience "Beady" Brazil along with her older sister, Mary Ann "Polly" Brazil, born in Arkansas about 1843, were orphaned daughters of Andrew Jackson Brazil.[2] They appear in the 1880 Census of Fayette County, Texas in the household of Mary Ann's husband, fifty-year old farmer John Holligan who married Mary Ann Brazil in Bastrop County on January 12, 1876. "Bedie" married first on August 30,1885, to John B. Votaw, a widower who was about fifteen years her senior. Before, at the 1880 Census, Votaw had married the former Nancy Gage, daughter of Jonas Gage. By 1895, Widow "Beadie" Votaw married Nathan " Nate" Barker, a local farmer. In 1900, "Beady" and "Nate" Barker lived on Barton's Creek in Bastrop County, next door to Edmund Sawyer. After their stay in Nix Community, Lampasas County, Nate and Obedience returned to Arkansas sometime before World War I.

Etheridge was good at baseball, swimming, climbing, and horseback riding. He regularly won Sunday races on Aunt Jane's quarter horse, "Tram," much to the resentment of his brother Lee who had only his dad's Percheon plow horse to ride. Etheridge even won the annual Bend horse race, held in May at the McAnelly Place, which featured a community picnic, lemonade, and a race. Etheridge used his agility at tree-climbing not only for robbing bee trees but in threshing pecans. His fearless skill at tree-climbing meant that Etheridge was always the chief pecan thresher.

EVENTS, 1913-1917

Etheridge trapped fur animals such as wild cat, fox, ringtail, skunk to meet his school expenses. He made enough money from trapping to buy himself a green suit and some perfume to impress his first girlfriend, Lizzy Towerton, at the Colony community. After Lometa, he went to school in San Saba where he enjoyed a very good teacher, Miss Goodson. He lived at his Uncle Moses's Sherrill Ranch just outside the town where he cut and hauled wood for them and plowed their fields. He also burned prickly pear in winter for the cattle since 1913 was yet another drought year.

Privates Shorty Myers and Etheridge Brazil, 1918

WORLD WAR I

As the new Federal law required, Etheridge had to register for the draft in the fall of 1917 along with his neighbor, Joe Wild, and his friend, "Shorty" Myers. In the spring of 1918, Etheridge took the train to Fort Worth, expecting to enlist in the U.S. Navy. Rejected for some face-saving reason, the Navy wanted skilled technicians, not more uneducated farm boys. Broke and having no means for getting home, Etheridge took a job in the Fort Worth stockyard where he cared for show cattle entered in the Fort Worth Fat Stock Show. Etheridge survived on milk from the dairy cows and cornbread from a local cafe. At last he rode a cattle train back to Rochelle and home.

Over Calvin's strong objections, Etheridge was drafted May 5, 1918, at age twenty-two. Ordered to report to the railroad station at San Saba, he was examined and certified fit by the doctor. Along with his wartime buddy from San Saba County, Dennis "Shorty" Myers, he went to the train station in Lometa where they met up with a troop train carrying other recruits to San Antonio. The train was so crowded that they had to be pulled in through the coach window. At Fort Sam they were sworn into Army service, given orientation lectures, uniforms, foot lockers, and shots for tetanus and small pox. They lived in tents until they were moved into barracks. As a Private, Etheridge's pay was one dollar a day. He managed to save some of his first pay--sixteen dollars--but someone stole it from his foot locker. After that, he locked it.

Assigned to 'G' Company, 3rd Division, Etheridge and his company were shipped to Eagle Pass for recruit training from June to August 1918. At daybreak, the recruits could hear the "Mexican canaries," ragtag Mexican militia's donkeys braying across the Rio Grande River. Barbed wire surrounded his camp. Only for guard duty could recruits ever leave their compound. Etheridge pulled guard duty on the International Bridge three times. Since the United States and Mexico were virtually at war, he could hear shots now and then as Mexicans attempted to sneak across the Rio Grande.

Not all recruits were enthusiastic about killing Germans. One German-American lad, Amil Heine, mouthed off about not wanting to fight the Germans. Taken to a horse trough and submerged, Amil was forced to recant. He was then given a "Kaiser Bill" moustache with wagon grease.

Oddly, not one officer or non-com appeared to notice. Another man named Breedlove from Kentucky asked for and got conscientious objector status. But rather than being returned home, the officers assigned Breedlove to every unpleasant camp chore including permanent laundry duty.

At boot camp, the soldiers drilled carrying eleven-pound Springfield rifles, trained in trench warfare, and made to climb rope netting in preparation for being shipped off to France. All the men in his squad slept together in one large tent including his drill instructor.

Texans and other farm boys had it easier in boot camp than most city boys. Their feet weren't pinched from wearing city-boy pointed shoes but flat and solid from habitual walking. The Texans were used to the heat and knew how to survive off the land, like how to get moisture from cactus fruit. Furthermore, the Army chow was much appreciated by the farm boys. There was plenty of good meat and they didn't have to kill or cook it themselves.

Walking back to Fort Sam Houston and San Antonio was an ordeal for everyone during those hot August days. At Del Rio, the soldiers enjoyed snack food at the YMCA and joined in morale-building song such as "*Over There*" and "*K-K-Katy.*" However, at Castroville, the soldiers weren't to make any anti-German remarks because of the large population of German-Americans living there. Etheridge's regiment made it on foot as far as Uvalde before the commander called for transport trucks from San Antonio to minimize heat casualties. The officers gave them barrels of lemonade sweetened with famous Uvalde honey. Then everyone stripped and jumped into the cool, refreshing Uvalde city water pond.

Back at Fort Sam Houston, the regiment was assigned to barracks duty awaiting orders for France. During those months of waiting, they had to listen to motivation lectures against the Germans on such topics as "Bleeding Belgium" and other Hun atrocities.

While on the target range at Camp Bullis outside San Antonio, the great influenza pandemic, "the Spanish Flu," struck in early autumn. Etheridge's symptoms started with chills. Back at Fort Sam Houston, he and other flu victims filled up the 7th Cavalry's barracks. The male nurses made them gargle with a Listerine-like solution but it did little good against the new, deadly strain of influenza. All night long Etheridge could hear the gurneys go by as dead soldiers were taken away. He himself was delirious through

October but recovered by November. Many civilians also died. Letters from home arrived full of flu death notices.

After recovering, his unit mobilized for France. They boarded the train in San Antonio, bound for embarkation at Newport News, Virginia, by way of Chicago. They turned in their footlockers and packed all their belongings in barracks bags. They were in route in Kansas when news of the Armistice on November 11,1918, reached them. A great celebration greeted them when they arrived in Chicago. Diverted to Camp Grant, Illinois, they waited to see whether the armistice would hold. Assigned to barracks duty at Camp Grant where, unknown to him, so many of Etheridge's old Saline County kin had been prisoners sixty years before during the Civil War.

At Camp Grant, Etheridge hated being a "barracks soldier" with little to do but attend drills and formations. Yet Camp Grant wasn't all drudgery. For example, he got a chance to ride toboggan sleds that winter. But the highlight had to be his five-day leave spent with Sally Moore in Frankfort, Kentucky. He had become pen pals with her through her cousin, his comrade at Fort Sam Houston. Sally and her grandmother met Etheridge at the train station in Frankfort and took him home. Her father owned a tobacco farm. Etheridge remembered him always carrying a squirrel rifle. Sally continued to write to Etheridge and made it clear she was ready to marry him but of course, Calvin forbade it.

In February 1919, Etheridge road the train to the Replacement Depot at New Orleans. From there, they sent him to Fort Worth and Camp Bowie where he received his honorable discharge and a free rail pass home. There had been many changes in his absence. Many had died in the epidemic- -Fanny Millican, Tommy Gage, Moses Brazil, and soldiers Walt Stafford and Jewell's fiancé, Eugene Tate. Others had died in action in France like as D. Ragsdale, Jimmy's brother, who was cut in two by a German shell. Cal Brazil's family took a rare non-business trip to Calvert to visit the Walls and celebrate the safe return of their son from the war.

William Wall, Martha Brazil Wall, and family

COLLEGE YEARS, 1919-1932

Etherege agonized throughout the summer of 1919. He felt guilty about his decision to leave Calvin and farm life for the ministry. Living in Lometa before the war and the Army showed him that he could succeed away from the farm. His Aunt Laura Brazil, hearing Etheridge in prayer over his future, counseled him to go for the ministry and so did William Gage who also offered him financial help for college. By now, Baptists wanted educated ministers, not just those who had been called and ordained. Etheridge was called by a church near Richland Springs and ordained by '"the laying on of the hands."3 Several other ministers were present, including his father, Reverend Calvin Brazil.

Etheridge enrolled at Howard Payne College's preparatory school on September 6, 1920. As a ministerial student, his tuition was free. His only expenses were food and lodging. As the minister of a small church between Zephr and Brownwood but having no car, he rode there on his bicycle. That's where he learned not to get into local squabbles since he had to mediate their disputes. Etheridge entered Howard Payne College in September 1922.

For whatever reason, Calvin withdrew his promise of financial support. Etheridge had to sleep on a bare floor in Reverend Tom McNeely's apartment. Cal visited him there and Etheridge told him he would make it on his own just fine. He took a job as a bicycle delivery boy for a Brownwood dry cleaners, picking up and delivering men's suits.

"Percy" Pierce Neece, a Brownwood native and his friend during the war, was now a fellow student. He was the one who pulled him and Shorty into the railcar in Lometa when they were drafted. Percy was supportive of Etheridge during that tough time. Neece and his new wife supported Etheridge's decision to go it alone without Calvin's help. Neece always smiled and said, "I've always believed in you, Brazil. I'll see the day when your life will be full and happy by serving others." He lived to see it.

Etheridge decided to take the necessary Education courses to be certified to teach in Texas schools so he could better support himself. He finished the required courses by correspondence and was certified to teach. He also accepted a position as pastor at Morris Ranch in Gillespie County between Fredericksburg and Kerrville.

In the summer of 1923, Etheridge taught school at Honey Creek in Bandera County. That's where he met Evelyn Price.   They were introduced by Jack Scott, pastor of First Baptist Church in Bandera. It was love at first glance. Jack had asked Etheridge to help with a revival at Pipe Creek. Evelyn was the pianist. They teamed up then and "never looked back."

Courtship at the Price home on Medina River, Bandera, consisted mostly of sitting on the front porch swing, talking for hours into the evening. "Boss" Price, ever the jokester, would break them up about 9:30 P.M. with some hint like " Well, preacher, you build a fire in the stove and I'll get my wife to cook us some breakfast."

Etheridge and Evelyn were married after Prayer Meeting by
Rev. Jack Scott on Thursday, December 20, 1923

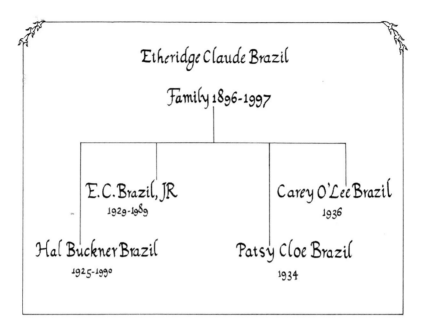

Etheridge Claude Brazil

Family 1896-1997

E.C. Brazil, JR
1929-1989

Carey O'Lee Brazil
1936

Hal Buckner Brazil
1925-1990

Patsy Cloe Brazil
1934

Etheridge and Evelyn both attended Howard Payne. They lived at Avenue C and Fisk Avenue where he worked for a Mrs. Jennings, a clothier and milliner. Etheridge pastored at Winchell Church in Brown County. After their firstborn, Hal Buckner Brazil, was born on January 4, 1925, they alternated classes so that one was always home with the baby. Hal was named for Hal Buckner, founder of Baptist Buckner's Orphan Home.

In the summer of 1927, after graduating Bachelor of Arts, Etheridge went back to Plainview Church in San Saba County. In September, they both took teaching jobs at Camp Verde, twelve miles from Bandera, where together they earned $150 per month. Evelyn taught grades one through four and Etheridge grades five through eight except they switched her fourth grade geography for his eighth grade algebra class. They bought a new Ford coupe because they had to sell their Model T Ford his senior year in order to eat.

In 1928, Calvin Brazil and family moved to Carrizo Springs. Only Otis and Ina Mae remained in San Saba County. That summer, Etheridge won the pastorate of the First Baptist Church at Pearsall, Texas, in part through their connections with the Rankin's and Reverend Walter Davis. Etheridge and Evelyn also taught school at Aurelia, a tiny rural school with only seven pupils. Etheridge C. Brazil, Junior, was born in March 19,

1929, at "the teacherage."   Etheridge got angry because, ironically, "the doctor was drunk."

Said Etheridge, "E.C., our second-born son, was always like a summer grasshopper! He just wanted to enjoy life and have a rollicking good time He was a funny, candid child, like his Uncle Lee. When E.C. was about five, his cousin Lorraine Brazil had just sung a quivering solo for a family gathering. It was met with an uncomfortable silence. Then E.C. blurted out, 'If I couldn't sing any better than that I'd just toot!' Everyone nearly died laughing, including Lorraine. He was a natural musician. It just seemed second nature to him. He truly loved music.

He also had another side--a stormy temper. You could push him so far and no farther. For example, he got mad at his tricycle once and kicked it very hard. Unfortunately, he was standing on the second floor by an open barn loft door. His pants leg caught in the tricycle and they both fell to the ground below. He was knocked unconscious for many hours which badly scared everyone."

From May to October 1929, Reverend Etheridge Brazil pastored the Black Creek Baptist Church, a well-paid pastorate and a viable country church where he baptized many converts. He was also able to save money for the seminary. Off to the Southwest Baptist Theological Seminary at Fort Worth, they rented a house near the Santa Fe tracks, spacious enough to have room for their milk cow and laying hens. They attended the Seminary from October 1929 to graduation in May 1932. Etheridge pastored Union Baptist Church in Navarro County, hosted by a principal deacon who was a cotton merchant. He gave the Brazils badly-needed goods during those hard Depression times.

Both Brazils thoroughly enjoyed their seminary days despite the Depression. The Leonard Brothers Store in Fort Worth, an emporium with food and other cheap goods, was a poor preacher's paradise. They sold bread for only three cents a loaf and were just as cheap on other goods. Above all they enjoyed the fellowship and support of other seminarians. "What depression?" their motto since all seminarians were poor in material things but rich "in the spirit of Christian love." Evelyn graduated with the highest grade point average of any female student since the seminary had been founded twenty-five years before. The couple were glad to be professionally-trained and completely self-reliant.

From 1932 to 1934, Reverend Brazil's next church was the First Baptist Church in Bishop, Texas, a nice, big-membership church with a parsonage. Since the Depression was at its depth, there was little cash but lots of produce. With Etheridge, the church fathers got a young seminary grad with no ties to old factions. Bishop was steadily losing farm population but the Brazil team was able to add about 200 new members.

Etheridge remembered various WPA projects around Bishop including food commodities but they didn't need them. He did take four of his cows at Carrizo Springs to be slaughtered in the Federal Relief Program in order to raise beef prices. Other Brazil cattle were also killed at only $2.50 per head. He also remembered good cotton crops plowed under by the same programs, shocking events to farm producers. Etheridge preached against the 20th Amendment repealing Prohibition but it passed anyway. Throughout, he and the family listened to President Roosevelt's "Fireside Chats" on the radio.

Calvin visited his son, Etheridge, at Bishop and was impressed with his success. The visit was worthwhile if for nothing else than to hear his father admit for once he was wrong. "My father was so impressed with my life, my family, my life's work that he actually did apologize to me for trying to persuade me to go into ranching and not the ministry." In those unhappy times, a small church clique headed by a Mr. Witt, a ginner, opposed Dad's ministry. That hurt Dad's feelings and he left Bishop without a fight.

On February 24, 1934, Etheridge and Evelyn's daughter, Patsy Cloe Brazil, arrived. Mom picked the name 'Patsy," and Dad "Cloe," a Biblical name. In 1934 into 1935, Etheridge and his growing family lived in a house at Carrizo Springs vacated by the Thompsons. There was no money anywhere. They just survived, hand to mouth. Poverty in her first years had a lasting effect on baby Patsy.

In October 1935, Etheridge pastored Central Baptist Church on Brady Creek in Brady, Texas. To supplement his small salary, he began selling family burial insurance for Commercial Union Life in Waco at $16.20 a year for an entire family. He felt good about this service because he was often thanked later by those who used its benefits.

Central Baptist Church was good pastoral work and had good attendance but little money. During this time, a $100 check in World War I veterans' benefits arrived for Etheridge. He bought their first Coldspot refrigerator and a Sears's washing machine. Etheridge traded an insurance policy for a shoat pig which he butchered and put into the new freezer.

Etheridge's sister, Madge, died in San Antonio on April 6, 1936. Said Etheridge, " Her son, Brock Faulkner, drove her body back to High Valley Cemetery in a cabless truck. A very sad funeral it was."   Once again, someone dies and someone else is born: on November 5, 1936, the Brazil's last son, me, arrived on a cold Thursday morning.

Etheridge moved back to San Saba in May 1937, where he helped pastor the Plainview Baptist Church. He also continued to sell insurance. The presiding minister at Plainview church, a Reverend Renfro, eventually pushed Etheridge out of his pastorate. " He was a vicious, imbalanced man who used shameless slander and empty promises to ease me out" said Reverend Brazil. Renfro only lasted six months as pastor. The church ultimately failed and eventually consolidated with the Algerita Baptist Church.

Mass Baptism on Richland Creek, Plainview Community, c.1938
(Reverend Renfro on the left officiating. Reverend Brazil on
the far right. I'm somewhere on the upper bank.)

Reverend Brazil had no pastorate from 1939 to1942 while he was busy building "the Rock House" and selling insurance. He traded insurance for the rock veneer and borrowed $1000 from the San Saba Building and Loan Association, using his two lots as collateral. His brother-in-law, Marvin Thompson, and he built the house from scratch on a lot that had a burned house on it. Salvaged materials from the burned house were used to build a temporary shelter shed out back. They installed the inside plumbing using a $32.44 package deal from Sears & Roebuck. Sears accidentally sent two sets and were amazed that Etheridge returned the extra set. He rented the construction shelter to an old couple whose rent paid Etheridge's house note. By 1940, he finished building our "Rock House" on Annex Street in San Saba. Etheridge also traded for a donkey to plow his garden. We had a cow and chickens and much produce from "the lower garden."

Chaplain Etheridge Brazil's family, 1942

WORLD WAR II

We heard about the attack on Pearl Harbor that Sunday after church, December 7, 1941. Fear, then anger spread over America. The Baptist Board in Atlanta approved Etheridge to join the U.S. Army Chaplains' Corps. He was sworn in, uniformed, and left for Harvard and chaplain's training on December 24, 1942. There were quotas from each denomination so

Southern Baptists, now the largest Southern denomination, enjoyed a large quota. They accepted only college and seminary graduates with at least two years of pastoral experience. His World War I experience was also helpful in getting his Army commission. Single ministers were the first to be sent overseas into combat zones. Etheridge stayed stateside for a time.

Etheridge attended the Army Chaplains' School at Harvard University from December 1942, to January 1943. At Harvard, Etheridge stayed in a Cambridge boarding house with other chaplains in training. There he met Lee Craig, an Arkansawer he knew from the seminary. They took such courses as *Military Courtesy, World Affairs* and *U.S. History* which centered on Totalitarianism, Hitler's Thousand Year Reich, and Soviet Communism. His professor correctly predicted the Cold War period that followed World War II.

After classes, he and Craig explored the Boston area together. Once while he and Craig were looking at some Civil War general's statue, Craig remarked, "Hey, Brazil. Let's go eat. That old so-and-so probably shot your granddaddy or mine anyway." From Harvard he went to Fort Benjamin Harrison, Indiana, awaiting assignment.

From March 1943 to February 1944, Etheridge served as Protestant Chaplain at Camp Millard, Bucyrus, Ohio, a facility of New York Central railroad shops. Headed by a Virginian, Colonel Cheshire, Etheridge's regimental commander had been with the Baltimore and Ohio Railroad before the war. Their mission was to covert American broad-gage locomotives to narrow gage that would fit European rails. Their destination: France.

Etheridge loved his work at Bucyrus but unfortunately, the combination of exposure to cold weather and coal smoke was too much for him and he had to be hospitalized with sinusitis.   He asked Colonel Cheshire for a transfer to some warmer climate and got it.

From February 1944 to June 1945, Etheridge's new post was Protestant Chaplain for the Army's 67th Replacement Regiment, Camp Blanding, Florida. His son, Hal, received his draft notice in Ohio so Etheridge drove to his new assignment by way of Camp Claiborne, Louisiana, where Hal had just finished basic training.

Chaplain Etheridge Brazil

Etheridge's duties as chaplain included holding regular divine services, visiting soldiers in the base hospital and jail, and much counseling during those stressful times. " The soldiers, the majority of them had been overseas already, were there to recuperate. They were assigned to replacement regiments waiting to go overseas again. They weren't usually eager to return to combat and would come to my office with various reasons to talk, most of them about dealing with this fear" Etheridge said. During this time, he was promoted to captain. Also during this time, his mother died on February 4, 1945. Etheridge tried to get back in time for the funeral but missed it because of heavy rain and thin wartime tires on our car.

On June 5, 1945, Etheridge boarded ship for New Caledonia at Camp Beal, near Marysville, California. Evelyn was there to see him off. The trip to New Caledonia took three weeks by the Island Mail route. From New Caledonia, he went to Guadalcanal then returned by plane to Hawaii by way of Kwajalein. On this new assignment, he had five other chaplains under his command. At Honolulu, assigned to the Sand Island Chapel, he also helped the head chaplain.

Back in Texas, Evelyn had a near-tragic experience thanks to a mix-up in names. The Breazeales in San Saba County had a son in the Army Air Corps named Hal B. Breazeale. Hal was killed in action. The Western Union messenger, about to deliver his death notice to Evelyn, the mother of Hal B. Brazil, when someone stopped him at the last moment.

I studied the Breazeale family early on because the two names, Brazil and Breazeale, were often mixed up in counties where the two lived together. It almost happened again in San Saba County in 1945.

On August 6, 1945, America dropped the atomic bomb on Hiroshima. The mass carnage shocked and horrified Etheridge. On "V-J Day" that soon followed, he attended the big victory parade in Honolulu and remembered seeing the members of the Hawaiian royal family heading the parade. Of his Hawaiian experience, Etheridge said,

"I loved Hawaii and would have liked to have stayed there. Colonel Koehee wanted me to stay with a promotion to major. I got word from the Red Cross and Doctor Felts in San Saba that Evelyn was bad off. The stress of it all got to be so much she had a breakdown. Patsy and Carey were little. E.C. was a teenager and needed his dad. The whole family needed me so I requested a stateside transfer as soon as possible. I knew that ended my Army career but my family needed me."

In October 1945, responding to Evelyn's pleas, Etheridge flew home to Texas to deal with E.C. Before that Colonel Koehee, his superior, the Texas officer who had sworn him into chaplains' service in 1942, had all but guaranteed he could continue his Army career after the war but E.C.'s emergency request killed his chances. After his last leave, he reported to Jackson Barracks, New Orleans. On April 1, 1946, Etheridge took terminal leave from Fort Sam Houston, Texas, where his discharge became final on April 12th.

Life goes on. On September 1, 1946, Hal married Ruby Head in Lometa, Texas.

Reverend Etheridge Claude Brazil, c. 1946

SANTA ROSA, NEW MEXICO

Through the influence of another seminary connection in July 1946, Etheridge took charge as pastor of the First Baptist Church in Santa Rosa, New Mexico. He described Santa Rosa as "a majority of Latinos but good climate and good people on famous Route 66." Santa Rosa is still an important stopping place along that fabled route.

Another feature of Santa Rosa were the Penatentes. These primitive Catholics dramatized Christ's crucifixion, sometimes with fatal results. Their religion was sanctified by neither the state nor the Catholic Church. Etheridge wrote, "The Pentatents were an offshoot of the Catholic church who were into pseudo-crucifixions, whippings, crawling over broken glass, demonstrating Christ's sacrifice. They had a small church out from town in the Pinion bush. They were frowned on by the Catholic church. Visitors were not welcome. "One day a Pentatente woman came, asking me to baptize her newborn infant since the priest would not but I refused to." Etheridge counseled her, converted her, and sent her on her way but with the infant still unbaptized. Baptists believe baptism is for persons no younger than their teens, old enough to be "converted" and to understand their baptism.

LANCASTER, MISSOURI

From the summer of 1948 to Christmas 1949, Etheridge pastored forty-five rural Baptist churches spread over eight northern Missouri counties. He bought a house on the Unionville highway in Lancaster, Missouri, a small town five miles south of the Iowa state line. Etheridge said of this experience, "The winters up there were brutal with icy, bad roads which I considered too risky for my family to drive. There was just too much snow for me to get around to all the churches very well. And the job was not what I thought it would be either. The attitude of the people was closed. They were still feuding about the Civil War! Their hearts were not open to hear about God's Word because they weren't over 'The War' yet."

Missouri was not a good fit for him or his family. Etheridge's parishioners reflected the still-potent cultural divide in that region, American Baptists versus Southern Baptists, very provincial and still reacting to Civil War horrors. We didn't understand their border-state prejudices. They weren't friendly like the Southwesterners we knew. The family income was somewhat better than Santa Rosa's but Reverend Brazil had a very large circuit to cover.

Once more, Etheridge got undermined by someone working behind his back who wanted his ministry. In this case, it was a local preacher who had returned to the area after failing at a California ministry. Etheridge sold the Lancaster house and bought a new, green International truck, which he loaded up with furniture, cat, and chickens and headed out for Texas. Christmas Dinner 1949 consisted of bologna sandwiches in Mills County, Texas. But they tasted better than any roast turkey and dressing because we ate them in Texas, our home.

Once again with no ministry, Etheridge resumed selling insurance for Commercial Union Life. He also received a seventy-five dollars per month training allowance from the Veteran's Administration which he used at the cabinetry school at San Saba. He made and sold cedar chests, coffee tables, and whatnot shelves. During this period E.C. Brazil, Junior, and Bill Kimple volunteered for the Army on promise of getting into the Fourth Army Band at Fort Sam Houston, San Antonio. Patsy Cloe Brazil married Bill and changed her name slightly to "Patti." Etheridge's furniture training and experience landed him a job at his next home, Killeen, Texas.

Etheridge and Evelyn Brazil, c. 1977

REVEREND BRAZIL'S RETIREMENT

In July 1952, Etheridge moved to Killeen and bought a house at 305 Cloud Street from Cousin Desdemona Brazil. He worked first for Bell Furniture Company on Highway 190 until 1953 and on weekends, pastored Youngsport Baptist Church. Later, from 1953 to 1964, he worked for a service company at Fort Hood called Moore Services. Evelyn taught piano in their home.

Etheridge and Evelyn thoroughly enjoyed their retirement years. They led a number of religious programs at Memorial Baptist Church in Killeen. After Etheridge retired from Moore Services in 1964, they continued their membership at Memorial Baptist but traveled widely with their camper trailer. While they were still able, they belonged to a travel club, the "Happy Travelers" chapter of the National Campers and Hikers Association. They went to Baptist encampment events around the region and visited nearly every national park. They belonged to birdwatcher groups and followed bird migration routes across North America.

After Evelyn died in 1994, Etheridge was taken in by Patti and Bill Kimple in Dallas where he lived out his days. He died there on July 15, 1997.

Early in April 1996, Etheridge wrote, "Now I live in Dallas with Patsy and Bill. I have a cozy home in their guest house and they pet me. I see the clan whenever we can all get together. Last year for my ninety-ninth birthday, we had a party at Carey and Nada's pretty new home in Austin. Ruby had a nice gathering this past Christmas."

A year later, Etheridge wrote, "My dear Evelyn is gone from me. She died in January 1994, but I think of her every day and at night, I dream of her and wake up crying. I dream of my boys Hal and E.C. who are gone too. Often I gather all four of the children up when they were little in my dreams. I dream of the happy, carefree times during the retirement years when Evelyn and I were in our 'Happy Traveler' years--camping and traveling all over the U.S., making friends everywhere. Those were the good years.

Looking back over it--100 years this month--I have been very blessed in my life. Life has been a pleasure. I still love people, flowers, prayer time-- and naps. I wonder why I am still alive after so many years—one hundred years in a few days. I feel like I am about ready to 'go across' now to my heavenly home. I go in comfort and peace and sweet assurance. I pray for God to guide my footsteps."

ETHERIDGE BRAZIL'S SIBLINGS

Family Reunion in Lampasas, c.1960
(L to R: Etheridge, Otis, Lee, Jewell, and Patsy)

ARMOUR (January 23, 1889 - November 29, 1972)

"Armour had more self-will, energy and initiative than all her sisters put together. She didn't marry until mid-life because no man could control her. Calvin allowed Armour to punish her younger brothers if she thought they were 'slackers' on the job. She had dark brown hair, greenish eyes, and the Brazil Scotch-Irish hawk nose and high cheekbones." Very social, Etheridge said she was most like her Aunt Ida Brazil Bolton.

Her husband, Pete Long (his Anglicized Greek name) owned a restaurant in Big Spring, Texas, where Armour lived out the rest of her life at their home on 606 Scurry Street. Armour traveled widely through Europe, Alaska, and the Northeastern United States. I adored Pete Long. With him began my lifelong bias for the people, food, and culture of the Mediterranean. Both Armour and Pete are buried in High Valley Baptist Cemetery.

MADGE (August 24, 1890 - April 6, 1936)

"Pretty Madge had light brown hair, blue-gray eyes, and a fair complexion. Similar to her Aunt Laura in her religious devotion, Madge loved to play Baptist hymns on the family's Jacob Doll piano. Madge believed that God would heal her of the uterine infection that plagued the last twelve years of her young life following her miscarriage in 1924. According to the doctors, a simple operation would have saved her life. In those hard times, no one offered to pay for the surgery, not even her father Calvin who could have easily afforded it at the time. By the time Madge did make it to the hospital in San Antonio twelve years later, it was too late and she died at age forty-six."

Madge earned a teaching certificate which she used at Hall's Valley near Richland Springs, San Saba County, until her marriage on September 6, 1914. She married Lewis Faulkner, a "mule-skinner" who Calvin hired for his four-horse team to haul onions to the railhead at San Saba. When she eloped, she wrote a note and slipped out the back window. They were married by a justice of the peace at Bend, Texas. Sometime thereafter, Madge returned to her father's farm, pregnant and hungry. She and Lewis rented a place on Calvin's farm. With her first baby almost due, she asked Etheridge for a good name. Ironically, he suggested *Brock* after an Army captain he knew and admired. Brock Faulkner grew up to become a distinguished Army officer. "She was a good mother and a comforting motherly influence to all in need" said Etheridge. Madge is buried at Carrizo Springs.

JEWELL (March 6, 1892 - September 13, 1973)

Said Etheridge, "Jewell, nicknamed 'Jewsy,' was a frail child. Her puberty was delayed to her late teens. Abby had her see the doctor about it. She went through menopause only in her thirties. Her high cholesterol lifelong farm diet may have contributed to the hardening of the arteries in her brain that forced her into a rest home in Mexia for the last years of her life. Jewell had dark brown hair, gray-green eyes, and a pretty, freckled complexion. Growing up, she was basically an optimistic tomboy. She married Marvin Thompson, a cousin of her Aunt Beatrice Sullivan's, wife of Richard Allen Brazil.

She and her husband Marvin bought a farm in Mexia. It was known within the family as "Gravel Hill." They earned the farm through her frugality and Marvin's competence at carpentry, farming, and running a dairy cream route. Their busy farm had chickens, cows, pigs, a fruit orchard and a mule-driven sugarcane mill. Jewell's fiancé, Eugene Tate, was drafted in 1917 and died in France during the influenza epidemic. Although she loved her husband dearly, she always remembered her early, tragic loss.

"Jewell was good at salvaging things, 'making something out of nothing,' anything innovative. She loved poetry and idolized her father and the Brazils. She was the mover behind the Brazil Reunions of the 1950's and 60's that were held every Fathers' Day at the Lampasas City Park."

WILLIAM LEE (January 8, 1898 - March 17, 1975)

"Named for his Uncle William Gage, He had a Gage-like physique. Relatively short, he wore tall boots to compensate for his height. He had dark curly hair. Lee was his parents' favorite. Lee was also a picky eater--he would only eat certain foods prepared in a certain way and served at certain times. As a child, when dinner wasn't ready when he thought it should be, he is remembered saying, 'Ma, if I don't eat soon, I'm just gonna fall behind the dresser.'"

Etheridge and Lee were lifelong friends. Lee had a good mind, hated farming, and always regretted that he was not able to break away from their father and attend college as Etheridge did. From his love of anything mechanical it's likely he would have made a good engineer. He was also an able carpenter. One of the several marks of his intelligence and spirituality was his winning of the highest degree offered by the Masonic Order. He was also a long-term deacon in the First Baptist Church of Lometa.

Lee had several female admirers when he was young and single, so many in fact that Lee later bragged that he "had to fight 'em off with my hat." Lee met his wife, Frances Ellis, when she was teaching at the Bend School. They courted for six years. It was a loving but not always easy marriage.

OTIS SALEM (March 8, 1900 - April 28, 1971)

"Otis showed much of his Scotch-Irish blood with his sandy-reddish hair, light skin, and blue-green eyes. Although his grandmother, Jane Brazil, called him "Prillaman," he also looked like his grandfather, Jesse Brazil. Otis was a hard worker, a natural farmer. He kept his family together during the Depression by keeping his farm, the old Jesse Brazil place, where he took in most of the family after the Carrizo Springs disaster. Otis had a quiet, deep spirituality. He preferred to stay in his community where he was well loved and respected within the circles of Bend and Chappel society. Otis was as much a nineteenth century man as twentieth century. He loved to talk history with Niel McAnnely, founder of Bend, Texas, and other old pioneers. Otis was very sensitive to teasing, especially from Lee. That's why he changed his middle name from "Salem" to "Calvin," not realizing until later what Salem meant to him, his Gage grandfather's middle name. He was closest to Madge, his gentle sister."

ELIZABETH JANE "PATSY"
(November 1, 1902 - August 7, 1996)

"Named for her two grandmothers, Sarah Elizabeth Nettles and Jane Prillaman. Patsy was given the nickname "Patsy," the traditional nickname for "Martha," by her father in honor of his aunt, Martha Brazil Hepple as well as her Aunt Martha Gage Brazil. Patsy she was often compared with Aunt Martha for her very social nature. Her nickname, "Patsy," stuck and she adopted it as her own.

Patsy had flaxen hair like the Burleson's, blue-gray eyes, pretty features, and a slender frame. She was a happy and giving person all her life. Never having children of her own, she doted on her nieces and nephews who naturally returned her love. Patsy took care of the High Valley Baptist Church as long as she lived in San Saba County. She made sure the earliest church records were preserved in the Southwest Texas Baptist Seminary in Fort Worth."

Although some of her siblings also got those easy-to-obtain Texas teaching certificates, Patsy was the only one to make teaching her career. She took her B.A. degree from Howard Payne in Education and taught high school English and Spanish successfully in Littlefield, Paint Rock, Rock Springs, and San Saba High School.

While she made her living by teaching, Patsy was a frustrated artist at heart. She loved to play the piano and paint still lifes and landscapes. A very intelligent woman, she read widely and owned a sizeable personal library. Like Armour, who sometimes went with her, Patsy traveled widely, especially to Northeast--Washington D.C., Niagara Falls, and Canada among other places. Patsy was a leader in her Chappel community, in High Valley Baptist Church, and at San Saba High School.

Patsy retired from teaching when she married Ausley Lackey in 1945. Although mature in years, Patsy's marriage to Ausley showed the naivety and optimism of any girl unfamiliar with the realities of marriage. She thought she could reform Ausley Lackey after they married. The prospects weren't promising. Ausley had served time for theft in his native Georgia. His first wife, a Miss Harkey, divorced him. And all he brought to Patsy's marriage was a run-down farm near Harkeyville and his difficult personality. He moved in with Patsy and her widower father who had lost his beloved Abigail only two months before. According to Etheridge, Ausley mistreated his old father-in-law. Patsy was caught between two men who hated each other, divided over their competition for Patsy's love and attention.

Patsy's judgment in men was not improved by the Ausley experience. When he died in 1969, Patsy still felt lonely. She married Martin Crutsinger in

1971. Their marriage lasted less than a year. She wisely divorced him when his character flaws became apparent even to her. Crutsinger, who was fifteen years her junior, was divorced by his first wife, Beverly, in 1968. He had been overheard bragging about Patsy, "I'm gonna marry that widow and get everything's she's got!" He did--but didn't.

Patsy, like her sister Jewell, was confined to a rest home in her last years, dying in Killeen on August 7, 1996. She, too, lies buried in High Valley Cemetery.

CHAPTER TWELVE

THE PRICES

The Prices introduced a welcome strain of a bright, talented, and conventional family into our genetic mix. Except for Evelyn Price, they were not particularly religious and brought a light-hearted, practical approach to life. The Prices didn't have to prove they were still aristocratic church leaders. They just enjoyed living.

Evelyn Price Brazil (1907-1994)

John Richard Price, Jr., Evelyn's father, was born January 28, 1881, at Florence, Texas. He married December 25, 1901, at Bandera, Texas where he died February 10, 1937. Mrs. Perlie Price of Hawley[1] said "J.R. Price was given his nickname, 'Boss', by an old Negro ex-slave that had belonged to his grandfather, Joseph A. Price. The old Negro, named 'Rafe', stayed with his former master after the Civil War because he didn't want to leave him."[1]

Price married Cora Leah White, daughter of David Fisher White and Melina Carolyn Estes. She was born March 17, 1881, in Osage Community, Coryell County, Texas, and died in Bandera on October 9, 1968.

John Richard Price, Junior, and Cora Price, 1929

THE WHITES

David White family
(Top R to L: Cora, Frank, Lily, Christopher Columbus, Manda,
Mary. Below:Margaret, Melinda, David, Henry)

David Fischer White was born near Dayton, Ohio, on July 12, 1830, the son of Henry and Mary White. David married Malinda Carolyn Estes at McKinney, Texas, on May 12, 1867, and died at Bandera, Texas, on January 11, 1908. According to his daughter, Cora, David's parents came from Holland.[2] Their name was originally *Weiss*, Anglicized to *White*. His middle name, *Fisher*, was his mother's maiden name.[2]

David White was a blacksmith. He never stayed long in one place. Soon after he and Malinda married in Collin County, Texas, they moved to Benton, Arkansas. In 1875, they moved to Falls County, Texas. In 1878, they went to Coryell County, Texas, and from there in 1885 to Bosque County. In 1886, they moved to Hamilton County and in 1887 to Erath County. In 1893, they went to Atascosa County. Finally, in 1896, they landed in Bandera County. David died there from 'Parapysis' according to the doctor who filed his death certificate.

In 1850, David White, 20, a blacksmith, born in Ohio, lived with his parents, Henry, 70, born in Virginia, and his mother, Mary, 55, also born in Virginia. Perhaps his parents came from Holland. All three lived in

Missouri. In 1860, David White, 30, was living with his brother, Jacob White, 38, a well-to-do farmer with assets of $5,480 real estate, $5,480 personal property, in Tussville, Henry County, Missouri.

David White was in Sparinaw, Benton County, Arkansas, when the 1870 census taker came around on August 11th. His wife, Malinda, 28, was born in Arkansas as were his two children, Mary, 2, and Henry, four months old.

David White appeared on the 1880 census of Coryell County as "D.F. White," aged 49. His parents' birthplaces were not given. His wife, "M.C.," 37, was born in Arkansas with parents born in Illinois and Alabama. His six children at the time all had Ohio and Arkansas as their parents' birthplaces, the first four children, Mary Rebecca, 12; Henry Blueford, 10; Margaret Ann, 7; and Amanda Minerva, 5, were born in Arkansas. The other two, Lillie May, 3, and Christopher Columbus White, one year old, were born in Texas. Cora and her brother, Benjamin Franklin White, weren't born yet.

THE ESTES FAMILY

Malinda Carolyn Estes was born April 19, 1842, in Arkansas, and died at Bandera, Texas, on October 3, 1940. She was the fifth of seven children born to Blueford Estes and wife, Rebecca. Blueford was born in Kentucky about 1803 and his wife was born in Tennessee about 1806. Their other six children were William H. Estes, born 1829 in Illinois; Polly A. , born 1836 in Missouri; Joseph, born 1838 also in Missouri; Leonard C., born 1839 in Arkansas; Christopher Columbus , born 1845; and Amanda M., born in August 1850, also in Arkansas. Amanda married Thomas Lee and died in Runnels County, Texas. Christopher Estes never married but died a Confederate soldier in the Civil War. Malinda Estes White was considered a "hell cat" by those who knew her, unlike David White who was considered a kind gentleman.

Blueford Estes was recorded in War Eagle Township in Madison County, Arkansas, in 1840. He was in his 30's with two sons in the ten to fourteen age range, and two under five. His wife, too, was in her 30's with daughters one ten to fourteen and two five to nine years old.

Blueford Estes, 47, a farmer, appeared on the Black River schedules for Lawrence County, Arkansas, on October 30, 1850. With wife, Rebecca, his seven children appear on the returns as described above.

THE PRICES

John and Cora White Price had six children:

Lenora Vineta Price, born November 23, 1902, at Bandera and married first Henry Mills and second, Thorton D. Woolfly.

Eunice Edra Price, born January 27, 1905, at Waltersville, Oregon and married Harold J.Young at Bandera on July 4, 1924.

Gladys Evelyn Price born May 19, 1907, at Bandera and married Etheridge Claude Brazil at Bandera on December 20, 1923.

Zella May Price born September 27, 1909, at Tarpley, Texas, and married December 25, 1932, at Bandera to Baird Foster. They were married by Rev. E.C. Brazil.

Glen Leroy Price was born in Wendling, Oregon, on August 20, 1912, and married first, Mrs. Nina M. Klaus on August 6, 1941, and second, Mrs. Pansy Fay Wilson Price, divorced wife of his brother, Carroll, on February 1, 1946.

Carroll Truette Price was born November 29, 1919, and married first, Pansy Fay Wilson, in New Braunfels and second, Lillian Hunnicut.

John Richard Price, Senior was born February 12, 1857, in Arkansas, and married July 11, 1878, in Gillespie County, Texas, to Elizabeth Passmore, daughter of Andrew J. Passmore and "Eppsy" Cato. John died on July 2, 1933, in Hawley, Texas. Elizabeth died in 1900 from typhoid fever caused by the Medina River Flood that year. She died in Devine, Texas. John Richard Price, Senior and Elizabeth Passmore had eleven children:

Miley Price burned to death at age nine months.

Viola Price, born May 24, 1879 or 80, in Doss Valley, Gillespie County, Texas and married in Oklahoma to W.P. Allgood.

John Richard Price, Jr. (1881-1937)

Pearl Price, born June 12, 1884, and married September 3, 1904, at Eastland, Texas, to Ross Price.

Charles Henry Lee Price, born May 16, 1886, in Doss Valley and married in Texas on December 25, 1909. to McCoy Thomas. He died in May 1946, in Brownwood.

Lottie Price was born at Doss Valley on June 27, 1890, and married to Jess Gardner.

Neva Corrine Price, born September 17, 1893, at Doss Valley and married January 31, 1909, at Brownwood to Ernest Davis.

Hershel Price was born February 14, 1896, at Velma, Oklahoma, and married at Hawley, Texas, in November 11, 1918, to Jessie Cook.

Donie Price was born in February in the 1890's at Alma, Oklahoma, and married at Brownwood, Texas to W.B. Withers.

Floyd Price was born at Devine, Texas, on March 27, 1901, and married to Velma Cook.

Lula Price died around two years of age.

John Richard Price, Senior's second wife, Roxie Ann Horton, was born August 16, 1877, and died at Salt Creek, Brownwood, Texas, on November 21, 1927. They had six children. The first four were born in Brownwood, Texas, and the fifth in Abilene while the sixth was born in Hawley, Texas: Harold Lee (1908), Walter Orville (1910), Adelia Inez (1918), Laura Mozelle (1915), Thelma Pauline (1917), and Mildred Orlena Price (1919).[3]

Joseph A. Price was born in Illinois in 1825 and married in Polk City, Arkansas, to Jane Waits who was born in Alabama on June 13, 1823. They were married September 1, 1844, in Polk County. Joseph Price died in Brownwood, Texas on March 13, 1916. According to Roxanne Harton Price, second wife of J.R. Price, Junior,[3] "Joseph and Jane Price, parents of her late husband, are buried at the Baptist Cemetery at Jenkin's Spring, Brown County, Texas about eleven miles southeast of Brownwood."

Jane Waits was the daughter of Humphrey Waits and wife, Elizabeth. They appeared on the 1850 Federal Census in Fordorn Township, Polk County,

Arkansas as Humphrey Waits, 66, a miller, born in South Carolina, with wife, Elizabeth, 63, also born in South Carolina, and their son, Augustus, 24, a farmer, born in Alabama.

Joseph A. Price and Jane Waits Price had five known children:

Rachael R. Price, born in Polk County, Arkansas, in 1849, and married July 11, 1878, to Wallace Lee Price. She died in Oregon.

Joseph H. Price, born in Polk County in 1852 or 1853 and married in Gillespie County on July 26, 1880, to Sarah Gibson.

Augustus Slaughter Price, born in Polk County on February 7, 1855, and married in Gillespie County on June 10, 1880, to Susanna Weatherby.

John Richard Price, Sr., born in Polk County in 1857 and married in Gillespie County on July 11, 1878 to Elizabeth Passmore.

Elizabeth Price, born in Polk County in September 1859.

John Price, born 1800 in Virginia, had three children by his first wife:

John Price, Jr. born in Illinois in 1817 and married Louisa.

William Price, born in Illinois in 1824 and married Nancy E. in Arkansas in the 1840's.

Joseph A. Price, born in Illinois in 1825, married Jane Waits in Polk County, Arkansas, on September 1, 1844, and died in Brownwood, Texas, on March 13, 1916.

In his 1910 Confederate pension application, #18849, Joseph Price said he was born in Illinois and lived in Texas for 40 years. He lived in Brownwood, Texas. He served in Texas' Company "H," Duff's Regiment, which he joined in 1862 and surrendered at the close of war. His affidavit was filed by Rachael Price, age 61, who resided in Eugene Lane County, Oregon. Joseph Price was her father, who enlisted January 1862, in Capt. Deld Hunter's Co. "A," 35th Cavalry Regiment and served during the war. She was his eldest child and was old enough to remember the war. "I would say applicant, viz. Joseph Price, is 'physically broke down owing to his advanced age (viz. 89 years)." The War Department confirmed Joseph served in Company "H," 33rd Texas Cavalry.[4]

John Price married second, Louisa by whom he had at least five children:

Martha C., born in Illinois in 1835

Rebecca E., born in Illinois in 1839

Lorina, born in Arkansas in 1842

James E., born in Arkansas in 1844

Louisa J., born in Arkansas in 1845

Federal Census of 1850, November 1, White Township, Polk County, Arkansas revealed:

Price, John	50 M	Farmer	Virginia
Louisa	34 F		Tennessee
Martha C.	15 F		Illinois
Rebecca E.	15 F		Illinois
Lorina	8 F		Arkansas
James H.	6 M		Arkansas
Louisa S.	5 F		Arkansas
Price, Joseph	25 M	Farmer	Illinois
Jane	25 F		Alabama
Rachael R.	1 F		Arkansas
Price, William	26M	Farmer	Illinois
Nancy E.	20 F		Alabama
Letitia A.	2 F		Arkansas
Caranda J.	5/l2 F		Arkansas

1860 Federal Census of Polk County, Arkansas, White Township, Dallas Post Office, July 17, showed:

Price, Joseph	36 M	miller 250-500	Illinois
Jane	35 F		Georgia
Rachael	11 F		Arkansas

Joseph H.	7 M	"
Augustus	5 M	"
John R.	3 M	"
Elizabeth	10/12 F	"

(living near Augustus Waits, also a miller)

1880 Federal Census of Gillespie County, Texas:

Price, Joseph	58 M	Farmer	Illinois- Kentucky-?
Jane	58 F		Alabama- North Carolina-Virginia
Joseph A.	28 M		Arkansas-Illinois-Alabama

1920 Federal Census of Bandera County, Texas-All north of the {Medina} river Precinct #1:

Price, John R.	38 M	Head	Texas-Texas-Texas
Cora	39 F	Wife	Texas-Ohio-Missouri
Linora	17 F	Daughter	Texas-Texas-Texas
Eunice	14 F	"	Oregon-Texas-Texas
Evelyn	12 F	"	Texas-Texas-Texas
Zella Mae	10 F	Daughter	Texas-Texas-Texas
Glen	7 M	Son	Oregon-Texas-Texas
Carroll	1/12 M	Son	Texas-Texas-Texas

Gladys Evelyn Price shared her testimony about her conversion to the Baptist faith:[5]

"My Testimony

When I was 11 years old {1919}, we were having the annual summer revival. My parents were saved when I was 6. . . .I came under conviction, realizing I was lost and needed a Savior. I remember going home from church with a girl friend who lived on a big ranch and had everything one could imagine to play with--but I was so miserable I didn't feel like playing with anything. Running through my mind was the fact: if I should die today I'd go to Hell. As the service passed, I became more miserable, and one Wednesday night I went forward. I thought that was what I needed to do. I was voted into the church. But instead of feeling better, I felt worse. We were to be baptized on Sunday afternoon so I thought, 'Surely I'll feel better after I'm baptized" But the baptizing came and went and nothing changed. I knew I was not saved and I didn't know what to do about it. I was ashamed to talk to my parents. . . . .

So I went to my organ and began to play. Always that made me feel better. But not so on this Tuesday following the baptizing. As I would play 'I am Thine, O Lord' or the words seemed to mock me. 'Have Thine Own Way,' 'Higher Ground' and many others but this only makes it worse. So I turned to 'Only Trust Him' and began to play, reading the words as I went along--'Come every soul by sin oppressed, and He will surely give you rest by trusting in his Word' and then the chorus 'Only trust Him, He will save you now.' I thought 'Could it be that simple?' And bowing my head, seated there at my organ, I turned everything over to the Lord. I remember telling the Lord if He would save me, he could have my life, my talents, my all for the rest of my life.

Such joy unspeakable flooded my soul, and I really went to playing the organ. It was easy to play then. I stayed there so long, my mother finally came in and chased me out of the house. I didn't mind for I went up on a hill near the house in a grove of trees, and continued thanking God for so great a salvation"!⁵

Evelyn's funeral announcement said, "Mrs. Brazil will be remembered most recently as the church organist at Memorial Baptist Church in Killeen from 1954 to 1981 and a piano teacher for many children in Killeen."

THE PASSMORES

Dictionary of English and Welch Surnames:

Local, of 'Pasmore'. Passmore. Adam= County Sommerset, England Edward III= Kirby's Quest, p. 243.

Andrew Jackson Passmore, born November 23, 1831, in Telfair County, Georgia, and married Mary Cato in Telfair.   He died in 1916 on Onion Creek, Gillespie County, Texas. Andrew Jackson Passmore's mother was Mary Candor Brooker who was born in Georgia in 1830 and died on Onion Creek July 28, 1896. Their children:

William Passmore, born in Georgia in 1850

Milam Passmore, born in Georgia in 1853

Lucretia Passmore, born January 16, 1855, in Florida. She married John Sembritzki in Fredericksburg, Texas, on December 21, 1885 and died in Clyde, Texas on April 8, 1928.

Susan Ann Passmore, born in Clay County, Florida, on April 10, 1857, and married Louis Gibson in Fredericksburg, Texas. She died on May 10, 1909.

John Passmore, born in Clay County, Florida, on March 25, 1859 and married Ida Webb in Custer County, Oklahoma. He died on August 1, 1906.

Elizabeth Passmore, born in Clay County on February 8, 1861, and married in Gillespie County on July 11, 1878, to John Richard Price. She died in Divine, Texas, on June 15, 1901.

Andrew Passmore, born July 22, 1863, and died in January 1865.

Charlotte Passmore, born April 5, 1866, and died in December 1872.

Daniel Passmore, born August 24, 1867, and died December 6, 1872.

Lucinda Passmore, born July 30, 1869, and died March 25, 1873.

Eliza Ellen Passmore, born in Texas on March 9, 1871. She married Alfred Sadler in Fredericksburg, in 1925. She died on February 5, 1936.

Lenard Passmore, born in Texas, on January 12, 1873, and married Rachael Banta. He died on December 28, 1936.

John Passmore, father of Andrew Jackson Passmore, was born about 1806 in Washington County, Georgia. He married Sarah Brooker, daughter of Joseph Brooker, born in Burke County, Georgia, also in 1806. Their children:

Robert Passmore, born 1829 in Telfair County, Georgia, like all the others

Andrew Jackson Passmore

Bryant Passmore, born 1837 and married Elisa E.

Emily Passmore, born in 1839

Narcissa, born in 1843

John Passmore, born in 1844 and married Claracey in Texas

Elizabeth Passmore, born in Telfair County in 1845

Andrew J. Passmore served in Company "D," 11th Florida Infantry, CSA.[6]

Andrew J. Passmore signed his will in Gillespie County, Texas, on April 21, 1904. He gave his son Leonard Passmore 340 acres of Survey originally granted to F. Rodriquez. He gave other bequests to his daughter Susan Ann Gibson, wife of Louis Gibson; the children of Elizabeth Price, deceased wife of J.R. Price; Lucretia Sembritzsky, wife of John Sembritzsky; Eliza Ellen Sattler, wife of Alfred Sattler; and John Passmore, "… all other lands I may own, and not herein specially bequeathed . . . ." He gave all the residue of my estate, one sixth to the above sons and daughters including Elizabeth Price's children "or if any of them should be dead then such shall go to his or her children."

"It is my will and I hereby so provide that whoever of my children or their descendants of this Will, shall not agree to be entirely excluded from receiving or inheriting any part of my Estate and such share herein bequeathed shall go to the others who take under this Will. . . "

Intelligent Andrew Passmore knew how to stop any squabbling over his estate before it began.

"The land herein included to be given to my children, Susan Ann, Lucretia, Eliza Ellen, John and Elizabeth's children, being all of Sur. No 323, containing 640 acres, originally granted to W.L. Cunningham and 320 acres of Sur. No. 326, originally granted to F. Rodriquez, all situated in Gillespie County. All land therein bequeathed being held in common with my deceased wife. My son Leonard, having improved the 340 acres herein set apart to him, wherefore I desire that all of my other children shall make no claim against the same as heirs of their mother and he in return shall not assent claim as such against the other lands. . . ." He appointed his son Leonard Passmore his executor.

#378 Inventory and Appraisement on the Estate of A.J. Passmore dated March 25, 1916:

"640 acres survey No. 323, grantee W.L. Cunningham ($12,800)

320 acres survey No. survey No. 326, grantee Francisco Rodriquez ($5760)

350 acres out of sur. No. 325 grantee Francisco Rodriquez ($6800)

Cash on hand ($936.61)

Sixty head of cattle ($2470)

Twenty eight head of horses and mules ($1260)

Five jacks and jennets ($210)

About thirty head of hogs ($195)

Farm implements consisting of one stump puller, one mower and rake, one Acme harrow, two disc-plows, one riding cultivator, one hand planter, two hand plows, one pitchfork, one fire showel, one crowbar, one garden rake, one posthole digger, one showel, five singletrees, one wire stretcher, one reaphook, one set of blocks and tackle, seven ropes ($141.75)

One farm waggon ($50)

One buggy ($20)

One Hack ($5)

One Rail road scraper ($4)

One saddle ($4)

One buggy harness ($5)

Two sets of double harness ($5)

One molasses mill ($5)

One set of pipe wrenches ($5)

One shoe repairing outfit (40 cents)

Fodder chopper ($7.50)

Brass Cylinder (50 cents)

Blacksmith tools consisting of: two vices, one leather bellows, one anvil, two forge hammers, several sets of hinges, bolts, screws, nails et. cet., one iron drill, three sets of screw plates with dies, wire clippers, three files, two cold-chisels, and minor implements ($25.45)

Carpenters tools: consisting of: three saws, one plane, four augers, carpenter compass, two squares, four chisels, two drawing knives, one turning lath, one brace and bits, two hand axes, one hatchet, one adze, one cross-cut saw, & minor implements ($8.40)

Kitchen furniture consisting of: one table, one kitchen-safe, one stove with pots & stewpans, three buckets, one washpan, twenty six cups, twenty two saucers, eight plates, two meat-platters, six glasses, five tin pans, one glass pitcher, two sets of knives & forks, seven jars, twelve fruit jars, and other odds & ends ($18.15)

Supplies consisting of: one sack of meal, five pounds of coffee, five lbs beans, five lbs sugar ($4.40)

Household furniture, consisiting of: three bedsteads, one cot, two feather beds, two cotton beds, fourteen quilts & blankets, two pillows, two trunks, five chairs, two lamps, one lantern ($17.40)

One sewing machine ($ 0)

Four pocket-knives ($1.25)

thirty three books et cet ($2)

Wearing apparel consisting of: one cap, one hat, two pairs of gloves, three pairs of wool socks, one overcoat, one suit of clothes, two suits of heavy underwear, five pairs of drawers, ten shirts, five pairs of pants, two coats & other minor articles ($14.60)

Total: $30,776.41" {about $650,000 in 2009}[7]

German-Americans in Fredericksburg, Texas, were careful to list every item of value in Andrew Passmore's estate.

The 1830 Federal Census of Telfair County, Georgia, showed:

> Passmore, John   males: 1 under 5, 1: 20-29
> 1: 20-29
>
> Passmore, Cilvey (Sylvia)   males: 1: 15-19
> 1:50-59
>
> Brooker, Joseph   males: 3 under 5, 2:5-9, 1:10-14, 1:40-49
> 1:10-14, 1:20-29
>
> Cato, William   males: 1 under 5, 1:20-29, 1:40-49
> 1 under 5, 1:5-9, 1:10-14, 1:15-19, 1:30-39
>
> Peterson, Jesse   males:1 under 5, 1:5-9, 1:30-39
> 2 under 5, 1`:15-19
>
> Peterson, John   males: 2 under 5, 2:5-9, 1:30-39
> 1 under 5, 1:5-9, 1:20-29

Federal Census of 1840, Telfair County, Georgia, included:

> Passmore, John   males: 1 under 5, 1:5-9, 1:10-14, 1:30-39
> 1 under 5, 1:5-9, 1:10-14, 1:30-39
>
> Brooker, Joseph   males: 2:5-9, 1:10-14, 2:20-29, 1:50-59
> 1 under 5, 2:15-19, 1:40-49
>
> Cato, Henry   males: 1:30-39
> 1 under 5, 1:5-9, 1:20-29

Cato, William   males: l under 5, 1:5-9, 1:40-49, 1:50-59
                       3:5-9, 1:10-14, 1:15-19, 2:20-29, 1:40-49

Brooker, Charles   males: 1:15-19
                       under 5, l:15-19

The Federal Census of 1850, Telfair County, Georgia: 348th District, page 372, Household 12-12 revealed:

Passmore, John	44 M	$200	Washington County, Georgia (actual place of birth)
Sarah	44 F		Burke County, Georgia
Robert	21 M		Telfair County, Georgia
Alexander	18 M		"
Bryant	13 M		"
Emily	11 F		"
Narcissa	7 F		"
Sarah Brooker	6 F		"
Elizabeth	5 F		"
John	6M		"

Fussell, Timothy	20 M	Irwin County, Georgia
Charlotte	16 F	Telfair County, Georgia

437th District, Households 55-56, 2 September 2, 1850

Joseph Brooker	66 M	Farmer $150	South Carolina
Cander	59 F		"
Richard	20 M	Farmer	Telfair County, Georgia
James	18 M		"
Cander	14 F		"
Henry	26 M	"Idiot"	"
William Cato	65 M	Farmer $100	South Carolina

Polly Ann	60 F		"
Cara Ann	27 F		Montgomery County, Georgia
Ginsey	26 F		"
John	21M	Farmer	Telfair County, Georgia
Olife	18 F		"
Cato, Cander	38 F		Montgomery County, Georgia
Epsy	20 F		Telfair County, Georgia
Polly Ann	18 F		"
William	16 M		"
Susan	11 F		"
Prissa	8 F		"
Jane	6/12F (twin)		"
"One boy"	6/12M (twin)		"

The Federal Census of Clay County, Florida. August 9, 1860 showed:

Chesowicke Community, 86-86

Passmore, A.J.	28 M	Farmer $550	Georgia
Epsy	30 F		"
William	10 M		"
Milam	7 M		Georgia
Lucretia	5 M		Florida
Susan	3 F		"
John	1 M		"

On the 1880 Federal Census of Gillespie County, Texas, we find:

Passmore, A.J.	48 M	Farmer	Georgia-Ga.-Ga.
Eppsy	50 F		Georgia-Ga.-N.C.
Lucretia	25 F		Florida-Ga.-Ga.
Susan	23 F		«
John	21 M		«
Elisa A.	9 F		Texas-Ga.-Ga.
Lenard	7 M		«

CHAPTER THIRTEEN

CAREY HAMILTON BRACEWELL (1936-   )

CHILDHOOD

I was born *Carey O'Lee Brazil* in Brady, Texas, on Thursday, November 5, 1936, at 5:20 AM. Common to early November births, my parents really didn't want another child. The Great Depression still depressed America. However "if it be God's will," they wanted another girl to be my sister Patti's pal, two boys and two girls. They named me for William Carey (1761-1834), an English Baptist missionary to India. My middle name was a combination of my two paternal uncles' names, Otis and Lee. I kept my first name.

Even though my parents weren't rich, they were wealthy in their love for each other and their children. They were dedicated to loving everyone and spreading the Baptist gospel. Any disagreements they may have had were settled privately, away from the children. Dad always played the Southern gallant to Mom. He called her "my lady" among other enduring terms. And he was a true stoic, never complaining to her or anyone about anything.

They never expressed what must have been one their greatest disappointments that none of their children stayed Baptist. Their kids suffered from the impossible task of modeling for others "the perfect Baptist children" with all the guilt and morbid focus on the Calvinistic afterworld. But at least three out of four of us wouldn't have changed our parents for anyone else's. E.C. Brazil, Junior, the typical second child, adopted the "Bad Boy" role to Hal's "Hero" image. If he could, he might have changed parents for someone "cooler."

When I interviewed my father in 1973 to get information for this book, I asked him about me just as I asked about all the other kinfolks. My father said he was surprised I was so bright as a child. But was it a compliment to me or an indictment of my siblings? He said I talked at ten months. My first words, sitting on Hal's lap while watching the night sky were, ironically, "moon, star, sky." My first sentence spoken at eighteen months, in reference to a big flood on the San Saba River, was "John, your piggies will get out!" as their pig pen floated down the river.

Father said I was "a sweet, calm, quiet, and philosophical child who reflected both Price and Brazil traits" having Boss Price's intelligence and determination and the Brazil height and quietness. "You were a quiet, sweet-tempered child who seemed to think things out carefully. You exhibited a spirit of self-reliance. You were always a studious boy who even as a child would choose big words with profound meanings. You had a mind of my own, not wishy-washy. You had long curly hair, quiet and deliberate, very dependable, obedient, and respectful. You were our largest baby so far, big and sturdy. You were absolutely adored by all, mama and sister both." Naturally I identified with a father who loved me so much.

Dad related an often-repeated story: "Once when he was about five you had some pet chickens. You would put them on the fence in a row and with your Bible, preach to your flock. One by one, the chickens would grow weary of this and hop down. You would repeatedly put them back up. Finally you got mad and lost your patience, saying 'All right then! Just go to Hell if you want to!'"

In 1938, we moved to the Harbor house just outside the town of San Saba on the San Saba River. Then in 1940, we moved into our Rock House on Annex Street in sleepy, small, conservative San Saba. Of our childhood there together, Patti said, " We played a lot together and we hid a lot from E.C. who seemed to be constantly annoyed by his younger siblings. You were always pretty quiet and didn't seem to need to socialize all that much. You were more of a dreamer, a thinker, even when you were very young. You are the smartest of the four of us. You are the most sensitive, too, I believe. From an early time you seemed to live in your own world. You thought about things, keeping your own counsel. I don't remember you running around with other kids so much, probably preferring your own company more. I treasure those years of ours together when it was just you and me against the world. Those years we moved around to a new town and a new school, especially during the war years. We had each other and we could count on that. You have always been quiet and thoughtful and kind."

Patti and Carey, c.1940

WORLD WAR II

On December 7, 1941, I was playing outside when the news came about the attack on Pearl Harbor. I was scared because my family was scared even though I had no idea at age five what had happened or where. In 1942, we Moved to Bucyrus, Ohio, where I started first grade. Ohio was like a new world. There was green grass everywhere, factories and people talking in strange accents.

My first crush was on my teacher, a lovely woman who loved her class. Like my mother who played classics on her piano, my teacher played classical music records for the class. She played for us Schumann's *Traumerei*, still my favorite.

In 1943, we moved to Keystone Heights, Florida, where Dad became the Protestant Chaplain at Camp Blanding. I remember the chapels and the temporary buildings. I also recall the lonesome G.I.s who gave candy and soft drinks to Patsy and me. Our house in Keystone Heights sat on sandy flatland with orange groves all around. I went to second grade at Keystone Heights. Poorly-trained, resentful, and overworked Florida teachers tempered my former love of teachers.

I remember the scary posters of bestial-looking Nazis and Japs posters at the camp. I also remember the "Buy War bonds" campaigns and the scrap metal drives that sent us scrounging for anything metal we could give to the war effort. The popular music, "*White Cliffs of Dover,*" and "*Praise the Lord and Pass the Ammunition,* " stay in memory because they were sung so early in my life with such emotion. I remember the government ration books for food, especially meat, sugar and butter. Our first use of margarine with the colored gel inside we had to mix ourselves. Our shoes, tires and gasoline were rationed.

D-Day, June 1944, had no impact on me at seven except that it worried my parents about Hal which in turn affected me. I wasn't too clear about what was happening overseas. However, launching of the first V-2 German flying bombs against England that year did bother me because they said one might someday hit America.

We returned to San Saba in 1945 to await Dad's return as World War II wound down. Meanwhile, we ate a lot of Spam (fatty, processed meat) and Karo syrup, both much too frequent in our diet. I still hate Spam. Before 1945, we at least ate well at Army camps until Dad went overseas and we were sent back to Texas.

President Roosevelt's death on April 12, 1945, affected me mainly because it so saddened everyone around me. Roosevelt had seen us through the most critical times in our lives. People reacted as though a trusted father had died. Germany's surrender the following month meant Hal's assured return and an end to half of my mother's worry. The other half was Dad's safe homecoming.

America dropped atomic bombs on Japan late in 1945. Her surrender a few days later in August ended World War II. Japan's capitulation made a deeper impression because it meant my father would now come back from the Pacific. Moreover, it meant an end to our fear of "those Godless Japs."

On V-J Day, September 2, 1945, all of San Saba erupted in celebration. Cars horns honked, the town fire siren howled, and we kids marched up and down the street laughing and yelling, beating on pots and pans in place of drums. Everyone welcomed the launching of the United Nations at the end of the war, naively hoping like our elders before us that such a league of nations would finally put an end to the horrors of war. Dad returned home early to deal with problems with E.C. Brazil, Junior.

AFTER THE WAR: A NEAR-DEATH EXPERIENCE

Although I had no way of understanding what happened to me (given my age and culture), I had a near-death experience in the summer of 1946 that changed my life and put me on the path to mystical understanding. Bathing in Cherokee Creek near Jesse Brazil's old farm, I slipped on a mossy rock and almost drowned in the murky green water. I panicked and went down three times before I disappeared. My father was fishing downstream when it happened. It took him several minutes to find me and pull me out. My cousin, Jesse Jim Brazil, and other witnesses couldn't understand why I was angry because I was rescued from drowning. I didn't want to come back.

It was a classical near-death experience. After the panic, I saw my body floating near the bottom of the creek. Next, I was surrounded by intense white light and felt profound love everywhere. I saw a group of smiling Light Beings waiting for me up ahead. I moved toward them. The first one stepped forward and embraced me. It was my late grandmother, Abigail Gage Brazil. We spoke to each other by thought. I pled with all of them to let me stay. However, they explained that I had to go back, that I had to grow up and become a man, get married and have certain children. They showed me the meaning of my life up to then and what lay ahead. I protested but next I found myself lying upside down on a big rock, getting the water pumped out of my lungs. I took a swing at the first person near me, Cousin Jesse Jim Brazil.

There wasn't anything in my experience at age nine or in Baptist theology that helped me understand the changes near drowning brought. After that, my whole perspective changed. I saw the golden white love light surrounding the heads of a loving old couple we knew, the Elmores. I felt deep peace with the whole world. Dad and our local pastor recognized my deepened spirituality and allowed me to join the church ahead of schedule. Ever since that near drowning, I may dread pain but I have never again feared death.

We lived in Santa Rosa, New Mexico, from 1946 to 1947 where Dad pastored the First Baptist Church. I was in the fourth grade. Santa Rosa, mostly Mexican and Catholic, was a small desert town on the Pecos River crossed by U.S. Route 66. My best friends were Beverly Bob Woodruff, my teacher's niece and my first actual girlfriend, and my buddy, Fred Wisner. Beverly lived with her aunt, my teacher, Miss Pansy Woodruff, a good Baptist parishioner. Beverly was an attractive girl but at our age, our romance never progressed beyond holding hands.

In 1948, Dad took the job as district missionary to forty-five rural Baptist churches in northern Missouri. I went to fifth grade in Lancaster, Missouri, five miles from the Iowa state line. I remember the dark woods all around, the cold weather and another girl friend named Ann Naggs. At Christmas, 1948, we returned to San Saba where I went to sixth grade.

Moving into adolescence spoiled my carefree days. It was a miserable time for us all. I escaped into adventure stories. Among other titles, I read all of Forrester's "Horatio Hornblower" series at the San Saba County Library, which inspirited me to one day join the Navy. And life went on. In 1950, when the Korean war broke out and it affected me twice: It took Hal out of my life except for the occasional visit on military leave and, with universal selective service, it made me start thinking about my own future military obligation. I was thirteen at war's outbreak and no one including me foresaw how long the war might last.

With the extension of the military draft the following June 1951, twenty-one year-old E.C. Brazil realized he would be drafted soon. He volunteered for the Army as a musician specialist. He was accepted because he studied music in college at the university in Kirksville, Missouri. He was assigned to the Fourth Army Band in San Antonio, Texas, where he became friends with another bandsman, Bill Kimple, of Dallas. He introduced her to Patti and on February 16, 1952, Patti and Bill married. I was jealous of Bill for taking away Patti and in awe of his wealth and sophistication.

Impoverished by the Texas Drought of 1950-57, we moved to Killeen, Texas. Dad and I found jobs at Bell Furniture Company. Later, I managed a Post Exchange beer garden at Fort Hood. Killeen was a small town before Viet Nam and later wars built up Fort Hood and next-door Killeen. Dry weather, scrub live oak and mesquite bushes scattered along otherwise empty, chalky hills, the Killeen area was poorly suited for farming except for the Leon River bottom lands. But the Killeen area made Fort Hood the best place in America for tank division training. Fort Hood is still the largest Army base in America.

Dad bought our first television set in Killeen, a bulky black-and-white model that had an outside rooftop antenna and received just three stations. Television changed our lives forever as it did for most Americans. Because I was still a kid, the tornado that struck nearby downtown Waco, Texas, on May 11, 1953, shook me hard. It was not so much that the tornado leveled the R.T. Dennis Building, killing more than a hundred people, as ghastly as it was to watch on TV. It was the looting and mutilating of bodies that followed. Looters cut off the fingers of some of the victims to get their rings. I began to realize that the world was not so safe and loving as this Baptist preacher's kid had once believed.

ADOLESCENCE

I bought my first car in Killeen, a '41 Plymouth. Gayle Mayhew was my first girlfriend. I dated other girls, then became attracted to Janet Bay. We dated at first with my friend, Jack McBride, and his girlfriend. Later, we went alone to Killeen's outdoor theater known as "the passion pit." We decided to get married after I fulfilled my military obligation. With our strict Baptist backgrounds and no safe birth control available, totally in love, we became engaged in the summer of 1954.

Meanwhile, Congress passed the Korean G.I. Bill of Rights that offered educational benefits and loan guarantees to veterans of the Korean conflict.

I realized my parents had little money so volunteering for the military was my best chance to get a college education. On August 31, 1954, I volunteered for the Navy to get the Korean War benefits. I was also ready to be on my own.

Carey Brazil, Aerographer's Mate, 1958

In my opinion, a stretch in the military can do a young man good if he can learn from it and keep from being injured or killed. With my good luck, the Korean War armistice held. I made friends in the service but I was homesick for most of my enlistment. After finishing basic training in San Diego, California, late in 1954, I was sent to the Naval Air Training Command in Norman, Oklahoma for aviation training.

After that, I took Aerographers Mate training in meteorology at Lakehurst, New Jersey, and that summer, 1955, got assigned to Aerial Reconnaissance Squadron Three on Guam in the Pacific. On my first hurricane-hunting mission, none of the crew told me about "St. Elmo's fire," the static electricity in high wind storms that made the plane look like it's on fire. I panicked, started looking for a parachute, and the crew had a good laugh at my initiation into hurricane-hunting.

In 1957, I returned to San Diego where I was assigned to the Fleet Weather Center on North Island in San Diego Bay. I Went home on leave and married Janet Bay on April 20, 1957 at the East Side Baptist Church in Killeen. We drove back to San Diego. Our honeymoon at our apartment in San Diego was enchanting. We-picnicked in Balboa Park, visited Disney World and toured Tijuana, Mexico. As the French say, "Things are always best in the beginning." I was honorably discharged on October 4, 1957, the day the Space Age began with the launching of Russia's Sputnik space satellite. Janet and I listened with wonder to the "beep-beep-beep" of Sputnik on our car radio as we drove back to Texas.

Starting at mid-term 1958 until mid-term 1962, I was an undergraduate student at the University of Texas, Austin, going to school on the Korean G.I. Bill. There wasn't enough money in the bill to make ends meet, so Janet worked at Internal Revenue Service and I worked at Fred Shriver's Exxon gasoline station and Studer's Camera Shop.

My undergraduate experience at University of Texas was one of the most positive, life-changing periods of my life even though it was a struggle for me both academically, financially, personally and spiritually. Academically, because my weak academic background was not ready for a major university challenge; financially, because I was self-supporting and the birth of two children meant the loss of Janet's income. However, we deeply loved our children and there was no question that Janet should be a stay at home mom in the best interests of our two babies. Personally, it was a struggle because the stress was almost too much for Janet and therefore for me.

Spiritually, it was a struggle because all my former comforting religious belief systems fell away in the face of modern enlightenment. The motto of the University of Texas, ironically Biblical, is "You shall know the truth and the truth shall set you free." All my early religious beliefs, except for an abiding faith in our Creator, gradually fell away as I studied advanced history and other social sciences.

The first semester I majored in pharmacy but my academic background was too weak to continue. I switched to the College of Arts and Sciences intending to become a history teacher. I majored in European history with a minor in geography.

THE PERSONAL CAREY

I am a scholar and mostly a loner. I have a good capacity for sustained concentration and a natural ability for solving complex problems that interest me. I have a lot of original ideas and insights related to my perceptions and observations of the world around me. And until I controlled my ego through meditation, I prided myself on my gifts of knowledge, logical thought, and objective reasoning.

I display a calm and cool objectivity. I can stand back and view life from a rational, objective perspective, even about those about whom I care. I am unusually self-sufficient and independent. I can function on my own. And I do need my personal space to be respected. I guard my space and privacy judicially. I'm not that easy to live with: in relationships, my closeness can be followed by periods of isolation. I need privacy for me to gather my thoughts and process the events of the day.

I maintain a low profile. I've a minimalist approach to life. I don't talk a lot. I don't require anything to live except the essentials. I don't put much put much emphasis on material things or are caught up in matters of status. In other words, I'm an Old Soul.

Emotionally, I'm also self-sufficient.   I'd rather understand through observation or by accumulating information than getting too deep into the emotional side of thing.   I'm good at maintaining a sense of calm in the middle of a storm. I give off a sort of "guru" aura that makes people want to seek me out for ideas, advice, and information. There seems to be a confidence and a sense of wisdom about me. Like my father's ancestors, it's easy for me to attract a spiritual following.

I know that I am here to serve others and work toward attaining higher consciousness. I am thoughtful, respectful of other's space, informed, likeable, ethical, calm, and insightful, forward thinking and creative, patient, and focused.

Then there's my shadow self.

I tend to over-analyze and it can take me a long time for me to act on my thoughts. The time it took to write this book is proof enough. I can be a world-class procrastinator. I have a knack for putting off things I don't want to do.

I can be too distant and detached. I need so much privacy or alone time, it may come across as overly disconnected behavior. Some take me as downright withdrawn, refusing to be part of the action or occasion. I can be a bit hard to reach. Why am I like that? I am cynical by nature. So until trust is built, I become preoccupied with what I am doing. And I have a stubborn streak. I can be so much in my head, I can lose touch with my heart. I'm not always tuned in to what others are feeling. Taking life rationally, I sometimes miss important emotional clues.

Although usually friendly and nice in the Southern manner, I can exhibit strain during prolonged conversation, especially casual social banter with people. I can be so uncomfortable or turned off that I opt out of conversation altogether. Boring subjects, idle chatter and silly small talk can leave me dead silent. But if a subject I like comes up, an extremely different, enthusiastic person will emerge.

When I am in my shadow self, I can be procrastinating, unresponsive, stubborn, cynical, preoccupied, close-minded, overly private, opinionated, distant, and overly analytical. But somehow people love me anyway.

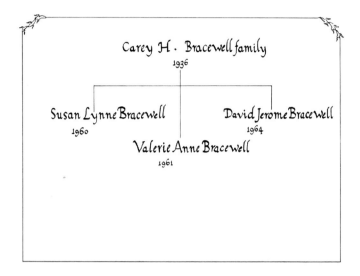

My first child, Susan, was born on April 22, 1960. Janet did not have an easy pregnancy. It was preceded by a miscarriage the year before and her moods swung wildly with Susan. Having an unplanned baby worked a financial hardship on us but we welcomed our first baby nonetheless. We were living in married students' housing on Lake Austin Boulevard, a collection of renovated Army officers' quarters known as Breckenridge Apartments. Many of our friends also had unplanned babies in those days before effective birth control. We were at the end of the famous postwar "Baby Boom." My senior year at the university, Valerie arrived on November 21, 1961. Valerie was still welcomed into our crowded apartment.

My first Texas Poll Tax receipt, last of Texas' Jim Crow voting requirements

I was twenty-four in my sophomore year, when I voted for John F. Kennedy for president. Twenty-one was then still the earliest age for voting. And it required a poll tax receipt, one of the last remains of Southern "Jim Crow" laws. Both Janet and I were enthusiastic supporters of Kennedy and reveled in the glamour of the Kennedy "Camelot" period. When Kennedy took office the following January, the full meaning of departing President Eisenhower's warning about the increasing power of America's military-industrial complex had not yet dawned on me.

After graduation in 1962, I took a teaching job in flat, dusty, windswept Levelland, Texas. It was a harsh physical environment for us all, especially for Valerie who was often sick from allergies. We decided to return to south Texas. From 1962 to 1968, I taught history and geography in junior high school and community college in Alvin, Texas, a small oil and gas-producing town south of Houston. I bought our first house, 1511 West Phillips, again using my veteran's G.I. Bill. My son, David, was born at Angleton, Texas, on December 21, 1964. He was welcomed by parents and siblings alike in those easier financial times.

In the summer of 1968, I finished my Master of Education degree at University of Houston and passed a Mid-Level exam for employment in the federal government. I took a better-paying job with the Army at Ft. Belvoir, Virginia, as a training instructor to Army engineering officers. We bought a single story house with basement at 1513 Hylton Avenue in Woodbridge, Virginia. It was located in the wooded, rolling hills just west of Chesapeake Bay. After six months at Fort Belvoir, I changed jobs and worked four years as a researcher for the Naval Personnel Research and Development laboratory at Anacostia Station, Washington, D.C. While there, going to school nights and weekends, I earned a Master in Management degree (MBA) from George Washington University.

Janet and children, Washington, D.C., c.1970
(L to R: Susan, Valerie, Janet, David)

CHILDREN

I loved my children and tried to treat them all equally. My model was my mother. She treated us as evenly as she could. She knew from her own experience what it felt like to be unwanted by her mother who also played favorites. Trained as a social scientist, I believed what psychology taught me and expected all three would be *tabla rasa*, blank slates upon which I could write my own hopes and ambitions for them. Reality turned out otherwise. Although I didn't know it when they were born, I learned in time that each new soul is born with their own agenda.

As we became parents, I wrote our *Principles of Parenthood*, a six-page typewritten set of fifty beliefs Janet and I tried to enforce. Some examples:

1. Recognize that no one procedure, practice, technique, or way of doing things makes for good or bad adjustment on the child's part. It is the attitude toward the child—love, affection, being wanted, appreciated, trusted, and accepted as a person that determines how well the child will adjust inside and outside the home.

2. Live in the best neighborhood possible. Unlike the adolescent or the adult, the child must select his friends from the immediate neighborhood in which he lives.

3. Recognize that the infant comes among us as a little savage and the first fifteen years of his life are in a very real sense the disciplinary years. . . .Children do not characteristically yearn to become civilized. They do not yearn to live orderly lives. They want to be free to make their own decisions. . . .but they are generally reluctant to make their decisions based on the basis of the greatest good for the greatest number. In short, they are reluctant to discipline themselves.

4. At every age, encourage the child to develop as broad a range of interests as possible.

5. Provide an adequate amount of good play equipment at every age, keeping in mind that too much equipment is just as bad as too little. A limited amount of well-selected equipment encourages the child to be more resourceful in his play and to be more social than when there is too much equipment.

6. Take care to answer fully and honestly every question the child asks during his 'questioning age' which begins around the third year and reaches its peak at the time he enters school.

7. Encourage the child to develop his vocabulary by reading to him, by teaching him words directly, and by encouraging him to listen to the radio and the television set.

41. If the child wishes it, provide music lessons for him at age seven years and thereafter. If properly directed, the child's interest in music may lead to one of his most popular leisure-time activities as he grows older."

Susan, my first born, "proved the breed." She has never disappointed me. She earned her degree from the University of Texas, married Mark Lyons who is now a high tech banking manager. Susan teaches advanced science classes at a local high school, helps run a mail order book business, and continues to live a productive, useful life. She and Mark gave me four wondrous grandchildren—Shannon, Stephanie, Michael, and Zachary Lyons.

Valerie, our second child, married a West Point graduate, Chris Wilson, and has two children, Sarah and Samuel Wilson. She is very much loved.

David also makes his father proud. He studied business at the University of Texas, worked as a lab technician for the Army, was involved in Army Reserve Officer Training Corps, and is now a successful technical manager for Orchard Soft, a software medical company in Indianapolis, Indiana. He and his wife, Michelle Oliver, a nurse, gave us a delightful grandchild, Rachel Bracewell.

Beyond this summary, I can't be more analytical about my own children as I have been with other relatives. They're too close to me.

The Lyons family, 2010
(L to R: Zachary, Mark, Shannon, Susan, Stephanie and Michael)

EVENTS, 1973-1983

My support of the war in Vietnam faded with my loss of innocence about the true nature of the war. In addition, my naiveté about federal careers in Washington, D.C. disappeared. It was disillusioning to realize how little most bureaucrats in Washington really cared about the public they served. But not all of them were like that.

I was impressed with the dedication of U.S. Marines. I got to know some of their best officers in a study I took part in that upgraded their Marine Headquarters in Washington from the German military model to a more efficient, computer-driven Systems Approach to management.

Janet wasn't happy staying home with our kids now they were in school so she took a clerical job with the National Health Service in Bethesda, Maryland. Our marriage had settled into a dull routine and although we didn't know it, we were gradually growing apart as our children were growing up. I took our children to many of the cultural exhibits and events in the Washington area. I also did a lot of genealogical research on site at the National Archives and in Richmond and Raleigh, much to Janet's resentment.

Early in 1973, I finished my master's degree in Management and returned to Texas, settling near Houston in a Pearland, Texas, rent house. I found a job in the accounting industry as Director of Personnel for Ernst & Ernst in downtown Houston. Located on the thirty-second floor of the Pennzoil Building, my office had all of downtown Houston at my feet. I bought a beautiful two-story home at 12415 Attlee Drive in West Houston and we moved in.

Does changing your name change your destiny? Later that year I changed our surname to *Bracewell* at a civil court in Houston on July 5, 1973. As a kid, I was teased about "Brazil nuts" and other unflattering taunts. The traditional Baptist teaching, "Turn the other cheek," soon grew stale because no one else practiced it. In addition, having discovered our true English heritage, I preferred our surname's original spelling to Hispanic-sounding *Brazil*. Mind you, it would not have bothered me to be Hispanic. It just is not who I am. At first, I tried to educate people on how the name *Brace well* should be pronounced as *Brazil*. However, later I gave up because the public insisted on pronouncing it "like it's spelled," pronouncing the "w." Universal education does have its drawbacks.

In 1986, in Austin, I changed my middle name to *Hamilton* since I disliked the Irish sound of *O'Lee*, a name given to me based on the mistaken notion we're Irish. We're originally Celtic but not Irish. I suspect certain Scotch-Irish ancestors like Jemima White gave my older relatives the impression we're Irish. I also believed that with *Hamilton*, my full name carried a higher spiritual vibration.

When the Supreme Court decided in *Roe vs. Wade* (1973), it had little personal impact on me since I had a vasectomy after David was born. All the same, Janet and I would never have considered having an abortion even though we both strongly supported a woman's right to choose. We had good genes and didn't mind passing them on. Discounting signs of a growing Fundamentalist insurgence in America and knowing that abortion was, until that time, primarily a Catholic issue, I had no inkling of the national abortion struggle and ideological divide that lay ahead for America.

The infamous "Oil Patch Bust" and mini-depression in 1974 caused Ernst & Ernst to abolish my director of personnel position. I then started my own business with Bill Kimple's help, the Quickway Convenience Store, in north Houston. Later, I sold that business and took a job as Training Director job for the Southland Corporation.

1976 was a year of celebration for America, our 200th Anniversary. However, it turned out a year of calamity for the Carey Bracewell's. Janet and I saw very little of each other because I worked very long hours at the Quickway. We divorced on June 24, 1976. Janet filed the suit but we were both ready for a new beginning. Still, we were stunned that it actually happened and tried many times to reconcile. It was the first divorce in either family.

I could find no answers in psychology that would account for the divorce. On a whim, I turned to a reading from a professional astrologer, Jeannie Long. Jeannie was English and had a British degree in astrology. She taught the subject at a local university in Houston. Her answer to me rang true: basically, Janet and I were high school sweethearts who were too much alike. It worked in high school because we were still finding ourselves. Another person like me made a good mirror. But a viable marriage needs both sameness and contrast. It was time to go. I sold the

Quickway to divide our community property and finished paying off my child support.

Janet and I made mistakes in our marriage. But in my view, the divorce was fated and inevitable. But whatever good I did before and after the divorce was forever lost on certain people who chose to follow Shakespeare's sad maxim, "Men's evil manners live in brass; their virtues we write in water."

Beginning in 1977, I worked for the Southland Corporation in Houston. My first job was a training director then I switched to group store supervisor. I was lonely and met Patricia Hines at a "Parents Without Partners" meeting. She was a lovely woman, younger than me, born in 1948. She reminded me of Janet. Her first marriage ended after it produced two children. She married first, barefoot in Jackson Park in New Orleans, to a man who came back from Viet Nam angry and addicted. Pat and I married in Houston on June 15, 1978. It was Pat's destiny to never hold a relationship together for long. Ours lasted five years.

In 1978, Pat and I moved to Austin, Texas, to get away from our bad memories in Houston. There I could only find work as a store manager. We were hardly well-to-do but I did manage to buy a house on Scenic Brook Drive. Pat encouraged me in my spiritual growth. She was part of the new Hippie generation. Our financial condition worsened and I declared bankruptcy. We divorced on August 2, 1983. Years later, I still wish her and her children all the best life can offer.

Although neither Nada nor I intended to remarry, I met Nada Kaye Hassen and we immediately fell in love. She was born in Hamlin, Texas, a lovely woman of Lebanese descent. She, too, had come off a difficult marriage and moved from Odessa, Texas, to Austin to get away from her sad memories. We were married in Austin on September 15, 1983. With her came two lovely stepdaughters, Gehan "Gigi" and Jana, who have always been very loving and supportive of me in all I do. Coming at the end of the worst period of my life, by marrying Nada, my best period began.

Carey and Nada's Wedding, 1983
(Gehan "Gigi" on left; the happy couple; Jana, Susan and Mark Lyons on right)

Nada and Carey, 1980's

Carey's faculty ID card at Austin Community College

LAST CAREER

I taught Management in the Business Department at the Austin Community College in the 1980's. And beginning in September 1984 until my retirement in December 2001, I also worked fulltime for the U.S. Postal Service in Austin as supervisor, trainer, carrier, and union steward. Nada's first job in Austin was a placement agent in a personnel agency. Her last job was as an executive distribution manager for Tokyo Electron Company in Austin. In 1992, we bought Nada's dream house at 1610 Lightwood Loop in South Austin.

SPIRITUAL GROWTH

Like Patricia, Nada always supported my spiritual growth. After living a conventional lifestyle up to 1976, I felt free enough to find what I felt was missing for me in traditional religion. In the 1980's and 1990's, I meditated regularly and became a meditation teacher. I studied and meditated upon the many approaches to God. I looked long for a guide because so many masters, after achieving God-consciousness and living only in right-brain awareness, unwittingly starved their bodies to death and died in obscurity. One master, Gadahar (1836-1886), who was liberated but fought the urge to remain in samadhi so he could guide other seekers. After his enlightenment, disciples flocked to him and wrote down in Pali all of his teachings. Given the honorary title, Shi Ramakrishna, he deeply influenced me along with other folks like Indian Prime Minister Nehru, Gandhi, and Martin Luther King, Jr. Ramakrishna's disciple, Vivekananda, brought meditation to America in the 1920's.

On July 16, 1987, Nada and I had a profound spiritual experience at the Sufi monastery near Blanco, Texas. It was a life-changing epiphany. We were gifted with a vision of the challenging future that lies ahead for us and for the Earth.

Carey in deep meditation at the Sufi Monastery near Blanco,
Texas, on July 16, 1987, at the Harmonic Convergence. Notice
the surprising red triangle that appeared on my forehead

In 1990, we bought our 75-acre farm at Hext Community near Mason, Texas, and began preparing for our future. Our farm is crossed by Five Mile Creek and is dotted with Live oak, red oak, and mesquite. During the warm months-- which is most of the year-- the only sounds one hears are cicadas, squabbling Scissortails, and Mockingbirds.

After retirement, we sold our house on Lightwood Loop and retired to Hext where we built a new home. It sat on a mesa about forty feet above the creek. We called the farm "The Sanctuary of Eagles," meant to be an intentional community for spiritual couples. Three other couples bought tracts from us. One couple built a home and lived near us for a few years. But as it happens with nearly all spiritual communities, ours failed. But we did have other successes.

MUSEUM ON THE SQUARE

The Carey Bracewell's helped found the Mason County Museum on the Square. The museum is a success. Carey helped with planning, tore out the old pharmacy fixtures, painted and generally helped out. Nada also helped in planning and was a great fund-raiser and organizer.

Museum on the Square crew

Carey and Nada on a cruise in 2007

TRAVEL

"Those were the best years of my life" my father said about retirement and camping all over North America with my mother. Traveling with Nada has also been the best time of my life. We have been to England and Europe. We made a special trip by Euro rail to Naples to visit the Roman ruins at Pompeii and Herculaleum.   Journeying east, we've been all around the Eastern Mediterranean to Egypt. We also spent two unforgettable weeks at Chouifat, Lebanon, Nada's ancestral village.

In this hemisphere, we spent a week in Mexico City, and stayed at resorts on both coasts of Mexico. We have cruised the islands of the Caribbean more times than I can remember and visited countries all the way down to Panama. We've taken other lengthy cruises to Alaska and Hawaii and rode the railroad to Denali. Between our travels together and separately in our careers, there's not much of the world we haven't seen.

RETIREMENT

In December 2001, relieved to be finally through with federal service, I retired and moved to Hext. For a time, I played at farming. I raised a small flock of sheep and grew a bountiful half-acre garden using old fashioned self-reproducing seeds.   But after a time, fulltime country living proved too much for both Nada and me. Boring, ultra-conservative neighbors and our harsh physical environment combined with the backbreaking reality of farm work for me and loneliness for Nada made country living harder than we expected.

Then in October 2002, I had a heart attack. I knew that heart disease would end this life but I didn't think it would begin so soon. I was rushed by ambulance to San Angelo where I underwent an emergency triple heart bypass surgery. Regardless of what the future may hold, we knew we had to return to the city for closer medical care.   In 2006, we bought a condominium in northeast Austin at 8600 Fathom Circle. With my Manx cat at my side, I finish this story where my adult life began, in Austin, Texas.

MY SIBLINGS

Carey's siblings: Carey, Patti, Hal, and E.C.

HAL BUCKNER BRAZIL (January 4, 1925-September 19, 1990)

The Hal Brazil family
(Donnie, Judy, Jerry, Ruby, and Hal)

Everyone loved my brother, Hal, and hated to see him leave for the Army in World War II. My sister, Patti, said, "Hal was the 'approachable daddy figure.' He was kind to me--watchful, caring, and warm. He loved me a lot and he was someone I trusted, much like Daddy. Hal had more time for fun." [1]

During World War II, Hal's outfit was the 84th "Rail-splitter" division. The division was mostly Southern men. It was organized about sixty miles north of Dallas at Camp Howze on January 4, 1943. On July 8th, Hal was drafted and joined the division for training at Camp Clairborne, Louisiana. His 16,000-man Army unit was set up as an armored division. They were sent to Camp Kilmer, New Jersey, and by October 1, 1944, arrived in England. They landed in Normandy on Omaha Beach on November 1, 1944.

Within a week after they landed, the Rail-splitters were attacking one of the strongest sections of the German's Siegfried Line. According to their commander, General A.R. Bolling, " At their first engagement, Lindern on the Seigfried Line, they behaved admirably. A German prisoner of war reported that 'they expected the 84th to behave as any new division but it fought them harder than any he had seen, including experienced troops in Russia."

Hal earned his first Army medal citation at Lindern, Germany, a Bronze Star: "For meritorious service . . .against the enemy in Germany, 3 Dec 1944. . . .During an attack on the enemy. . . .Brazil helped lay 1 1/2 miles of wire in order that communication could be established between the battalion command post and observation post. Though under constant enemy observation and shelling, Technician Fifth Grade Brazil maintained constant wire communication, thus enabling the battalion to complete its mission. A.R. Bolling, Brigadier General, U.S. Army, Commanding." The Germans shot at Hal with small arms and even 88-millimeter guns. Like his great-grandfather, Jesse Brazil, in the Civil War, he was wounded and carried metal shrapnel in his body for the rest of his life.

After Lindern, the 84th Division fought in the Battle of the Bulge, defending March-a-Femme and Rochfort in Belgium. General Bolling was proud how his division was surrounded by Germans but fought hard like a paratrooper division who were trained to fight surrounded. After the Bulge, the division went on to Devantame, Ourthe, Haven and Roer to the

Rhine Breakthrough in Germany, finally on to Restorf-Revestorf in late March 1945 when the war ended. Staff Sergeant Hal Brazil was honorably discharged on December 22, 1945.

The *San Saba News* noted his return from the war with these comments: "He took part in the Battle of the Ardennes, Rhineland, and Central Europe and wears the following decorations:

American Theatre Campaign, European Campaign with four Bronze Stars, Good Conduct metal with clasp, Purple Heart, Bronze Star with one oak leaf cluster, and World War II Victory medal."

Hanover, Germany, April 1945. Hal Brazil on the far left

In 1946 while we lived in San Saba, Hal had just returned home from the war and was sitting in his dark bedroom, recovering from what is now called "post-traumatic stress syndrome." A fire across the street broke out and burnt down a two-story home. As Patti related, "There was a huge house fire at the neighbor's house to the right of ours and across the street. The house was a large old wooden two-story. It went up in flames that turned the evening sky to orange and the sparks flew up for what seemed like miles into the sky. No one was hurt, but the teenager who lived there was crying, watching her home burn up. She kept saying over and over, "Oh, my clothes are all burning up! Oh my, all my clothes!' I felt so sorry for her." When asked why he didn't go watch the fire, Hal answered "Folks, I've seen whole cities go up in flames. What's one house?"

Hal used the World War II G.I. Bill to attend the University of Texas and majored in business. He also earned a commission in the U.S. Army Reserve Quartermaster Corps. After graduation he was hired as a sales person for Armour & Company, Fort Worth, Texas. Then, after two years where he successfully sold meat products to wholesalers and retailers, he was drafted back into the Army during the Korean War. Having already spent so much time in the military, he decided to make the Army his career.

Hal's last Army citation was The Legion of Merit, Oak Leaf cluster: "To Colonel Hall B. Brazil, Ordinance Corps: His unusual foresight, initiative, and competence contributed to the effective accomplishment of this command's mission. Given this 21st day of September, 1978, R.M. Shoemaker, General, U.S. Army Commander, U.S. Army Forces Command."

Hal and Ruby have grandchildren Jennifer and Matthew Hayes through their daughter, Judy Brazil Hayes, and Grant, Collin, and Sawyer Brazil through their son, Don Brazil.

E.C. BRAZIL, Jr. (March 19, 1929-December 16, 1989)

The BEARKATS

E.C. Brazil, Trombonist

In an E-mail, Patti Kimple related her memory of E.C: [2]

"He married the love of his life Barbara Bracht from Brownsville and they had three children, Mark, Kevin, and Claudia. E. C. was a proud dad, would attend the football games of his sons with great pride, and enjoyed seeing daughter Claudia at her swimming and diving meets where she excelled. He and Mark flew together in private aviation here in Dallas. He had a bond with Kevin that was always so sweet too.

E.C. and Barbara both played in the Austin and Richardson symphonies, Barbara taught private oboe lessons and E. C. worked constantly in several musical groups in Dallas. He tried some business ventures with Bill but music was always his strong suite and where he was the happiest since that was always where his talent was.

As an adult, E. C. was a marvelous raconteur, perhaps the best I have ever been around. He had at least five jokes on any subject that might come up in a conversation, and he told them as well as any stand-up comic I have ever heard. The jokes just slipped right into the conversation and left the group feeling really good and laughing long after he left the room. He was self-deprecating and that is always funny. He was ready to tell about incidents that happened to him where he didn't come off so well. Those who knew him on the road with the big band of the 1950's, members of Hal McIntire's Band, still smile when E. C.'s name is mentioned. He was so much fun everyone said. He was quick with a retort, could play all the voices and the dialog when he told a story. I think perhaps he learned very early humor was his contribution to any situation and he honed it to a polish.

E.C's son, Kevin, shared one of E.C.'s practical jokes: Once when E.C. was teaching a new Northern friend about Southwestern outdoor cooking, he explained to him how to cook a turkey on a grill. After careful instruction, he asked the new guy to check on the turkey after exactly half an hour. Then E.C. covertly switched the bird and disappeared for about thirty minutes, going out for more beer. When he came back, the newcomer was practically in tears. He though he had shrunk the turkey. E.C. had switched it for a Cornish game hen!3

Since E.C. associated mostly with musicians and barroom patrons, his humor was often bawdy. When E.C. was hospitalized, a doctor came in and asked him " Does it burn when you urinate?" to which E. C. replied, "Gee doc, I don't know. I never lighted it."

Barbara added, "E.C. was an aficionado of foreign sports cars and an excellent mechanic, a skill that he passed on to his sons Mark and Kevin. He and two other life-long friends opened Moth Motorsports in Austin in 1958 and it quickly became a gathering place for other devotees of racing, hill-climbs and road rallies. Later, in Dallas, he and two other musician friends founded International Recording Inc. producing award-winning musical commercials for many national clients. And oh, yes! He loved The Dallas Cowboys!!"

His love of sports he also passed down to his children and grandchildren. E.C.'s grandchildren are Leslie Lee Brazil (born 1990), Miles Etheridge

Brazil (1992) through his son, Mark, and Jason Zachary Brazil (1993) through his second son, Kevin Brazil.

He was a unique person, talented and funny, and we all miss him. Sadly, his last years were not good ones but he left an indelible mark on all of us who knew him.

E.C. Brazil family
(Barbara, E.C., Claudia, Kevin, and seated Mark)

The Bill Kimple family
(Children, L to R--Lisa, Cheri, Robin)

PATTI BRAZIL KIMPLE (February 26, 1934-   )

"I was born in Bishop, Texas, a small town near Corpus Christi. It was during the Great Depression but my parents said I brought sunshine to the hard times. A Mexican lady named Rosa took care of me while my mother recovered from delivery.

My first memories started when we lived in Brady, Texas. Dad was pastor of a Baptist church and as always, Mother played the piano for all services. My brother, Carey, was born there in 1936. Our relationship began with sibling rivalry: I remember Mother holding the new baby on her lap—"My place!"—and feeding him with a blue baby bottle. But Mother cleverly let Carey be my baby too so he and I soon became close, lifelong friends. My older brothers were tolerant of me. Hal, at least, liked me. When I was four, we moved to San Saba, Texas. I remember learning to tie my own shoes and the sash on my sun dress.

Mother was always the center of my world. She encouraged my learning and my independence. She let me wash the dishes. I stood on a chair and marveled at the beautiful bubbles. I loved to help her. Somehow Mother found the money to subscribe to a kid's magazine called *Jack and Jill*. Mother read its great stories to Carey and me.

I began first grade in 1940 at the old San Saba Grammar School. The building smelled like apples, chalk, and bats. My teacher was Miss Fannie Walker, tall, thin, with gray hair in a bun. Miss Fanny turned me on to reading. I'm still happiest with a new book in one hand and a fresh cup of tea in the other!

After the Japanese attacked Pearl Harbor and America entered World War II, Dad joined the Army in 1942 as a Protestant Chaplain. We moved to Bucyrus, Ohio—a cold town that smelled of coal smoke. Dad was resplendent in his uniform with chaplain's crosses on his lapels. In 1943, Dad was ordered to Camp Blanding, Florida—a paradise of warm water, orange trees, and sunshine. My parents loved Florida and so did we kids. E.C. had a job after school and we all went to school riding on the back of his Cushman motor scooter. Florida was magical to me, a gangly nine-year old. I found wild strawberries and a swampy orchid-type plant near our house in Keystone Heights. When it rained—which was often—little tiny tree frogs would hop up on the widows and sing their chorus.

Dad was sent overseas in 1945. Hal was in the Army. The rest of us returned to our familiar Rock House in San Saba. I was eleven years old and glad to see my old school chums again. It was also good to see my Brazil cousins once more—Wanda, Jessie Pat, and Billie-- my girl cousins. Gasoline was scarce but we could still see each other because, unlike Florida, they didn't live too far away.

After Dad returned from the Pacific and was discharged from the Army, he accepted a position as Pastor of the First Baptist Church in Santa Rosa, New Mexico in 1946. I liked Santa Rosa and found the people in the West to be open and accepting. My best friends were Barbara and Jane. We joined Girl Scouts together. Santa Rosa's library was across the street from the parsonage. I spent my summers in the fabulous world of books, devouring Nancy Drew mysteries and other girl books.

I was starting my growth spurt during those years. I shot up to 5'6" by age 13, a true Brazil. Mother would rub my growing, aching leg muscles. I was sure no boy would ever be tall enough for me, ever!

It was getting really hard to leave my friends during this time, but we moved again in 1948 to Lancaster, Missouri, where Dad was the District Missionary for forty-five rural churches. I did not enjoy it up there although I did make friends. Unlike the West, the people of Lancaster were suspect of strangers. As the new girl, I was like an exotic from far-away Texas. It wasn't sad to leave there and go back to Texas.

I entered San Saba High School, graduated in three years, and in 1950, I enrolled at Southwest Texas State Teachers College at San Marcos (now Texas State University) at age sixteen. I loved college and my new friends. My roommate, Martha Nell, and I are still close. My major was Elementary Education with a minor in Art. I auditioned and was accepted in the Acapella Choir. I enjoyed performing there for the two years I was in school. I also pledged a good sorority.

In 1952, during my sophomore year, I happened to call my brother, E.C. He was at Fort Sam Houston in San Antonio, a member of the 4th Army Band. A guy answered the phone named Bill Kimple who turned out to be E.C.'s good friend. In fact, E.C. had wanted Bill to meet me. He had already told me about Bill. Neither me nor Bill was particularly interested in following through with E.C.'s suggestion. But once we connected on the phone, we laughed and chatted together for forty-five minutes.

Bill sat down that night and wrote to me, asking me if we could date. My roommate was from San Antonio. That same week, she asked me if I wanted to go home with her for the weekend, so I told Bill "Yes." Bill and I went to a little Italian restaurant with the usual red-checked tablecloth, a candle in the center. We had a wonderful time together, a warm evening filled with lots of laughter and fun. It was love at first sight.

Bill and I were married only six weeks later, on February 16, 1952. It was a beautiful candlelight church wedding at the First Baptist Church in San Saba. My sister-in-law, Ruby Brazil, was my matron of honor, my cousin, Jessie Pat, my college roomie, Martha Nell, and two sorority sisters were my attendants. Bill and his groomsmen were splendid in their black tuxedos. E.C. was Bill's Best Man, our Cupid. My beautiful ivory satin wedding gown was worn first by Bill's sister, Kay—another bonus in my life. I carried white orchids and orange blossoms atop a little ivory-covered Bible given to me by Mr. Kimple's cousin.

My Dad gave we away. He was much calmer than me because he had performed at many weddings before. As I entered the church and took his arm, he gently guided me to walk slowly and elegantly. I was far too nervous to know what to do. Mother did a magnificent job of coordinating the wedding.

Bill and I, using his three-day Army pass, left on our honeymoon. We then settled in San Antonio for a year while he finished his tour in the Army. I happily entered into the new world of learning to be a wife. Armed with my new Betty Crocker cookbook and new pots and pans as wedding gifts, I created some truly spectacular disasters. The women in my life made it all look so easy but not so for me, at least at first.

We moved back to Bill's home town, Dallas, in 1953. Bill finished his degree from Southern Methodist University. While he did that, I took some classes in comparative religion and psychology, two lifelong interests of mine. Bill entered Dixie Wax Paper Company as a salesman and then went on the road.

Our precious first child, Cheryl Ann, was born on September 27, 1954. With her birth, a new chapter opened for me—motherhood—something I had always wanted. I found that, like cooking, mothering was a day-by-day learning experience. But with the help of a good pediatrician, Dr. Spock's baby book, fairly good instincts and a prayer now and then,

I learned how to do it and really loved being a mother. During that same year, 1954, we built our first home.

On December 17, 1956, our tiny Lisa Kay was born. She weighed only three pounds, three ounces, since she was premature by two months. She had to stay in an incubator at Baylor Hospital until she reached five pounds. When we finally brought her home, she turned out to be a good baby, 'our littlest angel here at Christmas.' She and Cheri were good friends from the beginning.

In August, 1958, we built another house at 1344 Bar Harbor Drive in a neighborhood where more children lived. It was a happy time for us all: our home was a mecca for kids, playing in our home and in the quiet, tree-lined streets. Bill was by now Plant Manager of the Dallas Plant of Dixico, Incorporated (the new company name) in Dallas. He was also President of the CePo Packaging in Jacksonville, Florida. While Bill managed the business, I joined two women's clubs, a garden club, and an antique study club. Flower shows were one of my favorite events.

On October 2, 1963, our third precious daughter, Robin, was born. She had blue eyes, curly hair, and was sunshine to Bill and me all the time. Our household now included a dog, cats, and a hamster named "Samantha." We took the girls camping in the summer and skiing in the winter. We enjoyed Stevens Park Christian Church where the girls were in Sunday School. Bill sat on the Board of Directors, and I was involved in women's groups, sometimes hosting them in our home. During this period, Bill and I got our pilot's licenses and flew our own plane, a Navion.

We lived on Bar Harbor Drive for sixteen years. During that time, Cheri and Lisa graduated from high school. We had to put Robin in private school--Tyler Street Christian Academy--because of unrest in public schools during the 1960's school integration crises.

In 1973, we moved to 3711 Princeton Street in Highland Park, Dallas, so Robin could be in a better school. We lived there for thirty-two years. After our girls were grown and gone, in February 2005, we sold the house on Princeton and moved into our present home. It is a high-rise condominium with no more maintenance problems, a carefree life for us at last.

I bought a gift shop, Handmade and Company, specializing in handmade goods. I purchased wholesale items from eighty different makers: stocking quilts, toys, baby items, and other household goods. After Bill retired from Dixico, he agreed to join me at Handmade and Company. We kept the business going successfully for twelve years.

Meanwhile, our girls matured and married. Cheri married Phil Travis. They live in Boulder, Colorado, and have a son, Dylan. Cheri is a children's counselor.

Lisa married an Englishman. They have three children: David, Michael, and Caroline. Caroline is married and has three little girls of her own, making Bill and me great-grandparents! Lisa still misses America but enjoys living in England.

Robin married Rich Ellis. In winter, they live in Alamos, Mexico, and summer in Santa Fe, New Mexico. Their daughters, Avery and Tess, are our youngest grandchildren.

Today, my grandchildren, children, and Bill are the center of my world. We have been married fifty-eight years and treasure our days. We still laugh at the same things, truly enjoying each other. Bill writes me a love note every day.

We have traveled the world, loved it all, and we're now in the quieter phase of our lives. He writes music, plays his piano and his saxophone. I still do oil paintings. But I have just retired after fifteen years of volunteering at Scottish Rite Hospital and we have given up delivering for Meals on Wheels since walking is not as easy as it once was. I just ordered a Kindle, a book reading machine, and some new books to go into it. We still enjoy going to the symphony and being with our friends.

I'm convinced I'm the most blessed person on Earth for which I thank God every day."[2]

CHAPTER FOURTEEN
THE BAYS

Janet Bay, 1956

The same "Blue Norther" that dropped the temperature and air pressure in dusty Brady and caused my mother to go into labor moved downstate to Killeen and two days later caused Joyce Bay to deliver her twin baby girls. I married the younger twin twenty-one years later. Having so much in common with Janet was good in adolescence when we were discovering who we were.

SCOTCH-IRISH IMMIGRANT, ANDREW BAY

"The Reverend Andrew Bay was born about 1700 in Ulster, Ireland, and came to America about 1720. 1 He was part of a large contingent of Scotch Irish that settled first in Pennsylvania and Delaware. Old family histories tell of this and the later movement 'across the river into Maryland.' One of the early Bay gravestones at Bethel, Harford County, is marked 'born in Ireland".2

In Webster's *History of the Presbyterian Church*, pages 573-576, there is an account of this first Andrew Bay. It states that 'Andrew Bay was a native of Ireland and a weaver by trade. He was ordained in the New Side presbytery of Newcastle before 1748 and was pastor of Round Hill, near York, and of Marsh Creek in Adams County, Pennsylvania. His brother, Hugh Bay, graduated at Nassau Hall in 1750 and was a physician at Herbert's Cross Roads near Deer Creek in Harford County, Maryland." [3]

The *John Bay Bible*, owned by Laura Bull, stated that the Widow Bay had sons Reverend Andrew Bay, William Bay, and Hugh Bay. Reverend Andrew Bay married Sarah Hall and had sons Elihu Hall Bay, Hugh Bay, and Andrew Bay. Elihu Hall Bay became the best known of the early Bays. He was a lawyer and famous justice on the South Carolina Supreme Court. Andrew Bay, Junior, "simply dropped from sight."

This Andrew Bay, Junior, who "dropped from sight" from Harford County, Maryland, was
my Janet Bay's ancestor, according to genealogist Tommy West.[4] Andrew Bay, Jr. was listed as a taxable in 1774 in the household of Thomas Bay in Bush River Lower Hundred, in Harford County, Maryland.[5] Another son of Andrew Bay, Jr. was Hugh Bay, who in his Harford County will left his son, John Bay, 200 pounds with the interest in his land "except $100 to be paid by him to my brother Andrew Bay."[6]

ANDREW BAY IN TENNESSEE

Sergeant Major Andrew Bay enlisted in Colonel John Williams' Ninth Regiment, North Carolina Line, on May 1, 1777, and was discharged in January 1778. He served at the battles of Brandywine, Germantown, and Briar Creek.[4] In a North Carolina Comptroller's Office record, Sergeant Major Andrew Bay is referred to as "Lieutenant Major Andrew Bay."[7]

Webster's *New International Dictionary* defines a sergeant major as an "adjutant who served either as a general assistant to the commanding officer or as a staff officer in charge of and responsible for all official correspondence except combat orders, all returns and records of personnel, strength reports, and the preparation and distribution of orders."

In 1780, Guilford County, Commissioner John White stated that he purchased "of Andrew Bay forty bushels of corn" on a promissory note for thirty Spanish milled Dollars at 6% interest. In May 1780, he was promised another 150 pounds. In 1783, he was paid L28-8-7 "for services through 1779." On March 12, 1784, sixteen pounds were paid to Andrew Bay of Salisbury District.[8] In the *Abstract of Army Accounts of the N.C. Line* is a record of Thomas Bay collecting L92-11-1 on the service of Andrew Bay, "SM." The new state of North Carolina, on May 8, 1784, granted Sergeant Major Andrew Bay Military Land Warrant #811 for 357 acres for his thirty months of service.

In 1790, he filed Claim #1351 for 357 acres on the waters of Spencer Creek "in Tennessee County, North Carolina," now Wilson County, Tennessee. The first permanent settlement in Wilson County was made about 1794 at the north end of Hickory Ridge "near a bold spring, the head of Spencer's Creek about five miles west of the site of Lebanon. . . "Lebanon, the county seat, is situated on the east branch of Barton's Creek, six miles from the Cumberland River, and thirty miles east of Nashville. Lebanon was named for the cedars that originally surrounded the spring at the town site."[9]

"In 1799, Kirkpatrick's and Motheral's, Gray's, Stewart's, Bay's, and Elias Morrison began meeting together each Sabbath to read Holy Writ and join in prayer. From this seed sprang old New Hope Cumberland Presbyterian Church, established near Spencer's Lick. . . . ." [10]

The Sumner County tax list for 1787-1794 shows that in 1789, Andrew Bay owned 357 acres. He still had those 357 acres as late as 1803. Wilson County, which was carved from Sumner County in 1799, contains an extensive and orderly set of deed records from Andrew Bay and allied families.

THE EDDINGS FAMILY

Thomas Bay, Andrew's son, and Robert Davis signed a $2500 bond "to be void if there be no lawful objection why Thomas Bay and Polly Eddings may not be joined together as man and wife in the holy estate of matrimony. Given under our hands and seals this second day of January 1815."[11]

According to Jewel Wilson Powers in Houston, Texas, her information based on a family Bible, Abraham Eddings was born in June 1724, and he died November 3, 1801. His wife, "old Mary Eddings" died the 22nd day of July 1786. William Eddings moved to Wilson County, Tennessee, in 1807. He was a Revolutionary War veteran. His application, filed in 1832, was # S3326.

Kenedy Bay married Fannie Barnett in Wilson County on October 6, 1806. Sureties were Keneda Bay and John Gray.[12] According to genealogist Tommy West, Kennedy Bay was Thomas Bay's nephew, son of John Bay.

Andrew Bay died intestate and his estate was sold at auction on November 22, 1833.[13]

THOMAS BAY'S SERVICE IN THE WAR OF 1812

Thomas Bay filed a bounty land application under congressional Act of March 3, 1855. He stated that he was a corporal in Captain John Hill's Second Regiment of volunteers in the war against Great Britain in 1812. On June18, 1813, he volunteered in Wilson County, Tennessee. In December, he was mustered into service near Huntsville, Alabama, and continued in actual service, serving in the Creek War. He participated in the Battle of Emuckfaw on the 22nd January 1814. Bay was issued a bounty land certificate for 160 acres of the public domain on January 5, 1857.[13]

Thomas Bay served under General Andrew Jackson against the Indians and was at the Battle of Talladega. In 1813, the Creek Indians, stirred by Tecumseh's oratory, rose up against the whites. On August 30th, the inhabitants of Fort Mimms, Alabama, were massacred. Shortly afterward, a general muster of the militia was called to ask for volunteers. Captain Bradley's company was called into service on September 24th. Its strength, including officers, was eighty-four men.

"On November 9, 1813, the Battle of Talladega took place at noon. Talladega was across the Coosa River and thirty miles to the south. There was no road. At one o'clock in the morning Jackson began to move the army over the river. The following sunset the men dropped in their tracks six miles from the beleaguered town. Jackson was ill with dysentery. While the army slumbered he sat against a tree in agony, questioning scouts who had been sent to ascertain the topography of Talladega, the disposition of the enemy and of the force he was to relieve. At midnight came an express from White saying he protected the fort. This left two hundred sick, all of the stores of the army and its line of communication at the mercy of the enemy. .Jackson ordered a crescent-shaped formation with the points toward the town, and sent three hundred mounted companies to raise the enemy and court an attack. The encircled Creeks fell in heaps--three hundred dead Indians versus only fifteen Whites dead".[14]

The federal census for January 31, 1820, Wilson County, Tennessee, listed:

Andrew Bay	males l under 10, 1:16-18, 1:18-26, 1 over 45 2:16-26, 1:26-45, l over 45 {p. 3}
Thomas Bay	males 2 under 10, 1:26-45 2 under 10, 1:26-45
William Eddings	males 1:16-18, 1 over 45 3:10-16, 3:16-26, 1 over 45, two slaves (p. 13)
Cannaday Bay	males l under 10, 2:10-16, 1 over 45 4 under 10, 2:10-16, 1:26-45, six slaves
William Eddings	males 2:10-16, 1:26-45

3 under 10, 1:10-16, 1:26-45, three slaves

By the late 1820's, Thomas Bay had moved to western Tennessee and settled in Haywood County northeast of Memphis.

The Bays appeared on the 1840 federal census of Haywood County as

Thomas Bay   males 1:5-9, 1:10-14, l:15-19, 1:20-29, 1:40-49
                    1:5-9, 1:15-19, 1;20-29, 1:40-49

W.H. Bay   males 1:20-29
                    2 under 5, 1:20-29

Their last appearance on the federal census for Haywood County, dated October 28, 1850:

Household 1176

Williamson,	R.W.	27 M	Farming	Virginia
	Elizabeth	25 F		Tennessee
	Mary	6 F		"
	Thomas J.	4 M		"
	James	2 M		"
	Maurice	18 M	Farming	"

1178

Duckworth,	George W.	29 M	Farming	North Carolina
	Dorcus	82 F		"
	Thomas	10 M		Tennessee
	Margaret	8 F		"
	Henry	6 M		"
	Mary C.	4 F		"
	Robert	6/12 M		"

1188

Jones,	Edward R.	48 M	Farming $8000	North Carolina
	Martha A.	23 F		Tennessee
	Henry	16 M	Clerk	"

___ C.	14 M			"
Daniel H.	10 M			"
Calvin H.	8 M			"
Anna M.	6 F			"
Edward W.	3 M			"

(Anna through Henry attended school within the past year.)

1194

Bay,	Thomas	57 M	Farming $1200	Tennessee
	Mary	60 F		South Carolina
	Rebecca	30 F		Tennessee
	James	29 M	Farming	"
	Joseph	23 M	"	"
	Sarah	21 F		"
	Thomas	12 M		"

1195

Bay,	William H.	35 M	Farming $800	Tennessee
	Cintha	37 F		North Carolina
	Mary	12 F		Tennessee
	Belinda	10 F		"
	James	8 M		"
	Jehilla	4 F		"
	Lucinda	2 F		"
	Joseph	8/12 M		"

(James, Belinda, and Mary attended school within the year.)

1197

Williamson,	Robert	30 M	Farming $300	North Carolina
	Mary J.	25 F		Tennessee
	Thomas	2 M		"
	Robert	1/12 M		"

GONE TO TEXAS

Hattie Bay Hoke, daughter of James Bay, shared this Bay information with me in 1960:[15]

"The Thomas Bay family immigrated to Texas from Tennessee in 1850. They settled in the Bay's Chapel area, which was then only a thicket. The family at that time consisted of Thomas and Mary Bay, their three married children—Andrew Foster Bay, William Harrison Bay, and Jane Bay Williamson, their five unmarried children—Rebecca, James, Joseph, Sarah, and Thomas Bay, Jr., and their son-in-law, George W. Duckworth. Duckworth, the widower of Cynthia Bay Duckworth, returned to Tennessee not long thereafter leaving his three orphans with Cynthia's mother's family.

William Harrison 'Hack' Bay had six children at the time he emigrated from Tennessee. He said they would go for just a short distance and then they would have to look out for loose rocks to put under the wagon wheels while they were crossing the hills of Arkansas. The trip took about three months. They made their first Texas crop in 1850. He was a very virtuous man. He was a foster father to the Duckworth children and took over his father's work in the church. Andrew Foster Bay's farm was adjacent to and just north of Bay's Chapel.

James Henry Bay was the only Bay to follow a political career. James served as a justice of the peace and was a friend of Sam Houston's. It was James Bay who killed the Dodd boy. The two Dodd brothers had tried to court one of the unmarried Bay girls shortly after the Bays had immigrated to Texas. The Bay girl wanted nothing to do with either Dodd. Her brothers finally warned the Dodd's to stay away from her. The Dodd's rode up to the Bay cabin one day and shouted a challenge to the Bay men. James Bay stuck a hat on a broomstick and exposed it in a window. The Dodd's answered with a shotgun blast. James then returned the fire, killing one of the Dodd's.

During the Civil War, Robert Williamson remained at home to look after the needs of the ladies. He took his task a bit too literally and seduced Margaret Duckworth Roberts. When Margaret's husband returned from the war, Williamson tried to murder him from ambush. He fired at Roberts but missed. Roberts gave chase and caught up with him just as

Williamson was about to run in his own house. Roberts shot and killed him on the doorstep. It was later discovered that Williamson had stolen $800 in gold from Margaret."

On October 2, 1860, Thomas Bay signed his will:

. . .I desire after my death that my funeral expenses and just debts shall be paid, I also desire that my wife, Mary Bay, shall have the tract of land on which I now reside, and same which I purchased of Cumberland Polk, also to have the household and kitchen furniture, and my stock of cattle, hogs, oxen, one mule, one bay horse, wagon and all my farming utensils also the crop that may be on hand at my death, also my negro woman Mary and her child Joanna. . . .I desire that after the death of my wife Mary Bay, the land, negroes, and all other property devised to her by me under this will shall be sold by my executors on a credit of twelve months and the money when collected to be divided equally between my children, William H. Bay, Andrew F. Bay, James H. Bay, Thomas B. Bay, Rebecca E. Worsham, Elizabeth J. Williamson, Sarah J. Sandel, and my three Grand Children, Thomas L. Duckworth, Margaret Duckworth, George R. Duckworth, and to receive one eighth part of the same, to be equally divided between the three. . . .I also desire that my son Thomas B. Bay, shall remain with his mother ande manage the farm for her as long as it is agreeable to both of them. And in consideration of his services he is to have all the profits arising from the farm after supporting his mother. I desire that my son, Thomas B. Bay have one bed and its furniture which all my children have had except himself. I also desire that my son James H. Bay and my Son in Law, M.L. Sandel, shall be appointed my executors.   Thomas Bay[17]

Thomas Bay died on February 14, 1861, and buried in Bay's Chapel Cemetery. His tombstone states that he was born January 28, 1793. His epitaph, 'Farewell.' His wife's tombstone next to his is broken and only "Mary Bay" and "Farewell" can be read.

On March 28, 1861, the following obituary appeared in The *Texas Christian Advocate*:[18] "Thomas Bay was born in Davidson County, Tennessee, January 28, 1793. He married Mary Eddens 1820 in Wilson County. Immigrated to Texas in 1850, settling in Montgomery County. Served under General Andrew Jackson against the Indians in 1813 and was at the Battle of Talladega. Joined the Cumberland Presbyterian Church in 1820 and by letter to the Methodist Church in 1827. Was an official member some 30 years and remained in that capacity until April 1860 when he resigned his office as steward and his son Harrison was appointed in his place." 18

The following inventory was taken April 5, 1861, on the estate of Andrew Bay:

Land, 358 acres at $10 per acre	$3580.00
Negro Mary and Child Joe Anna	1000.00
1 Mule	80.00
1 Horse	70.00
1 Black mule (sold)	65.00
1 Yoke of oxen	60.00
1 Wagon	50.00
11 Head of Cattle at $5 per head	55.00
Stock of Hogs	60.00
Farming utensils	10.00
Household and Kitchen furniture	100.00
Bee gums	18.00
By one note	1300.00
By one note	35.00
By open account	180.00
By cash on hand	302.25
3 bales of cotton (at $45 per bale)	135.00

————————

$7100.25 19

BAYS IN THE CIVIL WAR

On April 21, 1862, Thomas B. Bay, 30, enlisted as a Private in Company ""I", 20th Texas Infantry Regiment, at Red Top (Prairie Plains), Texas, for three years or the duration of the war. Included in his service record, this letter:

Prairie Plains

Grimes Co. Tex.
Nov. 25, 1864
Lt. Col. Thos. M. Jack
Senior Asst Adjt General

Dear Sir- - -

We the under Signed Soldiers families do most earnestly petition Maj General Walker to grant us a detail for thirty days of Thos. B. Bay private in Co. I 20th Tex Inf and Sgt. G.C. Thompson of the same Co. and Regt. For the purpose of saving meat for another year-- We have never called for help before from the army, but there are no men left in our section able to gather our hogs for us—We have at least 100 head to kill, that are now fat upon the mast and will be a total loss to us which we are ill able to sustain. The men asked for know the range & these hogs are very wild-- We have entire confidence in their energy to serve us, and we will be ever grateful for the kindness-- As soon as the detail is over we pledge ourselves that they will return to camp without delay.

Among the twenty-two signers: Mrs. C.P. Bay, M.A. Bay, M.P. Bay, Margaret Duckworth, Rebecca E. Worsham, Sarah C. Bay, Mary Bay, Mark Hoke and R.M. Hoke. The company commander forwarded this "citizens' application" to his superiors, stating that Bay and Thompson "are good efficient soldiers." The asked for leave was granted.

James H. Bay, 19, enlisted in Thomas B. Bay's unit at Red Top on May 3, 1862, for the duration of the war. His medical records show that he was admitted to the Confederate General Hospital at Houston on July 22, 1863, suffering from *febris Int.*, malaria. A week later he returned to duty.

On August 28, 1863, William H. Bay, 49, enlisted in Company "C," 17th Cavalry Brigade, at Montgomery, Texas. He joined the service with a horse valued at $700, weapons valued at $75, and equipment valued at $40.

James H. Bay, age 41, enlisted the same day in Company "B" in the 17th Brigade of Texas Volunteer Infantry at Camp San Jacinto near Huntsville, Texas.

ANDREW F. BAY

Andrew F. Bay hired A.P. Bray as his substitute for military service during the Civil War.[20]   He was in his forties when the war broke out and almost too old for the Confederate draft.

1870 Federal Census of Montgomery County, Texas—

Bay,	Harrison	54 M	Farmer $600-400	Tennessee (place of birth)
	Cynthia P.	56 F		North Carolina
	James H.	27 M		Tennessee
	Sibebia	24 F		Tennessee
	Joseph W.	20 M		Tennessee
	John C.	14 M		Texas
Bay,	Andrew F.	50 M	Farmer $2300-500	Tennessee
	Elizabeth	47 F		North Carolina
	Roda A.	22 F		Tennessee
	Rebecca A.	20 F		Tennessee
	Lucy	18 F		Tennessee
	Mary H.	16 F		Texas
	William A.	14 M		Texas
	John	11 M		Texas
	Cordelia F.	9 F		Texas
Bay,	Thomas	38 M	Farmer $1000-800	Tennessee
	Caledonia	28 F		Tennessee
Bay,	Mary E.	79 F		South Carolina

On March 11, 1878, Andrew Foster Bay signed his will: [20]

1st—I desire that all my debts shall be fully paid.

2nd—I give and bequeath unto my wife, Elizabeth Bay, 200 acres of land, part of the Matthew Harris Survey and part of the Ben Johnson Survey, and to run the lines thereof as to include my residence, orchards, field, lot, out houses, and other improvements, and I hereby designate the same as the Homestead.

3rd—I give and bequeath unto my wife, Elizabeth Bay all my household and kitchen furniture Four Cows and Calves Two mules Wagon and gear all the corn fodder hay seeds and all the pork, bacon, and lard and all the groceries now on hand and the entire stock of hogs and all my farm tools, & c.

4th—To. . .my son John Bay a certain gray horse (the same that he now claims) a Saddle and Bridle one cow and calf, one bed and bedding the same as my other children have had.

5th--. . . .that my son John Bay shall take charge of and direct the management of the farm on said Homestead secure for and give his mother the said Elizabeth Bay, a good and decent support and take to himself the balance of all the rents and profits of said farm as pay for his services. . . .

6th—I hereby make and declare my grandson James O'Neal, to be a full heir to share equal with my children in the distribution of all my property and I hereby name and appoint Thomas B. Bay, his Guardian, to manage his property.

7th—I direct that after the death of my wife, Elizabeth Bay and all her debts have been paid the Homestead tract of land shall be equally divided among all my heirs.

8th—I direct that all my other lands, property, and claims not hereinbefore designated shall be bequeathed and divided equally among all my heirs so soon as possible.

9th—I hereby constitute and appoint my son, William A. Bay, and Luther W. Blount, Executors. . . . A.F. Bay

On April 25, 1878, Andrew F. Bay died. He was buried in the Bay's Chapel Cemetery. His tombstone gave his birthdate—April 1, 1817-- and his date of death. His epitaph: "Remember me as you pass by – As you are now so once was I -- As I am now soon you may be -- Prepare for death and follow me"

THE LIGHTSEYS

The year 1878 saw both Andrew F. Bay's death and the marriage of his son, William A. Bay, to Piedy Almira "Myra" Lightsey. Myra was born in Walker County, Texas, on November 7, 1862, the eleventh and last child of David Lightsey and wife, Orlena Tubbs Lightsey. It is thought that the Lightseys introduced some Indian blood into the William Bay family.

According to his tombstone in the Ebenezer Cemetery, located on State Highway 45 about seven miles west of Huntsville, David Lightsey was born March 3, 1818, and died June 11, 1874. His wife's stone reads "Our Mother, Orlena, wife of David Lightsey, Daughter of Jeremiah and Celia Tubbs. " She was born in September 1824 and died in October 1882.

David Lightsey was born in Georgia and his wife, Orlena, was born in Perry County, Alabama. On the 1840 federal census of Perry County, David Lightsey was a newlywed with one white male in his twenties and his bride, Orlena, was in her teens. There were ten families headed by a Tubb family, none of them named Jeremiah. On the 1830 federal census Jeremiah Tubb was listed with himself and wife in their thirties and nine children including five girls ranging in age from two under five, two five to nine, one of them doubtless Orlena, and another girl aged ten to fourteen.

David Lightsey appeared on the 1860 federal census of Walker County, Texas, as:

Lightsey,	David	42 M Farmer $7401	Georgia (owned four slaves)
	Orlena	36 F	Alabama
	George W.	16 M	Alabama
	William	14 M	Mississippi
	Mary E.	11 F	Mississippi
	John A.	9 M	Louisiana
	David C.	7 M	Louisiana
	Sarah A.	6 F	Arkansas
	Victoria	4 F	Arkansas
	Daniel W.	2 M	Arkansas

Orlena	F (two weeks old)		Texas

The different birthplaces of their children suggest which states they lived in before coming to Texas.

On the 1870 federal census of Precinct #1, Walker County, taken on July 5th, David appeared as:

Lightsey,	D.	52 M	Farmer $2000-700	Georgia
	Orlina	44 F		Alabama
	John A.	19 M		Louisiana
	David C.	18 M	At School	Louisiana
	Sarah A.	16 F	"	Arkansas
	Victoria	14 F	"	Arkansas
	Daniel W.	12 M	"	Arkansas
	Frances O.	10 F	"	Arkansas
	Piety	8 F	"	Arkansas
Irwing,	A.	26M	Teacher	Virginia

By the time of the federal census of 1880, David Lightsey was dead and his widow was living with her son-in-law, John C. Hardey, husband of Orlena's daughter, Sarah A. Hardey. On those returns, Orlena's birthplace was recorded as South Carolina as were both her parents.

AFTER THE CIVIL WAR

Also by the time of the same census of 1880, Andrew Foster Bay was dead and his widow lived with her daughter, Frances Neil.

"Frances Bay Neille married William Neille, a likeable person but he and Frances quarreled a great deal. After having served in the Civil War with 'Hack' Bay, he returned to Bay's Chapel only to desert Frances and the children and was never heard from again."

The 1880 Federal Census of Bay community was recorded on June 4, 1880, by J.H. Bay, a Montgomery County census official. His results for Election Precinct #5, page 5, line 38+:

Bay,	Elizabeth	60 F	Head	North Carolina-N.C.-N.C. (place of birth for self, father, and mother)
Neil,	Francis	37 F	Daughter	Tennessee-N.C.-N.C.-N.C.
	Rhoda	11 F	Granddaugher	Texas-N.C.-N.C.
	Thomas	7 M	Grandson	Texas-N.C.-N.C.
Bay,	William	23 M	Farmer	Texas-N.C.-N.C.
	Almira	18 F	Texas-Alabama-Alabama	
	Bony	1 M	Texas-TX-TX	

According to Hattie Hoke, William Bay's wife:

"William Anderson Bay was very straightforward and honest although his relatives were worried about him because he would not join the church. He first lived at his father's place by the church. After his marriage, he moved farther north of the community where he rented some rather poor land. He became discouraged finally and moved away to Hamilton County.

Almira Lightsey Bay known as 'Myra' had a beautiful dark complexion and was a good, quiet woman. She, like the other Lightseys, was a devout Baptist. She named her son Bony Bay after the physician who delivered him, Bonaparte Napoleon Keisler, M.D."[21]

The William A. Bay family, Bay's Chapel, c. 1882
(L to R: William-Bony-Heddy-Almira Lightsey Bay)

To continue the 1880 census:

Bay,	Harison	65 M		Farmer	Tennessee-Tenn.-S.C.
	Cinthia	67 F			North Carolina-N.C.-N.C.
	John	26 M			Texas-Tennessee-N.C.

Bay,	James	38 M		Farmer	Tennessee-Tenn.-N.C.
	Nancy	27 F			Arkansas-Tenn.-Tenn.
	Cinthia	7 F			Texas-Tenn.-Ark.
	Andrew	5 M			Texas-Tenn.-Ark.
	Armilda	3 F			Texas-Tenn.-Ark.
	Hattie	9/12 F (born in September)			Texas-Tenn.-Ark. (our informant)

Bay,	John	23 M		Farmer	Texas-Tenn.-Tenn.
	Stacy	20 F			Alabama-Tenn.-Tenn.

Bay,	Joseph	30 M		Farmer	Tennessee-Tenn.-Tenn.

	Margarett	24 F		Texas-Ala.-Ala.
	Ida	6 F		Texas-Tenn.-Tex.
	Allice	4 F		Texas-Tenn.-Tex.
	Lelia	2 F		Texas-Tenn.-Tex.
	Dink	8/12 F (born in October)		Texas-Tenn.-Tex.
Bay,	James	58 M	Farmer	Tennessee-Tenn.-Tenn.
	Sarah	48 F		Tennessee-Tenn.Tenn.
	Andrew	14 M		Texas-Tenn.-Tenn.
	William	12 M		Texas-Tenn.-Tenn.
	Malinda	10 F		Texas-Tenn.-Tenn.
	James	6 M		Texas-Tenn.-Tenn.

On February 3, 1898, Elizabeth B. Bay, widow of Andrew F. Bay, died and was buried in Bay's Chapel Cemetery. Her tombstone states that she was born March 17, 1820.

To find Bay's Chapel from Houston, go north on IH 45 to Conroe. At Conroe, turn west (left) on State Highway 105. At Plantersville, turn north (right) on FM 1774. At Anderson, turn east (right) on FM 149. Beyond Anderson about five miles, turn left (south) at the 'Bays Chapel' road signs.

According to her obituary, Almira Lightsey, [25] "Myra" married William A. Bay at the age of sixteen and moved to Hamilton County shortly after her marriage. They lived there until 1896, when they moved to Coryell County and settled in the Tama Community. There, their eldest son, Bony Anderson Bay, married Lucy May Kattes in the New Hope Church on April 30, 1899. The family then moved to Killeen when their property was incorporated by Camp Hood in 1942. William A. Bay died November 9, 1928, and was buried in the Tama Cemetery in Coryell County. After Camp Hood incorporated Tama he was reburied in the Killeen City Cemetery.

THE KATTES FAMILY

Lucy May Kattes was born February 23, 1881, in the Dogridge Community about three miles from Belton, Texas. She was the third child of Eli Paul Kattes and his wife, Harriett Jane Reid. Eli Kattes, her father, was the son of Joseph S. Kattes who was born in Salem County, New Jersey. There Joseph married Elizabeth Aarons on March 27, 1829. Their first child, Eli, was born in Salem County on July 10, 1830. The family later moved to Missouri.

Eli Kattes was an adventuresome soul. He took part in the California gold rush but found he could make more money, ten dollars a day, cooking for the miners rather than digging for ore. In a letter he wrote his mother from Nevada City dated February 21, 1851, he reassured his mother that he hadn't forgotten about her and he would be home soon. He ended the letter with a print of Nevada City from Prospect Hill and a warning to his sister, Elizabeth Kattes, then fourteen years old:

I hope you will be a good girll and mind your mother in every particular for she certainly knows how you should be better than you yourself and you are the oldest girll   you should try to set a good example before the younger ones. I give this advise as a brother who loves you you are now nearly a young woman and you should try to keep from bad habits of every kind   keep good manners and keep out of bad company etc [23]

A drawing of Nevada City, Nevada, Eli Kattes sent home in 1851

Like so many Missourians, the Civil War killed off the older men in Eli Kattes' family. All his brothers were killed fighting for the South except his youngest brother, George Washington Kattes, born January 3, 1846. George and his father, Joseph Kattes, were killed by Bushwhackers as they were trying to protect some livestock from the thieves.[24]

After the war, Eli Kattes moved to Bell County, Texas, where he met and married Harriett Jane Reide.[25] Harriett was born April 18, 1843. As of the 1860 federal census, Harriett lived with her grandfather, Able Bland, and her mother Sarah Reide with Harriett's siblings near Lewisville, LaGrange Township, in Lafayette County, Arkansas:

Bland,	Able	72 M	Farmer $1000	North Carolina (place of birth)
Reed,	Sarah	45 F		Indiana
	Samuel	21 M		Texas
	Emory	17 F		Texas
	Harriett	13 F		Texas
	Benjamin	15 M		Texas
	Chili	10 M		Louisiana

This last person was a female named Shelly, not *"Chili."* Sarah Reid's children, Lucy and Ben, were born near Buckner, Arkansas, not Texas, according to Lucy Bay.[26]

In Texas, Eli Kattes earned his living as a lime-burner. He died from lung cancer contracted in that business on December 13, 1885. After Eli died, Harriett married George Sharp. He lived only eighteen months and died of asthma. She then married William E. Hall. Harriett died of typhoid fever on November 8, 1901. She was buried originally in the Tama community cemetery but when Camp Hood took over that area, Harriett was also reburied in the Killeen City Cemetery.

THE KILLEEN BAYS

Bony Anderson Bay was born at Bay's Chapel, Montgomery County, on February 27, 1879, and married Lucy May Kattes at the New Hope

Church in Coryell County on April 30, 1899. I was lucky that he and his wife were still clear-minded when I interviewed them during the late 1950's. Bony Bay died in Killeen on February 14, 1962, and like the others, is buried in the Killeen City Cemetery.

Bony and Lucy had eight children, six of whom lived to maturity. They were more fortunate with boys than with girls: the first, Inez Bay, lived only three days in May 1917. Their second girl, Ima May, lived less than eighteen months, from January 1906 to June 1907. Their third girl, Illa, never married.

Bony Bay Family
(L to R: Bony, Arthur (standing), Bill, Lucy Kattes Bay)

All five of Bony and Lucy's sons lived to maturity. They were prominent in Killeen business affairs. The first, Arthur Bay, was born in 1900 and married Laura Marshall. The second, William Anderson Bay, "Bill," was born in 1902 and married Jewell Marshall. The third, Orville Bay, was born in 1908 and married Ellen Campbell. The fourth, R.Q. Bay, was born in 1912 and married Bessie Harris.

Bony Bay Family, c.1960
(standing, L to R: Ted, R.Q., Illa, Orval, Bill, and
Arthur Bay; seated, Lucy and Bony Bay)

Their fifth son, Ted Bay, was father of my first wife, Janet Bay, and David Bracewell's grandfather. Ted was born February 11, 1914, in Tama Community, Coryell County. He married Mattie Joyce Shelton in Coryell County on October 26, 1935.

Ted and Joyce Bay had three daughters:

Pearl Janice Bay, born November 7, 1936, in Killeen, married Lt. Colonel James H. Rohrabaugh, Jr on May 11, 1957; her twin, Polly Janet Bay, whom I married;

and Judy Lynn Bay, born in Lamesa, Texas, on December 27, 1947, and married first, Demuel Cleo Roberts in Mexico on August 8, 1965.

Ted died in Killeen on January 21, 1997, and his widow, Joyce, died there on November 29, 2002.

Ted Bay and the twins, Killeen, c. 1937

Mattie Joyce Shelton, c. 1936

THE SHELTONS

Mattie Joyce Shelton was born January 5, 1918, at Hubbard, Coryell County, Texas, the daughter of Luther A. Shelton and Frances Laverne Stovall. Luther Shelton was born in 1878 and married Frances in Coryell County on October 18, 1899.

Luther was the fifth child of Nehemiah "Nim" Howard Shelton who was said to be born in Alabama in 1848 and married Lydia A. Johnson. Nim died in Coryell County in 1921. He was the son of Kesikiah and Mary Shelton.

Nim's family appeared on the July 16, 1860 federal census for Owl Creek, Coryell County as:

Shelton,	Kesikiah	48 M	Farmer $1300-300	Tennessee (place of birth)
	Mary	43 F		South Carolina
	James J.	23 M	Farmer $150	Alabama
	Stephen N.	21 M	Laborer $150	Alabama
	Elizabeth L.	19 F		Alabama
	Mary C.	17 F		Alabama
	Caroline	14 F		Alabama
	Nehemiah	11 M		Texas
	Mary F.	17 F		Kentucky

Nehemiah "Nim" Howard Shelton (1848-1921)

Nim was a newlywed when he appeared on Coryell County federal census of 1870:

| Shelton, | Nehemiah | 23 M | Farmer $95-565 | Alabama |
| | Lydia | 20 F | | Texas |

By 1880, the census of Coryell County showed how much their family had grown in ten years:

Shelton,	Nim	30 M	Farmer	Alabama-Ala.-Ala.
	Lydia A.	29 F		Texas-Ala.-Ga.
	Eva	9 F		Texas-Ala.-Tex.
	James A.	9 M		"
	Leroy	6 M		"
	Horace	3 M		"
	Luthur	2 M		"
	Iva	1 F		"

Lydia A.J. Johnson (1850-1934)

Lydia A.J. Johnson, Nim Shelton's wife, was born in Tennessee in 1850 and married Shelton in Coryell County in 1870. She died in Coryell County in 1934. Lydia was the daughter of John Johnson who was born in Tennessee in 1805. John Johnson appeared on the 1860 census for Coryell Creek, Coryell County as:

Johnson,	John	55 M	Blacksmith	Tennessee
	Charlotte	50 F	$500-1500	Tennessee
	James	19 M	Herdsman	Tennessee
	Joseph	16 M		Tennessee
	Lidia A.J.	13 F		Tennessee
	Ben	6 M		Arkansas

After Lydia had married, John Johnson appeared again on the 1870 census of Coryell County as:

Johnson,	John	60 M	Farmer $800-1500	Virginia
	Charlotte	60 F		Tennessee
	Benjamin	16 M		Arkansas
Johnson,	Joseph	25 M	Farmer $400-700	Tennessee
	Rebecca	18 F		Texas
	William S.	1 M		Texas

THE STOVALLS

Frances Laverne Stovall was born in Texas in 1882 and married Luther A. Shelton in Coryell County on October 18, 1899.[27] She was the second child of William H. Stovall and Mary Clifford Lanier. William was born in Tennessee in 1854 and married Mary Lanier in Coryell County in 1878. He died in Coryell County August 1, 1935.

William H. Stovall was the third child of John Stovall and Elizabeth Webster Stovall, both born in Tennessee. According to Laverne Stovall Shelton, her father, William Stovall, was born in Shelby County, Tennessee, and moved to Bell County, Texas in 1874. In 1892, they moved to Owl Creek Community in Coryell County.[27]

Laverne Stovall Shelton showed me a power of attorney with more information on William H. Stovall's background:

"WHEREAS, I, W.H. Stovall, heir of Jonathan Webster & Joel H. Webster, owner of lands in Tennessee. . .granted by the state of Tennessee to the following grantees—Jonathan Webster, Joel H. Webster, Jonathan S. Webster, Lucretia V. Webster, Virginia W. Webster, Moses M. Cass, Goldman Green, and James C. Jones. . . .being principally wild and unimproved lands being recorded at the office of the Registrar of the Mountain District formerly located at Sparta, Tennessee. . . ."

William Stovall authorized a lawyer to examine these claims.

William H. Stovall appeared on the 1880 census of Howard Community, Bell County, Texas, as:

Stovall,	W.H.	24 M	Farmer	Tennessee-Tenn.-Tenn.
	M.C.	19 F		Alabama-Ga.-Ga.
	Luther A.	1 M		(blank)

Laverne Stovall Shelton, said her mother, Mary Clifford Lanier, was born in Montevallo, Alabama. Mary's father, Green Tillman Lanier, was a schoolteacher in Montevallo, Alabama, after the Civil War. Green Lanier was born and raised in Macon, Georgia, the home of Southern poet Sydney Lanier to whom he was presumably related.

Green Lanier appeared on the City of Montevallo, Shelby County, Alabama, on the census of 1860:

Lanier,	Green	28 M	Farmer $250	Georgia
	Mary K.	24 F		Georgia
	John R.	7 M		Alabama
	Mellrill(?)	5 M		Alabama

Green T. Lanier appeared in the Howard Community in Bell County, Texas, on the census of 1880 as:

Lanier,	G.	53 M	Farmer	Georgia-S.C.-S.C.
	Mary K.	45 F		Georgia-S.C.-S.C.
	Frances	14 F		Alabama-Ga.-Ga.

H. (W) G.   11 M   Alabama-Ga.-Ga.

Laverne's great-grandmother, Mary K. Warren Lanier, widow of Green T. Lanier, filed a successful Confederate Pension Application for Green Lanier.[28]   Mary K. stated that she married Green T. Lanier in Gordon County, Georgia, in September 1852.   By 1855, they lived in Sinclair County, Alabama.   Green enlisted at Montevallo, Alabama, in Company "B", 2nd Alabama Cavalry, in March 1862, and served to the end of the war.[28] He died April 14, 1899.

Mary K. Warren was born in Georgia in 1834, the daughter of John and his wife, Melissa C. John was born in Georgia in 1808. His wife was born in South Carolina in 1814. They appear on the 1850 census of Murray County, Georgia, as:

Warren,	John	42 M	Farmer	$600	Georgia
	Melissa S.	36 F			South Carolina
	Mary A.	16 F			Georgia
	Martha F.	11 F			Georgia

CHAPTER FIFTEEN

DAVID JEROME BRACEWELL (1964-   )

David J. Bracewell

CHILDHOOD

I was the third and last child born on December 21, 1964, in Angleton, Texas, to Carey and Janet Brazil.[1] I had two older sisters, Susan and Valerie, who preceding me. At that time the family lived in Alvin but Angleton was the closest hospital for deliveries. My earliest memories are not from Alvin but from our next home in Woodbridge, Virginia, just south of Washington, D.C.

We had the typical family arrangement for those times. My father worked all day away from home while mother worked all day at home. I find that old fashioned way still quite appealing. It's a shame it isn't as common or practical as it was for my generation.

Growing up in Woodbridge, I remember going to the Smithsonian museums, Prince William National Park, and monuments and battlefields in and around Washington, D.C. Weekends, to give Mom a break, Dad would take us kids on an outing, usually one of our own choosing.

On Sunday afternoon we would gather around the old black-and-white Zenith television set to watch Tarzan movies starring Johnny Weissmuller and eat exactly thirty-three malt balls. Why exactly thirty-three? The malt balls came in a bag of 100 and with three competitive kids who can count, the only solution was for a parent to eat the 100th lest it start a war!

In those days, TV was pretty boring so mostly we played outside with our friends. Some of the people I recall were the Careys, Armee, Jill and her brother, and Mary Ann Harpine-- my first kiss. No one ever forgets their first kiss. We played games like *Red Rover, Mother May I, Freeze Tag, Wacky Racers* and a game we made up called *ACK,* essentially a noisy game of tag played in a giant tree full of screaming elementary school-aged children. *Wacky Racers* was our version of the TV show on bikes, tricycles, or anything that moved. To this day, my sister Valerie has a permanently-crinkled big toe nail from getting it caught between the chain and sprocket playing *Wacky Racers*.

As a boy, I tended to gravitate more to my father as I think most boys do so most of my parenting memories about my parents come from interactions with him. He was stern but fair, could have a temper at times, yet was more tolerant than mother. I would wait for him to come home every day, staring out from behind our chain linked fence, looking for his green Ford to pull in. He believed in spanking. I think I may have received half a dozen spankings in my lifetime, most of which I earned by such antics as pounding the aluminum gutter downspouts flat with a hammer. I will never forget being punished for door slamming. My punishment was to open and close the door ten times correctly, an eternity when your friends are on the front lawn having a good time. I don't have as many memories of my mother during childhood other than her battle to kill roaches with a broom. To me, it seemed quite funny.

Susan, my eldest sister, was probably the most motherly person I have ever known. Not a single stray animal or person could come across her path without her snatching it up and mothering it. I was no exception. She treated me as much as a her own offspring as a brother. She looked after everything from dressing, feeding, and looking out of me. I suppose, given our age differences, it was only natural she act that way. But in many ways she was as influential as any woman could ever be to me.

With Valerie, my middle sister, our relationship was more antagonistic. Being so close in age to both Susan and me had to have been difficult for Valerie. I think being a middle child, not the baby or the biggest, probably was a difficult role to play. I wasn't always in conflict with Valerie but there was more than a fair amount of strife between us.

ADOLESCENCE

We moved from Woodbridge to Houston, Texas, where I attended the third grade at Ashford Elementary School. We lived in a neighborhood called Ashford South off Dairy Ashford Boulevard.   My first year was chaotic, not because of the move but because the school was run by a bunch of ex-hippies who had the grand idea to create an "open school," a school with no walls between classrooms. And in "not wanting to stifle creativity," the children were given few boundaries, creating a learning environment that seemed to me chaotic and stupid. I made many new friends at Ashford Elementary.   One of Susan's new friends was Mark Lyons who later became my brother-in-law and a life-long friend.

While living on Dairy-Ashford, my father opened a convenience store and things seem to change for the good. But in the long run, things got worse.

The business seemed to raise our economic fortunes and we moved to a larger home. But the price we paid as a family did not seem worth it. The amount of hours both my mother and father poured into the business on top of other factors eventually led to the dissolution of our family.

Mom, I and my two sisters ended up in Killeen, Texas, living in a rental property owned by my maternal grandfather, Ted Bay. We lived in Killeen for about a year then moved back to Houston. There, the family further splintered again with Susan moving out on her own at a very young age and Valerie moving in with our Aunt Janice Rohrabaugh for good. I bounced back and forth a bit between Mom and Dad, eventually settling in with Mom in some run-down apartments off Wirt Road in Houston. I was in the seventh grade. We lived at that address for two years, then Mom remarried.

Fortunately, my friends I had fallen in with had one healthy obsession and that was baseball. We couldn't afford to join the league so we made up one ourselves. We would wait until all the night games of "proper" teams had concluded and left the fields then break into the light controls, relight the fields, and play baseball into the early morning hours. In sharp contrast to how things are now, the Houston Police Department would actually watch us from time to time and not once did they ever comment about us having turned the lights back on or playing on a field to which we were not entitled. I think at that time the police had the logic and latitude to use their heads and ten to twenty unsupervised boys playing all night baseball was far better than ten to twenty unsupervised boys running amok. To pay for my baseball equipment I took my first job as a paperboy for our ramshackle apartment complex. Paper delivery at that time meant waking up around 5:30 AM, rolling the papers, putting them in a stolen shopping cart and zipping around the complex making sure to hit as many doors as possible to the irritation of *Houston Chronicle* subscribers.

Between the summers of my ninth and tenth grades, my mother remarried Rene Pernoud. Rene was an engineer for the city of Houston and designed most of its sewers systems and waterways. My sisters didn't know Rene very well and their opinions were not particularly favorable. However, having gotten to know him better than they did, I saw a much different side to him. He was an engineer in every way you can imagine an engineer. Rene was stubborn, methodical, logical, and impossible to argue with. Rene was of French Louisiana birth, born in the 1920's. Rene was also kind in a practical, non-emotional way, honest, sincere and candid to the point that sometimes shocked those who didn't know him well. He knew who he was, wore his opinions on his sleeve, and didn't give one damn bit about anyone who disagreed with him.

ADULTHOOD

I had three options when I graduated from high school: one was to live at home and to go to the University of Houston; the second to get a job; or third, join the Armed Forces. I joined the Army since having little or no boundaries for nearly a decade, I thought a little extra structure would probably be a good thing.

I left for Army boot camp two days after graduating from high school and ended up in an ancient World War II vintage barracks--actually a tank hill-- in Fort Jackson, South Carolina. The Army experience was pretty much what I expected. And while I wouldn't say I enjoyed everything the Army had to offer, on the whole it was a positive experience. I made some additional life-long friends such as Richard Varnis, a street- wise third generation Irish-American from South Philadelphia and Vito Forchione from Bridgeport, Connecticut.   I also fell in love (or so I thought) and was briefly married to another soldier, one Carol Smith. It didn't take long for either Carol or me to figure out that we didn't have a whole lot in common so luckily we divorced and both of us moved on with minimal damage.

My duty stations were Fort Jackson for basic training; Fort Sam Houston, San Antonio, for AIT School; Fort Leonard Wood, Missouri, as a duty station; Fitzsimmons for Reserves; Fort Riley, Kansas, as advance camp; and Fort Benning, Georgia, for airborne training.

After the military experience, I moved back to Texas and began working odd jobs, using my military benefits for college. I worked just about any job that would make extra money. I was a construction worker with Uncle Jim Rohrabaugh, a forklift driver at my stepmother Nada Bracewell's IBM computer warehouse along with cousin Kevin Brazil, a phlebotomist doing phlebotomy jobs around Austin. I was usually broke but happy.

I spent a good portion of my college years rooming with my classmates from the University of Texas Army Reserve Officer Training Corps. My roommates and friends, mostly from ROTC, were Johnny Lenz, Johnny Welch and Shawn Mohle. We all lived together in a ratty, rented condo on the east side of Austin. Most of the guys I knew at the University of Texas ROTC had prior military service. Shawn and I also had prior service so we tended to room together since our life experiences seemed to differ from the non-prior service cadets.

At the end of our ROTC training during my senior year, the first Gulf War had just ended and the Army underwent a drastic demobilization and cost-cutting period. I was attached to a reserve unit, the 549th MI, and saw several things that changed my idea about a military service career. The first was how terrible Army Reserve and National Guard units actually are. The thought of risking a deployment with those units did not sit well with me as they were and are essentially incompetent.

Next we received a new company commander, a captain, who had been a tank commander with the 2nd Armored Division. In contrast to the normal cadre of reservists, this guy was not just good. He was excellent. He was everything you wanted in an officer and yet here he was stationed in a backwater reserve unit, drilling with them once a month. He went from an active duty combat arms tank commander to reserve headquarters company reservist for a marginal unit because there were simply no jobs of any kind for him to fill on active duty to finish out his career. I didn't want to follow in his footsteps.

The other shoe dropped when all the ROTC seniors were called in the last semester and told "anyone can leave and you will owe nothing in terms of commitment or money." Between seeing the prospects of my current commander to now being able to walk away free and clear from all Government obligations, it's no surprise that me and just about every other prior-service person jumped at the chance to resign. I spent three years at the University of Texas but eventually ran out of money. I then took a full time day job and finished up college later at a private school.

My first well-paid non-military job came after I finished school, passed the AMT registry exams, and became a laboratory technologist for Southwest Regional Cancer Center in Austin, Texas. That organization later became US Oncology (USON). I worked at USON for ten years, going from technologist in Central Texas to regional laboratory and operations manager.

I have not mentioned any significant female friends to this point since, while there were a number of them, I don't think any of them were particularly memorable no matter how long I may have dated them. Since Carol, I had pretty much given up on the idea of marriage. And although I dated, I usually would find some reason not take any of them too seriously.

At this time I had a friend who had been nagging me to take this girl out that she knew who was "perfect for me." I had only been on one blind date in my life, the result of Cousin Tracy Robert's {daughter of Judy Bay Roberts} prompting back in junior high school, and that blind date seemed one blind date too many. My friend, Belinda, was not one to give up so after several weeks of hounding me, I relented and called the girl, believing it would probably be another disastrous blind date. That girl is now my wife, Michelle.

Belinda was right. After one date with Michelle, I knew she was the one. I had dated before and even been almost serious with some others but with Michelle, it just all came together. In addition to having identical beliefs and goals, we had oddly parallel lives, growing up fairly close to each other but going to different high schools. We didn't date very long—only about eight months--but I never had any doubts she would be my wife. We were married August 15, 1990, in Hyde Park Baptist Church in Austin.

Michelle was still in school studying nursing when we married. I was managing the four laboratories for USON in and around Austin, Texas. We moved into a small apartment in south Austin and starting saving for our first house. We bought a small three-bedroom house on Willow Way in Round Rock, Texas, but from our point of view, it was our *Taj Mahal.* Michelle graduated from nursing school and I got her first nursing job at my company, USON. We moved from Willow Way to Honey Bear Loop also in Round Rock, thinking we might need room when we started a family. Michelle decided to switch from cancer patients to labor and delivery and I decided that I wanted to try something other than managing people.

I left USON for Orchard Software Corporation. I had done business with this laboratory software company and was impressed with the product so I left my comfortable job with a publically traded company and became employee #13 with a new, smaller company--Orchard. I started off doing laboratory software installations for all of Texas. It meant twenty-five weeks of travel per year. I have been with Orchard for eleven years now and have held a number of positions: field engineer, HL7 engineer and my current position, managing thirty employees ranging from call center, internal systems and the post-go-live transition group. It would seem some people just can't escape management.

Michelle and I enjoy our careers, but the love of our life is each other and our darling daughter, Rachel Katherine Bracewell, born in Noblesville, Indiana, on December 19, 2001.

We follow the Baptist faith.

David, Rachel, and Michelle Bracewell

EPILOGUE

In this book, I traced David Bracewell's paternal lineage from medieval Yorkshire to modern Indiana. I followed David's direct ancestry from Edmund Bracewell, born in Grantham, Lincolnshire c. 1510 to the birth of his child, Rachel, in Noblesville, Indiana in 2001.

His spiritual leadership lineage began when the Church of England granted holy orders to his tenth great-grandfather, Reverend Robert Bracewell in 1631. Why have David's ancestors been Protestant religious leaders through all these centuries, proclaiming the gospel from Episcopal, Quaker and Baptist pulpits? Was it the influence of father upon son or some higher cause? Why did Valentine Bracewell's grandson, Richard Braswell (c.1732-1799), out of more than one hundred other Braswell males alive on the Eastern coast in his generation, decide to be the first Braswell to cross theAlleghanies and spread the Baptist gospel westward? Why, untl they tasted the sweet life of slave-owning aristocrats in Arkansas from 1825-65, did David's ancestors cling to the old Quaker lifestyle of of "Being on the Earth but not of the Earth?" Like most research, my findings solved one problem—in this case, David's ancestry—but raised others. Maybe I'll find these answers in the afterworld.

What began as a hobby in 1958 turned into a lifelong passion. My life is but a moment in history, and the genealogist's best is soon washed away as the stream of knowledge grows. Fifty years of happy association in the pursuit of family history has come to an end. I will miss this absorbing purpose that gave even deeper meaning and purpose to my life. Where the story goes from here is in God's hands.

REFERENCES AND NOTES

CHAPTER ONE

Ref. 1: Bardsley, Charles W.E. *A Dictionary of English and Welsh Surnames*. Oxford University Press, New York: 1901, p. 126.

Ref. 2: The full set of repeats (or alleles) for Rev. Robert Bracewell's DNA lineages as of 2010 are: DYS 393—13, DYS 390—24, DYS 19—14, DYS 391—10, DYS 385a—11, DYS 385b—14, DYS 426—12, DYS 388—12, DYS 439—12, DYS 389-1—13, DYS 392—13, DYS 389-2—29, DYS 458—17, DYS 459a—9, DYS 459b—10, DYS 455—11, DYS 454—11, DYS 447—25, DYS 437—15, DYS 448—19, DYS 449—30, DYS 464a—15, b—15, c—16, d—17, DYS 460—11, GATA H-4—11, YCA-IIa—19, b—23, DYS 450—16, DYS 607—14, DYS 576—17, DYS 570—18, CDYa—36, b—40, DYS 442—12, DYS 438—12, DYS 531—12, DYS 578—10, S-1a—15, b—16. DYS 590—8. DYS 641—10, DYS 472—8, DYS 6S1—10, DYS 511-10, DYS 425—12, DYS 413-a—16, b—23, DYS 557—16, DYS 594—10, DYS 436 12, DYS 490—12, DYS 534—15, DYS 450—8, DYS 444—12, DYS 481—24, DYS 520—20, DYS 446—12, DYS 617—10, DYS 568—11,

DYS 487—13, DYS 572—11, DYS 640—11, DYS 492—12, DYS 565—12.

Walt Gabennesch, whose wife is a Carver descendant, had our DNA tested farther and revealed that our haplotype is R1b1b2a1a2f, with SNPs L21, M529, and S145.

Early discoveries in the Rev. Robert Bracewell haplotype set involve the descendants of William Braswell, Jr. who died in Nash County, N.C. in 1785. They carry two variations of the haplotype,—1 marker at GATA H-4 and +1 marker at DYS 570. Descendants of Richard Bracewell of Laurens County, Georgia, from the lineage of Richard Bracewell (d. 1758) all carry +1 marker at CDY-b.

The DNA numbers for Richard Braswell, son of Susannah Burgess Bracewell and Richard Towle(y), to sixty-seven markers are: 13-22-15-10-14-14-11-14-11-12-11-29-16-8-9-8-11-23-16-20-30-12-14-15-15-10-10-19-21-14-14-17-18-35-40-11-10-11-8-15-15-8-12-10-8-9-9-12-22-24-15-10-12-12-16-8-13-25-20-13-13-11-12-11-11-12-11

The DNA string for descendants of James Braswell, son of Susannah Burgess Bracewell, follows the same DYS sequence as before: 13-24-14-11-11-15-12-12-12-14-13-30-18-9-10-11-11-24-15-20-29-15-16-17-117-11-11-19-23-16-15-19-14-38-40-12-12.

Ref. 3: Letter from William F. Bracewell of Austerfield Manor, North Doncaster, to Carey Bracewell, dated March 13, 1960

Ref. 4 : Graham, Stanley Challenger. 10 East Hill Street, Barnoldswick, Lancastershire, England BB18 6AH. Graham's series of articles appeared in *The Barnoldswick and Earby Times* from March through May, 2004 under the headline, *"A Brief Account of*

Some of the Bracewell Family in Barnoldswick, Earby, and Salterforth From 1539 to 1914."

Ref. 4: *Grantham Parish Register.* LDS Family History Library file #009406. Baptism records are missing from 1571-1572 and November 13, 1573-February 1579 when Richard Bracewell (died 1641 in London) was likely born.

Ref. 5: Graham to Bracewell, E-mail, 1999

Ref. 6: Swan, Conrad. College of Arms, Queen Victoria Street, London to James G.W. MacLamroc, Greensboro, North Carolina, letter dated May 19, 1969. "The will of Edmund (or Edward) Bracewell gives weight to the probability of the link between the London and Grantham Bracewells, and I do not think there is any ambiguous evidence."

Ref. 7: Notestein, Wallace. *The English People on the Eve of Colonization, 1603-1630.* Harper & Brothers, New York: 1954. pp.21-23

Ref. 8: Parish Registers – Vol. II, No.2, p. 4, Parish Records of Baptisms, Vol. 1, 1558-1623 St. Andrews, Holborn, London (MS 6667/1)

Ref. 9: Notestein, *Ibid.*

Ref. 10: Foster, Joseph. *Alumni Oxennienses: The Members of the University of Oxford, 1500-1714.* Oxford:1888

Ref. 11: Foster. *Ibid.*

Ref. 12: Swan, Conrad to James MacLamroc in Greensboro, North Carolina, a letter dated 1969. Swan was York Herald at Arms, genealogist at Guildhall Library, Aldermanury, London EC2P 2EJ

Ref. 13: Carter, Rev. Charles Sydney. *The English Church in the Seventeenth Century.* Longmans, Green and Co., New York: 1909. pp.61-64

Ref.14: Tatum, G.B. *The Puritans in Power: A Study in the History of the English Church from 1640 to 1660.* Cambridge University Press. Oxford:: 1913. p. 74, pp.88-90

Ref. 15: Wills, Deeds, Etc. Vol. I, 1662-1715, p.426

Ref. 16: Fischer, David Hackett. *Albion's Seed – Four British Folkways in America.* Oxford University Press, New York: 1989

Ref. 17: Fischer, *Ibid.*

Ref. 18: Nott, H. E. and E. Ralph. *Disposition Book of Bristol.* Vol. II, 1650-1654, "Bristol Record Society's Publication," p. 54

Ref. 19: *Henning's Statutes of Virginia.* Volume I, p. 378

Ref. 20: *Isle of Wight County, Will & Deed Book I, Vol. 1,* p. 9

Ref. 21: *Will & Deed Book I,* Vol. A, p. 52

Ref. 22: *Ibid.,* Vol. 2, p. 55

Ref. 23: *Isle of Wight County, Wills and Deeds, Etc., Vol. I,* p. 457-458

Ref. 24: *Will & Deed Book I, Vol. 2,* p. 81

Ref. 25: *Record of Wills, Deeds, Etc. Vol. 2, 1661-1719,* pp. 80-81

Ref. 26: Wills & Deeds, Vol. 2, p.567

Ref. 27: Boddie, John B. *Southside Virginia Families,* 2-257

Ref. 28: *Record of Wills, Deeds, Etc. Vol. 2, 1661-1719,* p. 367

Ref. 29: Robert Eley II, born c.1643 in Isle of Wight County and married Jane Bracewell Stokes c. 1678, he died before 1680. Their son, Robert Eley III, was born c.1679 and married Martha Doughtie, daughter of James Doughtie in Nansemond County, Virginia.

On December 9, 1706, Robert Eley III sold 400 acres of land " which descended to me as heir at law of my grandfather Robert Eley." His wife, Martha, appointed her father James Doughtie as attorney to surrender her dower rights. (Isle of Wight Deed Book 2, p. 56) Robert Eley III made his will in Isle of Wight County in September, 1738, leaving part of it to his son, Ely Eley (Isle of Wight County Will Book II, p. 233).

Ely Eley, born c. 1710 in Virginia married Ann Lawrence and had Samuel Eley, born c. 1736. Ely Eley's estate is recorded on April 27, 1741. (Isle of Wight Will Book IV, p. 324)

Samuel Eley was born c. 1736 in Virginia and married Mary Jordan Hilsman. Sam's will proved November 13, 1771 in Bute County, North Carolina (Bute Will Book A, p. 194). Their daughter, Ann Eley, is mentioned in Bute County Guardian Accounts, 1751-1772 and 1770-1778.

Ann Eley was born in 1767 in North Carolina and married John Johnson (1764-1828) in 1786. They moved to Olgethorpe County, Georgia. Their son, Jesse Johnson (1795-1856) was born in Georgia, April 28, 1795 and married Lucy Webb Barnett (1798-1857) in Greene County, Georgia, in 1817. He died in Lockhart, Texas, on May 15, 1856. (on 1850 Caldwell County, Texas, Census)

Their son was Samuel Eley Johnson, Sr. who was born in Alabama November 12, 1838, and married Elizabeth Bunton (1849-1917) in Lockhart, Texas, on December 11, 1867. Sam died February 23, 1913. (on 1860 and 1870 Caldwell County, Texas, Census, the 1880 Hays County and 1910 Gillespie County, Texas, Census)

Samuel Eley Johnson, Jr. (1877-1937) married Rebeckah Baines (1881-1959) and were parents of President Lyndon Baines Johnson (1907-1973). (on 1910 Census of Gillespie County as "S.E. Johnson, 32, and wife, Rebeccah Johnson, 28, with Lendon, aged 1.")

A well-known North Carolina lawyer, the late James MacLamroc, found Jane Bracewell's connection to President Johnson and placed it in a folder of his findings in the Lyndon Baines Johnson Library in Austin, Texas. I read the folder. Later, I asked a librarian to find it again. He couldn't. Some Austin research libraries operated on the honor system until several records and artifacts simply disappeared during the 1960's and 70's. For instance, I've heard of a number of colorful and irreplaceable Mexican land grand certificates that now mysteriously adorn certain office walls.

Ref. 30: Boddie. *Ibid.*

Ref. 31: Boddie. *Ibid.*

Ref. 32: *Isle of Wight County, Record of Wills, Deeds, Etc., Vol. 2*, pp.490-491, 503

Ref. 33: Neither Robert, Jr. nor his brother, Richard, were twenty-one or older when their father's will was signed February 15, 1668. And under the terms of the will, both of them had to be at least of legal age when Robert sold his brother-in-law, James Bagnall, a part of his father's estate on February 3, 1674. Therefore both brothers were born between 1647 and 1653. (Isle of Wight County, Wills and Deeds, Vol. 1, p. 299).

We know from Mary Burgess Skinner's acknowledgment of April 20, 1669 (Surry County Deed Book 1, p. 332) and other documents that Robert married Susanna Burgess, his peer. That the marriage took place before April 18, 1679, is proved by the will of Joyce Cripps (Isle of Wight County, Wills and Deeds, Vol. 2, p. 202) in which she left a shilling to "Shusan Braswell my Sisters Daughter." Mary married third to John Colling, Sr.

We also learned from the will of Richard Towle (*Ibid.,* p.323), Towle fathered more than three of Susannah's "Braswell" children, "the three youngest of whom" were Richard, William, and Elizabeth. All three were born after 1675 since none had yet "attained to the age of seaventeen years . . ." when he signed his will in 1692. As noted, Richard Towle(y)'s descendants have been shown to carry different DNA from Rev. Robert Bracewell's known offspring.

Susannah's will, signed October 22, 1714 (Will and Deed Book 3, p. 304) proves that, in addition, she also had a son, James Braswell; a granddaughter,

Elizabeth Braswell; a daughter, Ann; and a grandson, John Riggs. That her daughter, Ann, was born before December 11, 1674, is proved by the will of John Newman (Wills and Deeds Etc., Vol. 2, p. 368) signed on that date in 1695, which Ann witnessed as "Ann R(iggs?) Brassell." That Robert and his legal marriage to Susanna survived until at least March 27, 1696 is proved by his power of attorney on that date (Deed Book 1, p. 202).

James Braswell was evidently younger than Towle's offspring. He remained in Isle of Wight County until at least January 25, 1729, proved by Samuel Kindred's will on that date which James witnessed (Will Book 3, pp. 166-168). DNA tests on James' known descendants prove that his father was neither Towle(y) nor Robert Bracewell.

That both of Susanna's sons, Richard and William Braswell, remained in Isle of Wight County at least until December 25, 1731, was proved by the deed, Richard Braswell to Richard Jordan, Senior, (Deed Book 4, p. 201) by which Richard conveyed sixty acres he inherited from his mother, Susannah Braswell, "adjoining to the dividing Line of William Braswell . . ."

> Ref. 34: *Isle of Wight County, Wills and Deed Book 1, Vol. 2*, p. 323
>
> Ref. 35: Isle of Wight County order, dated October, 1694, in *Deed Book 1, Orders 1693-1795*, p. 51
>
> Ref. 36: *Deed Book I, 1688-1704*, p. 202
>
> Ref. 37: *Will & Deed Book* I, p. 81
>
> Ref. 38: *Virginia Land Grants, Vol. 7*, p. 293

CHAPTER TWO

> Ref. 1: Isle of Wight County, Will & Deed Book l, Vol. 1, pp. 307-308
>
> Ref. 2: Secretary of State. *The Colonial Records of North Carolina*, Vol. 4, p.523+}

Strong circumstantial evidence that our first American Richard's wife Sarah's surname was Valentine. This "Sarah Valentine opinion" was first expressed by Katherine Edwards, County Clerk of Isle of Wight County, Bracewell descendant, and professional genealogist. Given the prevailing custom of naming a younger son after his mother's family, it would stand to reason that the unique naming of one of his youngest son Valentine has family significance.

In addition, there were other Valentine families in Richard Bracewell's vicinity. A John Valentine was granted two tracts, one for fifty acres "lying in an Island called the Long Ponds" and another for 119 acres "lying before the ragged Islands commonly known by the name of the Long ponds," both near St. Luke's church between Isle of Wight and Nansemond counties. Valentine family members were elsewhere in Tidewater Virginia at the time of marriage. That "Valentine" was such a unique name, not a popular name, is proved by the list of Bertie and Edgecombe venire men cited above in which only one "Valentine" appears on this list of 470 adult men— "Vall Brassell."

Ref. 3: Boddie, John B. *Seventeenth Century Isle of Wight County, Virginia*. Chicago Law Printing Company, Chicago: 1938

Ref. 4: *Will & Deed Book 1, Vol.1*, p. 299

Ref. 5: *Ibid.*, p. 307-308

Ref. 6: *Ibid.*, p.304

Ref. 7: *Ibid.*, pp. 309-310

Ref. 8: *Ibid.*,_p. 325

Ref. 9: Fox, George. *The Journal of George Fox* (1694)

Ref. 10: *The Handy Book for Genealogists,* 2nd Edition, p. 238

Ref. 11: *Will & Deed Book 1, Vol. 1,* p. 466

Ref. 12: *Deed Book 1, 1688-1704,* p. 103

Ref. 13: *Deed Book 2,* p. 5

Ref. 14: *Deed Book 1 1688-1704,* p. 351

Ref. 15: *Deed Book 2,* p. 131

Ref. 16: Isle of Wight County, *The Great Book,* p. 174

Ref. 17: *Isle of Wight Deed Book 4,* pp.40-41; 43-44; 379-380; and 385-386

Ref. 18: *Will Book 4,* p. 64

Ref. 19: Deed Book 4, pp. 379-380. John and Alice Braswell sold Joseph Cobb, Jr., the two hundred acres he was granted September 28, 1732, "the garden only excepted" for a nominal five shillings. According to Cobb historians, John's daughter, Susannah Braswell, married Joseph Cobb. He died in 1753 in Northampton County, North Carolina.

Ref. 20: North Carolina Grants & File Folders, State Archives, Raleigh: Book 1, p. 173. William Bracewell was granted 1,280 acres on Cypress Swamp "issuing out of Morattuck {Meherrin} River.

Ref. 21: William C. Fields, Fayetteville, North Carolina

Ref. 22: *Bertie Deed Book C,* p.19

Ref. 23: *Halifax Deed Book 3,* pp. 177-180

Ref. 24: Governor's Office, *Council Journal,* 1755-1764, pp. 130-131; also printed in *Colonial Records of North Carolina,* Vol. V, pp. 994-995

Ref. 21: *Isle of Wight Deed Book 1, 1688-1704,* p. 401

Ref. 22: *Isle of Wight Great Book*, p, 174

Ref. 23: *Halifax Deed Book 3*, pp. 177-180

Ref. 24: Governor's Office, *Council Journal*, 1755-1764, pp. 130-131; also printed in *Colonial Records of North Carolina*, Volume V, pp. 994-995.

Ref. 25: *Edgecombe County Court Minutes, 1744-1746.* State Archives, C.R. 037.301.1

Ref. 26: *North Carolina Colonial Court Papers, Criminal Papers, General & Assize Courts, 1745-1749.* CCR 178, Archives, Raleigh

Ref. 27: *General Court Papers – Dockets – 1745-1746*, CCR 126, Archives, Raleigh

CHAPTER THREE

Ref. 1: *Isle of Wight County Will Book 3, 1726-1733*, pp. 149-150

Ref. 2: Bell, Mary Best. *Colonial Bertie North Carolina.* Vol. I, *Abstracts of Deed Book A, 1720-1725*,B-107. Henry Pope of Virginia to John Pope, "my son," ninety acres on Beaverdam Swamp

Ref. 3: The *'Quaker Manuscript'* in the Suffolk County, Virginia Clerk's Office

Ref. 4: *Chowan County Deed Book B, Part I*, pp. 126-128. "Swamp" then meant not "a lowland region saturated with water" but simply "a lowland with flowing water".

Ref. 5: *North Carolina Land Grants, Patent Book 3*, p. 39. North Carolina Archives, Raleigh

Ref. 6: Bell, Mary B. *Abstracts of Deeds, Colonial Bertie County, North Carolina.* Vol. 1, p. 4 (A-64)

Ref. 7: *Chowan County Deed Book F-1*, pp. 185-187

Ref. 8: Bell, *Ibid.*, p. 4 (A-63)

Ref. 9: Bell, *Ibid.*, (A-61)

Ref. 10: *General Court, Higher Court Minutes*, p. 364. North Carolina Archives, Raleigh

Ref. 11: *Ibid.*, Section 5, p. 321

Ref. 12: Secretary of State. *The Colonial Records of North Carolina.* Vol. 2, p. 807

Ref. 13: Byrd, William. *History of the Dividing Line,* republished by Dover Publications, Inc. as *William Byrd's Histories of the Dividing Line betwixt Virginia and North Carolina.* New York: 1967, p. 92-94

Ref. 14: *Ibid.*, p. 146

Ref. 15: Hoffman, Margaret E. *Abstracts of Deeds: Edgecombe Precinct, Edgecombe County, North Carolina, 1732-1758* (1969), Vol. 5, p. 462.

Ref. 16: *Ibid.*

Ref. 17: Map, *The Southern Boundary of the Lands granted the 17th day of September 1744 by his Majesty King George the Second to . . . Earl Granville"* at the North Carolina Archives Map Collection, Raleigh

Ref. 18: SS 680, *Land Entries, Warrants & Surveys, Johnston, 1746-1762*, North Carolina Archives, Raleigh

Ref. 19: *Ibid.*, Johnston 1746-1762

Ref. 20: Secretary of State, Granville Land Grants, Johnston County, SSLG 71-D. North Carolina Archives, Raleigh

Ref. 21: *General Court Papers, Dockets, 1752-1753*, North Carolina Archives, Raleigh

Ref. 22: *Granville County Deeds, Vol. 5*, p.23

Ref. 23: SS 702 – *Land Warrants, Orange: 1755-1789*

Ref. 24: SS 435 – Secretary of State, *Land Entries: 1747-1905*

Ref. 25: Grant 161, SSLG 88-K, PB14:391—North Carolina Archives, Raleigh

Ref. 26: *North Carolina Patent Book 12*, p. 20; *Survey Book 5*, p. 350. North Carolina Archives, Raleigh

Ref. 27: File T.O. 105, North Carolina Archives, Raleigh

Ref. 28: DSCR 207.320.l, *Salisbury District Court, Miscellaneous Papers, 1755-1756,* Folder #2, 1756, NC Archives, Raleigh

Ref. 29: *Ibid., Trial & Appearance Docket, 1755-1756*

Ref. 30: *Salisbury District Court, Execution Docket 207.318.1*, NC Archives, Raleigh

Ref. 31: All Bladen, Orange and Chatham counties deed records up to 1771 were lost in courthouse fires. Such missing records are a great loss to other genealogists who are still trying to sort Valentine Senior's descendants. Given the absence of wills and many Braswells with the same names and only fragmentary records to identity them, it was impossible for me to arrange a complete Valentine pedigree.

CHAPTER FOUR

Ref 1: James Smith Bible Record:

The Bible once belonged to James Smith in Utah. He was
born August 25, 1829, in Gipson County, Tennessee,
the son of Diana Braswell Smith, grandson of
John Braswell and great-grandson of Richard and
Obedience Braswell. The information in the Bible
is in the form of a dairy, written in Utah sometime
after April 8, 1884, its printing date.

Smith shared what he knew about his family from family
records and memory, mostly about the Smiths.
He probably learned most of what he knew from
an earlier Bible and about the Braswells, from his
mother, Diana. She died about ten years at the
writing. She passed away in Herber City, Utah, on
March 8, 1875. Smith may have consulted other
members of his family for some of the information
because a few names were added after he made the
original listing. As a family member would, Smith
used nicknames in place of Christian names in the
cases of "Robin" (Robert), "Vaul" (Valentine) and
"Birdence" (Obedience).

Smith's credibility is made stronger because he wrote
the dairy as a serious Mormon religious obligation.
He made only a couple of errors in reference to the
Pruitt and Braswell families out of a wealth of precise
information—names, dates and relationships.

The first sentence hints that Richard Braswell (c.1732-
1799) was the son of Richard Braswell, son of
Valentine: "the name of Richard Smiths wife <u>father</u>
{scratched out} Diana's Grandfather was Richard
Brasuell." Note he heard the surname pronounced
brasul.

The diary now belongs to a Smith descendant in Provo. A microfilmed copy is in the LDS Archives in Salt Lake City. Cite *GRE Smith Bible,* page 76.

A translation:

"John Brasuell was a son of Richard Brasuell Borned in the state of South Carolina <u>about</u> {scratched out} Grinvill Co. about the year 1752

Richard Brasuell brother to

John Brasuell

George Brasuell married Polley Morgan.

James Brasuell married Nancy Maxfield

Robin Brasuell

Vaul Brasuell

Serah Brasuell

Elizabeth Brasuell married James Buttler

Nancy Brasuell not married

Birdence Brasuell married David Hall

Richard Brasuell son of John Brasuell Borne 1792 South Carolina

Diana Brasuell borned South Carolina October. 9.1797 and married Richard Smith December.11.1817."

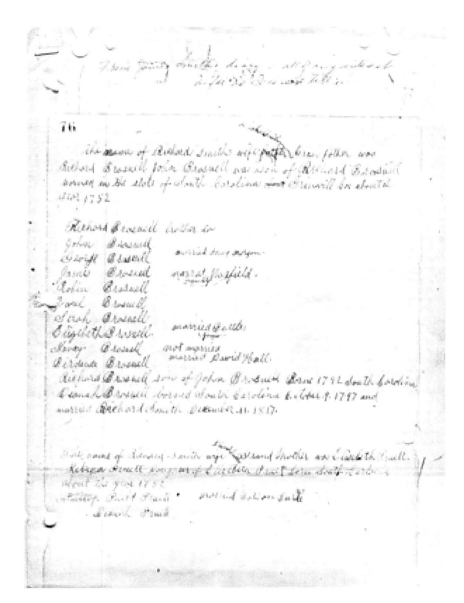

The James Smith Bible, Provo, Utah. Circa 1884

Ref. 2: Paschal, G.W. *History of the Baptists in North Carolina*. Raleigh: 1930

Ref. 3: *Minutes of the Orange County Court of Common Pleas and Quarter Sessions*. State Archives, Raleigh

Ref. 4: Paschal, *Ibid.*

Ref. 5: *Records of the Cherokee-High Valley Baptist Church, 1875-1920: Articles of Faith (1883)*. Frontispiece. Library, Southwestern Texas Baptist Seminary, Fort Worth, Texas

Ref. 6: Paschal, *Ibid., pp. 386-387*

Ref. 7: Evidence linking Richard and George Braswell to the Deep Water Church in Orange County and the Baptists in Little River, Montgomery County=

I. Church Evidence—

Richard and Obedience settled on Baptist Fork of the Little River in Montgomery County, North Carolina, in Rev. Shubal Stern's first commune sometime after moving his Deep Water Church there from Chatham County in 1758.

Baptist church records from South Carolina prove that Richard Braswell was a leader in the church by the 1790's. For example, he represented Tyger River Baptist Church as Messenger to an associational meeting in 1796. This would suggest he had been a member for some time.

II. Evidence Based on Affiliation with Certain Individuals—

RANDAL CHEEK

In February, 1761, the Orange County Court appointed Randal Cheek and 17 others—including

Valentine, Henry, Richard, and William Braswell to "lay out a Road . . . from the County Line to near Andrew Shepherds, to Henry Braswells and thence to Johnston County Line."

On the 1787 State Census of Montgomery County, Randal Cheek appears in JAMES Butler's Second District near Butler (who married Elizabeth Braswell) and Clarks Creek.

(2) ISAAC COOPER

In February, 1761, the Orange County Court appointed Cooper to the same road jury as mentioned above.

In July, 1774, the Anson County Court order Isaac Cooper and twelve others including George Braswell and John Cheek to work on the road "from Clarks Creek . . . . to Mark Allens Store on the Cross road near the ford of Little River . . . ."

WILLIAM LUCAS

William Lucas signed the Regulator petition of October 9, 1769, immediately after (#38) Richard Brassel. On the 1782 tax list for Capt. Rowland Judd's District in Wilkes County, North Carolina, William Lucas is listed only one name away from John Hall, Sr. whose son, David Hall, married Obedience Braswell.

(4) JOHN USSERY

In 1764, John Ursery in Orange County sold a 139-acre tract to Roger Adkinson.
John, James, and William Ussery appear on the 1763 tax list of Anson County.

John Ussery, Senior appears on the 1782 tax list of Montgomery County. On the 1787 State Census of Montgomery County, John Ussery is also in James Butler's 2nd District.

On January 30, 1790, again in Montgomery County, a pioneer entered for 148 acres "on Clarks Creek Joining . . . Sias Billingsby and John Ussery s line"

Ref. 8: Leflter. Hugh T, and Albert R. Newsome. *The History of a Southern State: North Carolina* university of North Carolina Press, Chapel Hill: 1963

Ref. 9. Saunders. *The colonial Records of North Carolina.* Vol.VIII,1769-1771. pp. 80-86

Ref. 10: Clarke, Walter. *Colonial and State Records of North Carolina.* Nash Brothers, Goldsboro: 1899. Vol. 8, p. 240

Ref. 11: *Ibid.,* Lefler & Newsome, *North Carolina: The History of a Southern State*

Ref. 12. Perdue, Jack L. " History Helps: The Regulator Movement" in *The Guilford Genealogist* Vol. 14, No. 2, pp. 80-82

Ref. 13: Paschal, G.W. *History of the Baptists in North Carolina.* Raleigh: 1930. Chapter XVI, "The Exodus of the Baptists"

Ref. 14: *North Caroline Land Grants,* #3187. State Archives, Raleigh

Ref. 15: *Anson County Deed Book K,* p. 340

Ref. 16: *Anson County, North Carolina: Minutes of the Court of Pleas and Quarter Sessions, 1771-1776.* LDS Film #4576, Part 1

Ref. 17: This is how Morgan Braswell appeared on the
1850 Census of Walker County, Alabama. Notice
the significance of his children's names:

#396 Brazel,	Morgin	70 M	Farmer $1000	Unknown ("dumb", unable to speak)
	Sarahan	57 F		Virginia (place of birth)
	George	33 M	Farmer	Tennessee
	Obedience	28 F		Tennessee
	Mary	28 F		Alabama
	Sarah	23 F		"
	Tomas	19 M	Farmer	"
	Morgin	16 M		"
#182 Brazel, Richard	29 M Farmer $150		Alabama	
	Milla	35 F		"
	Mary An	4 F		"
	Thomas	1 M		"

Given their strong preference for family names, it seems intriguing that
George Brazle (#11) and likely his son, Taylor Brazle (#16) were on a list of
fifty-one "delinquents who have not paid their poll tax for the year 1804"
(reported in *Records of Anderson County, Tennessee,* a WPA Project on LDS
microfilm #5566. p. 173). Who was "Taylor Brazle" named for?

They had already left Anderson County, Tennessee, the year before. George
and Morgan Brazzell were in Wilson County, Tennessee, on the 1804 tax
list.

"Morgin Brassell" reported one free poll in a Rutherford County, Tennessee,
tax list of 1809. {*Middle Tennessee Journal of Genealogy and History,* Vol.
XV, No. 1, Summer, 2001. pp. 10-11). The following year, George Brazel

in that county was credited with l male under 5, l:10-14, 1:15-25, and 1:26-45 plus white females l:15-25 and l:26-45. (Federal Census). George and children were in Morgan County, Alabama, early on as witnessed by Morgan 'Brazeal's' entry for government land in Morgan— Sec. 29, Township 13, Range 9, on February 12, 1825. (Federal Land Records)

Ref. 18: McBee, May Wilson. *Anson County, North Carolina: Abstract of Early Records*

Ref. 19: *Montgomery County Land Grants, 1779-1795*. North Carolina State Archives, Raleigh. S.S. 956

Ref. 20: McBee, *Ibid.*

Ref. 21: *Anson County Deed Book K*, p. 18

Ref. 22: Richard Brazil's personal Bible, an inscription on the back flyleaf of his 1834 free edition Bible published by the American Bible Society. It's last know owner was E.G. Hillin in Lometa, Texas.

Ref. 23: Buchanan, John. *The Road to Guilford Courthouse*. John Wiley & Sons, Inc.: 1997

Ref. 24: Wyche, Kathleen B. "North Carolina Militia Paroled by Lord Cornwallis in 1781" in *The North Carolina Genealogical Journal*, Vol. IV, No. 3, (August, 1978), p.150

Ref. 25: Revolutionary War application record of David Hall, National Archives, Washington, D.C

Ref. 26: Mrs. Palmyra Spencer, 3104 E. 21st Street, Sioux Falls, Sioux Falls, South Dakota, who has a copy of Millian Hall's will

Ref. 27: *Washington County Court of Pleas & Quarter Sessions, Vol. I, 1785-1798*, p. 163

Ref. 28: *Genealogical Society of the Original Wilkes County*

Ref. 29: *South Carolina Land Grants*, South Carolina Archives, Columbia, South Carolina Vol. 20, p. 142

Ref. 30: *Greenville District Deed Book B*, p.153

Ref. 31: *Heads of Families at the First Census of the United States Taken in the Year 1790*, National Archives, Washington, D.C.

Ref. 32: Townsend, Leah. *South Carolina Baptists, 1670-1805*. The Florence Printing Company, Florence, South Carolina: 1935

Ref. 33: *Post-Revolutionary War Plats*, South Carolina Archives, Vol. 22, p. 238

Ref. 33: Townsend, *Ibid.*

Ref. 34: *Knox County Deed Books C2V1*, p. 63, 75

Ref. 35 : *Greenville District Deed Book L*, p. 188.

Ref. 36: 1800 Federal Census schedules, National Archives, Washington, D.C.

Ref. 37: Steele, Isabella Brazil. *Bible Record*

CHAPTER FIVE

Ref. 1: Knox County Deed Book C2V1, p. 63

Ref .2: *Ibid.*, p. 75. Drury Woods Breazeale's family, formerly of Long Cane Creek, Abbeville County, South Carolina, had settled in Knox County before the Braswells and was better known to the county clerks. Given the similarity of names and usual casualness about spelling, it's little wonder Braswells were often called "Breazeales" in early East Tennessee records.

Ref. 3: Harper, Lillie D. "Outlaws of Cave-in-Rock", *Colonial Men and Times*. (1916)

Ref. 4: Brazeale, John William McNairy. *Life As It Is . . .* Chapter XVI , "History of the Harps," Knoxville: 1842: pp. 136-151. The early records of Knox County (which contained Anderson County until 1803) have both Breazeale and Braswell records. The two surnames were often confused. The mix-up between the two similar names had already begun in South Carolina by the late 1700's.

The Breazeales came from Huguenot France. Their chateau still exists. Driven out by Louis XIV, they took refuge in Bristol, England, then settled near Richmond, Virginia, in the 1680's. A grandson of their Immigrant settled in Abbeville County, South Carolina, the patriarch of most Southern Breazeales.

Luckily for both family's genealogists, the two families are easy to separate in the records, beginning with DNA: Breazeales carry a different DNA profile from the Bracewell's, Type "I," Norman. Type "I" is common in their ancestral French chateau in Brittany, settled by Normans and wherever else the Vikings roamed. The early Breazeales also used certain unique Christian names that help separate them from Braswells like *Aiken, Griffin, Kennon, Willis, Kinsman, and Archibald.*

Ref. 5: Spencer, Palmyra. Mentioned in a letter from Mrs. Glen Brasel of Wartburg, Tennessee dated September 1,1971, to Mrs. Spencer. On July 24, 1817, David Brasel, Jr., son of the murdered James Braswell, was married to Anna Clarkson, daughter of Constantine Clarkson, who was ancestors to my long-time colleague, Palmyra Spencer in Sioux Falls, South Dakota.

Ref. 6: Moore. *Records of the Tennessee Militia*

Ref. 7: Mrs. Eunice Young located in LDS records an 1804 Wilson County, Tennessee, tax list listing George and Morgan "Bazzell." Morgan Brassell was listed with one free poll on an 1809 tax list for Rutherford County.

In Pollyanna Creekmore's *East Tennessee Historical Society Publications*, #23 (1951), Creekmore assigns one poll to each man. That is, one voting male aged twenty-one to fifty. About Richard Brazil's land, Creekmore says it was "on Clinch River, below Clinton. Much of this land is now in the Atomic Energy Commission Reserve." About James Butler, she says "he was one of the first justices of the peace and formerly a captain in the Knox County militia, 1799."

The results of the 1802 Anderson County tax list, arranged by militia company leaders, were:

Captain Haile's company—Richard Brazil

Captain Davis' company, compiled by Captain James Butler, Esquire—Valentine Brazil, William Brazle (100 acres, Wolf Valley), George Brazle (100 acres, Clinch River), Robert Brazle (89 acres, Raccoon Valley), David Hall, and James Butler (200 acres on Clinch River)

Ref. 8: *Records of Anderson County, Tennessee,* WPA Project, Genealogical Society Microfilm #5566, p.94

Ref. 9: *The Larry Steele Bible*

The Bible belonged to Larry Steele who in 2000 lived in Dallas, Texas. He believed his great-great-great-grandmother, Isabelle Brazle Steele wrote the Bible record about 1850 just before moving from Kansas to Texas. The record is also drawn from an unidentified earlier source, the accuracy of Isabelle's record can be readily verified using other sources:

"James Brazle . . . was slane by the harpes the 29th of July 1799" agrees with local newspaper accounts.

"James Butler died Aug. Ỵe 21st 1803" agrees with county records which show that Elizabeth Braswell Butler, widow of James Butler, applied for letters of administration a few days later in Anderson County, Tennessee.

"Robert Brazle a son of Rob[r] Brazle Ser. was b. June Ỵe 25th 1807" was confirmed by his tombstone inscription in the cowboy ghost town of Mercury, Texas.

Isabelle's Oldest Records—

"Richard Brazle died April ye 16th 1799 and Obedience Brazle his wife died Oct. ye 28th 1805

James Brazle thir son was slane by the harpes the 29th of July 1799

Robert Brazle was born Sept the 17th 1773 and was married to Isabelle Lester the 31st of Jan. 1797

Ann Brazle a daughter of Robert Brazle and Isabelle his wife was born Dec. ye 11th 1797

N.B. {note well} Jeney thir sister was born Sept. ye 25 1799 and Elizabeth thir sister was b. July ye 18th 1801

James ther brother was born May ye 11th 1803

James Butler died Aug. ye 21st 1803

Robert Brazle a son of Robt. Brazle Ser. was b. June ye 25th 1807

William Brazle his bro. was b. Dec. the 16th 1809

George Brazle thire bro. was b. Aug. ye 15th 1812

Charlie Brazle thire Sis. was born Dec. ye 4th 1814

Janey Brazle died April ye 2ⁿᵈ 1819

James Brazle died April ye 27ᵗʰ 1819

Elizabeth Archer died July 8ᵗʰ 1819 {Elizabeth Braswell had married Moses Archer}

Isabelle Brazle the wife of Ro. Brazle d. March 1823"

Isabelle's Later Records—

"Lucy McCollum daughter of John F. McCollum was b. 2 June 1819

William McCollum her brother was born Feb. 16ᵗʰ 1821

John V. McCollum his bro. Was born Dec. 22, 1822

Jimmey St. John a daughter of Cattish St. John was born Nov. 1820

Anna Chilton wife of M. Chilton deceased on the 16ᵗʰ of Dec. in the year 1827

James Chilton son of M. Chilton and Anna his wife died May 3, 1841

Wm M. Chilton was m. to Catherine See on the 17ᵗʰ day of Feb. 1842

Lucy L. Chilton was born the 4ᵗʰ day of Feb. 1843

James P. Chilton her brother was b. on the 24ᵗʰ day of Feb. 1845"

Ref. 10: *The Larry Steele Bible, Ibid.*

Ref. 11: *St. Clair County Marriage Book B*, p. 361. Polly Brazil, daughter of Valentine, married Andre St. Jean on January 9, 1806

Ref. 12: *Records of Anderson County, Tennessee, Ibid.*, p. 307

Ref. 13: *White County Court Minutes, 1806-1811.* Genealogical Society Microfilm #5794. p. 74. Richard Brazel served on a jury.

Ref. 14: *Tennessee Grants*, State Archives, Nashville: #1629, GB-501

Ref. 15: *White County, Tennessee Deed Book E*, p. 71

Ref. 16: *Ibid*, p. 251

Ref. 17: *White County Tax Book, 1811-1815*, Genealogical Society Microfilm #5798

Ref. 18: *Vital Records of Randolph and Washington Counties, Illinois, 1809-1870.* L.D.S. Film #599,051

Ref. 19: *Federal Census*, Clear Creek Area, p. 82.

Ref. 20: P.T. Chapman. *A History of Johnson County, Illinois.* "In May1818, the county court ordered that a new court house be built at what was to become Vienna, Illinois. It was 'to be built of logs of good size to be hewn down outside and in, twenty-four feet in length and eighteen feet in width, with two doors and three windows . . . .'" In July 1818, George Brazel submitted the lowest bid for the above construction contract, and was awarded it.

In June 1819, the county court ordered that George Brazel be paid for building the court house and jury rooms. In May 1825 George Brazil was appointed a justice of the peace and was a candidate, also, for county commissioner. He was mentioned as the owner of Lot #46 in Vienna. *(Illinois House Journal 1824*, pp. 154 and 175)

In May 1825, George Brazell's property was mentioned as being on the boundary of School District #1. He was a patron of this first free school district in Johnson County. On October 12,1827, George Brazel was again commissioned a justice of the peace. (*Executive Record*, 1818-1838, Vol. 1, p.166)

1818 Territorial Census: (p. 75)

George Brasele 1 male 21 & up, plus eight other whites

1820 Federal Census of Johnson County, Massac Township:

George Brazil 1 under 10, 2:10-15, 1:16-25, 1:26-44

Females: 3 under 10, 1:10-15, 1:26-44 one person engaged in Agriculture

George died after 1825 near Vienna, Illinois.

1830 Federal Census of Johnson County, Illinois:

Mary Brazell 1:10-14 1:60-69 (females only)

G. W. Brazell 1 under 5, 1:15-19

Females: 1:10-14, 1:30-39

Jesse Brazell 1 under 5, 1:5-9, 1:10-14, 1:30-39, no females

Jesse Brazell was in Union County, Illinois, by 1850 where he died July 10, 1881. Some members of his family remained in Union County into modern times. (From Carolyn Geittmann, 1333 Copper Drive, Cape Girardeau, Missouri 63701)

Ref. 21: *War of 1812 Records,* Captain Owen Evans' Company of Mounted Militia, Illinois Territory. National Archives, Washington, D.C.

Ref. 22: *Delinquent Tax Lists, 1821-1826,* Wayne County, Missouri. They showed Richard, Senior; Robert, and Valentine Brazil still had lingering claims to pre-empted property even though they no longer lived there.

Ref. 23: Reported in the *Arkansas Gazette* in 1954 and shared by Carole Mayfield

Ref. 24: *Bethel Association: United Baptist Churches of Jesus Christ 1816-1941*. Farmington News Print Company. Microfilm: Arkansas History Commission, Little Rock

Ref. 25: McLeod, Walter E. *Centennial Memorial History of Lawrence County*. Russellville, Arkansas: Russellville Printing Company, 1936

Ref. 26: *Wills and Administrations of Lawrence County, Arkansas, 1816-1834; and Minutes of the Circuit Court, 1816-1830*

Ref. 27: Office of the Circuit Court, *Lawrence County Circuit Court Record Book D*, pp. 52-53, 63

Ref. 28: *The Benton Courier, History of Saline County, 1836-1936,* its Centennial Edition by local authors

Ref. 29: Rogers, James B. *History of Arkansas Baptists*: 1948

Ref. 30: *1830 Census of Pulaski County, Arkansas.* National Archives and Records Services, Washington, D.C. Microfilm Roll 5

Ref. 31: *Records of Pulaski County, Arkansas*

Ref. 32: *Ibid.* Richard Brazil, Jr. owned $100 in improvements, 1 poll, two horses over three and eighteen head of cattle over three.

Valentine Brazil had one mare over ten, one poll, three head of horses and five head of cattle.

Robert Brazil owned $100 in improvements, one poll, four head of horses and four head of cattle.

Moses Brazil owned $100 in improvements, one poll, two head of horses and two head of cattle.

Richard Brazil, Sr., owned $100 in improvements, one poll, two horses and ten head of cattle.

Ref. 33: *The Territorial Papers of the United States, Volume XXI, The Territory of Arkansas, 1829-1836*. Carter, Clarence E., editor. Government Printing Office, Washington: 1954. pp. 866-869 Joshua Chilton, Pension application dated 1871, National Archives. Washington, D.C.

Ref. 34: *Records of Pulaski County, Arkansas*. Ibid.

Ref. 35: Mary Dale Fornier, a 2002 letter to the author

Ref. 36: *The Benton Courier, Ibid*.

Ref. 37: *Ibid*.

Ref. 38: *Saline County Deed Records*

Ref. 39: *Saline County Marriage Book A*, p. 36

Ref. 40: *St. Clair County Marriage Book B,* p.361

Ref. 41: Leona Soladay, Freeport, Illinois, a genealogist and St. John descendant

Ref. 42: Sweet, William Warren. *Religion on the American Frontier*, Vol. 1, *The Baptists*, 1783-1830

Ref. 43: Carter, Clarence Edwin, Ed. *The Territorial Papers of the United States,* Volume XVI, "The Territory of Illinois, 1809-1814". pp. 188-189. Government Printing Office, Washington, D.C.: 1948.

Ref. 44: Military Service Records of Volunteer Organizations, Records of the War of 1812, National Archives, Washington, D.C.

Ref. 45: Brink. *History of Fayette County, Illinois*. pp. 25, 68-67. Philadelphia: 1878.

Ref. 46: Nancy Brazil's pension application, War of 1812, confirms the marriage

Ref. 47: Election Returns, Vol. 4, p., 55 and Vol. 7, p. 47

Ref. 48: Pictures of headstones; other sources including Rejected Bounty Land File 133987, 1850, National Archives, submitted by his wife, Nancy, on War of 1812 service of Valentine Braswell

Ref. 49: *Larry Steele Bible, Ibid.*

Ref. 50: Sweet, William Warren. *Ibid.*

Ref. 51: Illinois State Archives, Springfield, Illinois: Executive Record, 1809-1818, Vol. 3, p. 51

Ref. 52: *Ibid., Executive Record*, 1818-1832, Vol. 1, p. 7

Ref. 53*: Larry Steele Bible, Ibid.*

Ref. 54: An 'elder' is a licentiate, someone allowed to preach and perform other priestly functions but not given the full authority of an ordained minister.

Ref. 55: *Records of Anderson County, Tennessee.* WPA Project, Genealogical Society Microfilm #5566

Ref. 56: Joshua Chilton, Pension application dated 1871, National Archives. Washington, D.C.

Ref. 57: *Fulton County Deed Book 2*, p. 32

CHAPTER SIX

Ref. 1: The enumerator of the 1850 Federal Census of Saline County recorded the date of marriage for each couple.

Ref. 2: Hubbard, Lois Skinner. *The Allen's-A Southern History, 1577 through 2000.* According to Darren Altom, the book is based on a Bible record given to

Barbara Mason in 1940. It was her mother's Bible and had all the information back to Annanias Allen.

Ref. 3: Pease, Theodore C. *Collections of the Illinois State Historical Library*, Volume XXIV "Illinois Census returns, 1810, 1819", Springfield: 1935

Ref. 4: *Saline County Will Record A-l, 1836-1861*, p. 14

Ref. 5: *Ibid.*, p. 30, 45

Ref. 6: Volume 1, *Fulton County Marks & Brands Register*, Lewiston, Illinois

Ref. 7: Master index, Illinois Archives, Springfield, Illinois

Ref. 8: *Fulton County Deed Book 1*, p. 417

Ref. 9: *Ibid.*, p. 430

Ref. 10: *Ibid.*, p. 515-516

Ref. 11: April 25, 1836. Valentine Brazil and George James bought the NE fraction ¼ of Sec. 1, 1S 17W (224.55 acres: $280.69) from the Federal Government under the Preemption Act of 1834. Patented June 6, 1840, under Act of August 3, 1846. Certificate #1365. Vol. 10, p. 23. April 25, 1836. These and all other Federal land purchase records were copied from the plat books at the Bureau of Land Management, Washington, D.C.

Ref. 12: April 25, 1836. Richard Brazell, (Jr.) and Robert Brazell bought the NW1/4 of Sec. 27,1N 16W (160 acres, $200) under the Preemption Act of 1834. Patented October 11, 1839. Certificate#1368. Vol. 6, p.473.

Ref. 13: Federal military service is filed as "Called out for the protection of the Saline Frontier (during the Cherokee Indian Removal)—1836—under authority of General Gaines . . ."

National Archives, Washington, D.C.

Ref. 14: *Index to Compiled Service Records of Volunteer Soldiers Who Served During Indian Wars and Disturbances, 1815-1858."* National Archives, Washington, D.C.

Ref. 15: *Arkansas Gazette* of December 21, 1842. Reported by James Logan Morgan, Arkansas Records Association, 314 Vine Street, Newport, Arkansas

Ref. 16: *Federal Census of 1860, Saline County, Arkansas, Mortality Schedules.* National Archives, Washington, D.C.

Ref. 17: Bounty Land Warrant Application of Richard Brazil 13001-80-55, National Archives, Washington, D.C.

Ref. 18: Saline County Marriage Records

Ref. 19: The enumerator for the 1850 Federal Census of Saline County asked married couples when they were married and recorded their answers. He was chastised in writing by his supervisor for not following the rules. His mistake was our blessing. Nowhere else do we find the wedding date for Moses Brazil and Matilda Allen and many other Antebellum couples.

Ref. 20: Records of the U.S. Postal Service, National Archives, Washington, D.C.

Ref. 21: The $1200 value represents Real property (real estate) and $4000 Private property (other valuables, mostly slaves). In 1860, Moses Brazil owned two black male slaves aged twenty and seventeen.

Ref. 22: Confederate Service Records, National Archives, Washington, D.C.

Ref. 23: *Ibid.*

Ref. 24 *Ibid.*

Ref. 25: From *The Saline,* Vol. 2, #1 (March, 1987) written by his wife, Mariah, in 1885

Ref. 26: Records of the U.S. Postal Service, National Archives, Washington, D.C.

Ref. 27: A letter to the author from Mrs. Walter Havens, 1400 Sycamore, North Little Rock, Arkansas

Ref. 28: *The Benton Courier, "History of Saline County"* by the Works Project Administration, authors of the Centennial Edition, 1836-1936

Ref. 29: Personal testimony to the author, Richard Allen Brazil

Ref. 30: 1870 Federal Census, Bastrop County, Texas, p. 304

Ref. 31: Bastrop County deed records

Ref. 32: Probate Records, Fayette County, Texas

Ref. 33: Personal testimony of Rev. E.C. Brazil to the author, Woodbridge, Virginia, in 1972

Ref. 34: Index to Probate Cases of Texas, #206—San Saba County, January 30, 1866-June

28, 1939. Works Projects Administration, September, 1940

Ref. 35: Rev. E.C. Brazil, *Ibid.*

CHAPTER SEVEN

Ref. 1: *Saline County Marriage Book*, Vol. 1, Saline County Clerk, Benton, Arkansas

Ref. 2: *Centennial History of Arkansas*, Vol. 1

Ref. 3: Testimony of Richard Allen Brazil (1877-1968)

Ref. 4: *Saline County Marriage Book 1*, p. 75

Ref. 5: *Pulaski County Deed Book* C-2, p. 385-386

Ref. 6: *Saline County Chancery Book* A, pp. 256-257. *Records of Judgments, 1839-1845*

Ref. 7: *Pulaski County Deed Book* 2, pp. 422-423

Ref. 8: *Saline County Deed Book* F, p. 396

Ref. 9: Workers of the Writers' Program of the Work Projects Administration. *Arkansas: A Guide to the State.* Hastings House, Publishers, New York: 1941

Ref. 10: From *The Civil War in Arkansas*, an online database

Ref. 11: *Compiled Military Service Records of the Confederate States of America*, National Archives, GSA, Washington, D.C.

Ref. 12: Letter to the author from Mary Dale Fornier, January 25, 2002

Ref. 13: Mary Dale Fornier, *Ibid.*

Ref. 14: *The War of the Rebellion: a Compilation of the Official Records of the Union and Confederate Armies.* Washington, D.C., 1880-1901

Ref. 15: Library, Hill College History Complex, Hillsboro, Texas

Ref. 16: *The War of the Rebellion: Ibid.*

Ref. 17: Johnson, Ludwell H. *RED RIVER CAMPAIGN: Politics & Cotton in the Civil War.* Kent State University Press, Kent, Ohio: 1995. p. 258

Ref. 18*: Compiled Service Records, Ibid.*

Ref. 19: Richard Allen Brazil, *Ibid.*

Ref. 20: *Collin Deed Book* P, p. 798

Ref. 21: See Chapter Six, *"Bastrop County, Texas, 1869."* Microfilm of Bastrop County tax list for 1869, Texas State Archives, Austin, Texas. Jesse arrived in Texas with a taxable estate of five horses worth $150, four head of cattle worth $16, $52 in cash and $318 worth of personal property.

Ref. 22: Gacy, Simner, and Gentry: *Early Texas Births, 1838-1878*

Ref. 23: *Records of the Cherokee-High Valley Baptist Church, 1876-1920*, Southwest Texas Baptist Seminary, Fort Worth, Texas

Ref. 24: Precinct #4. Vol. 28, Enumeration Dist. 114, Sheet 3, Line 20

Ref. 25: Blind Supplemental Schedules

Ref. 26: Richard Allen Brazil, *Ibid.*

Ref. 27: E-mail from Joanne Aman of 2708 Woodland Drive, Waco, Texas 76710

Ref. 28: Testimony of Ida Brazil Bolton, his niece, who was present

Ref. 29: Jesse's granddaughter, Patsy Brazil Lackey

Ref. 30: Letter to the author from Ida Brazil Bolton, dated August 15, 1958

Ref. 31: *San Saba County Probate Records*: Jessie Brazil, deceased, filed July 15, 1892. Case #123

Ref. 32: Interview with Rev. E.C. Brazil, 1513 Hylton Avenue, Woodbridge, Virginia, by the author, April, 1972

CHAPTER EIGHT

Ref. 1: www.familysearch.com

Ref.2: Steinemann, Ernst. *"List of 18th Century Emigrants from Canton of Schoffhausen to the American Colonies, 1734-1752"*

Ref. 3: Rupp, Daniel. William Tiffin, Captain *Thirty Thousand Names of German, Swiss, Dutch, French and other Immigrants in Pennsylvania From 1727 to 1776*

Ref.4: Rogers, Ellen Stanley. *THE PRILLAMAN FAMILY: An Account of the Descendants of Jacob Prillaman, Sr. (1721-1796) of Franklin County, Virginia*. Hyattsville, Maryland: Mimeograph (1959)

Ref. 5: *Pittsylvania County Deed Book 2, 1770-1772*

Ref. 6: *Virginia Tax Payers, 1782-1787*

Ref. 7: Fothergill, A.B. and J. M. Nagle

Ref. 8: *Franklin County Will Book 5, 1837-1845*, pp. 74-75

Ref. 9: Rogers, *ibid.*, pp. 15-16:

Ref. 10: Research report from Albert Levengood, Rhea County, Tennessee

Ref. 11: Federal Census report

Ref. 12: *Rhea County Marriage Book 1*, p. 424

Ref. 13 : Twyla Edwards, Genealogist

Ref. 14: Mary's descendant, Gale Clements

Ref. 15: *1850 Federal Census of Saline County, Arkansas*

Ref. 16: Richard Allen Brazil, *Ibid.*

CHAPTER NINE

Ref. 1: Calvin's daughters, Armour and Patsy, supplied the chronology

Ref. 2: Unless otherwise noted, facts and quotes are from his son, Reverend Etheridge C. Brazil, recorded at1503 Hylton Avenue, Woodbridge, Virginia, in April 1972.

Ref. 3: *High Valley Baptist Church Minutes*, Southwest Texas Theological Seminary, Fort Worth Texas

Ref. 4: Martha Gage Brazil's testimony

Ref. 5: *High Valley Baptist Church Minutes, Ibid.*

Ref. 6: *Ibid.*

Ref. 7: *San Saba County deed records, Vol. 31*, pp. 227-229

Ref. 8: Patsy Lackey's personal papers, given to author

Ref. 9: *Lampasas Deed Book 5*, pp. 186-189, dated November 13, 1900. Cal and Moses Brazil bought the 1476 acres out of the R.D. McAnelly survey in Lampasas County from Rhoda A. Evans, a widow in Jeff Davis County. She was paid $2750.00 ($2000 down, $750 on notes).

Ref. 10: Letter from Patsy Lackey to Carey Bracewell dated July 10, 1972

Ref. 11: *High Valley Baptist Church Minutes, Ibid.*

Ref. 12: Transcripts Office, Baylor University, Waco, Texas

Ref. 13: Purchases from February to September, 1927, in Concho County deed records: From C.W. Arthur in Survey 171, J.C., W.L., and Otis C. bought 402.75 acres (DB 107 p. 638);From Rainwater in the same

Survey 171, JC bought 149 1/2 acres. L.D. Head sold JC another 50 acres (DB 132, p. 158);From Survey 172 Wincel Mott sold JC, Lee, and Otis 174 acres (DB 111, p.630);

Sales: J.C., W.L., and Otis to L.D. Head, 403 9/10 acres in Survey 170 (DB128, p. 351); J.C. and Oris to Monty Brown, 99 3/10 acres in Survey 171 (DB132, p. 279); Same parties, to Monty Brown, 50 acres in Survey 643; JC and Otis to Monty Brown, 402.75 acres in Survey 171 (DB 139. p. 356);Same instrument and seller JC to J.M. Wagstaff, acreage in Survey 643.

Ref. 14: Dimmit County Clerk, Deed Records: " Two purchases are in Vol. 40, p. 114 Montie Brown and Vol. 52, p. 154, from W.E. Shepperd. In Vol. 59, p. 608/615 there is a foreclosure suit from 1931, Oppenheimer Vs. Winter Garden Land Company, naming J.C. Brazil and several others. J.C. Brazil was cited but did not appear. This property is on or near the Lake Espinosa and is now known as "Cross-S Ranch" properties. Thousands of acres cut up into 10-acre tracts. There were also foreclosures on much of this land."

Ref. 15: Postcard, October 10, 1937: Calvin Brazil in San Saba, Texas, to Miss Patsy Brazil, Paint Rock, Texas

Ref. 16: Texas Death Certificate. Cal died of " cardiac failure, severity."

Ref. 17: Patsy Lackey's personal papers, *Ibid.*

CHAPTER TEN

Ref. 1: In a letter from Larry J. Gage dated December 29, 1969, he shared the Bible record now in the possession of Miss Marilda Abigail Gage, 508 W. Pecan Street, San Saba, Texas

Ref. 2: Mrs. Edna L. Boyd, 1348 E. Speedway, Tucson, Arizona

Ref. 3 Jillson, W.R. *Kentucky Land Grants*

Ref. 4: Shipman, Daniel. *Frontier Life: 58 Years in Texas* (1879)

Ref. 5: *Bastrop County Probate Records*, Book C, p. 7

Ref. 6: *Saline County Deed Records*

Ref. 7: *Bastrop County Probate Records,* Book C, p. 20

Ref. 8: Ibid., Book C, p. 36.

Ref. 9: Ibid., Book B, p. 302

Ref. 10: Ibid., Book C, p. 62

Ref. 11: Ibid., Book C, p. 143

Ref. 12: *Fayette County Probate Records*

Ref. 13: *Bastrop County Probate Records*, Book C, p. 27

Ref. 14: *Sunlight on the South Side: Lunenburg County, Virginia: A List of Tythables of Lunenburg County in 1748*. Aaron Burleson and Jonathan Burleson, 1 tithe each on "the mouth of Falling River Upwards."

Ref. 15: *Western North Carolina* (1914)

Ref. 16: Cert. #28016. *Fayette Marriage Book l*, p. 248

Ref. 17: Gage, Clyde. *The North Carolina Gage Family*, 2nd edition. September,1966

CHAPTER ELEVEN

Ref. 1: Unless otherwise noted, Etheridge Brazil told his own story through his forty-two hour interview with me in Woodbridge, Virginia, in 1972 and through his many written stories.

Ref. 2: Young Obedience Brazil and her sister Mary Ann are listed in their father, Andrew Jackson Brazil's, household on the 1860 Census of Brazil, Arkansas {See Chapter Six, *Moses Brazil (1803-1872)*. Just before them was the household of Sarah F. Miller which included a child with the rare name "Organ C.," evidently part of the "four sets of Civil War orphans" Moses and Matilda Brazil brought to Texas in 1869. Organ later became the wife of their Texas neighbor, Dan Sawyer. As he described on the first page in this chapter, Organ was Etheridge Brazil's midwife. Dan is thought to have been a son of Robert Sawyer who was born in Arkansas about 1820 and is buried in the Sawyer Cemetery probably alongside Moses and Matilda.

Ref. 3: *High Valley Baptist Church records*, Southwestern Baptist Seminary, Fort Worth, Texas

August 8, 1920. "By motion the church liberated Brother Etheridge Brazil and Fred Gage to preach the Gospel as they feel God has called them to do."

CHAPTER TWELVE

Ref. 1: Testimony of Mrs. Perlie Price, Hawley, Texas, with the author

Ref. 2: The White family probably originated in Holland but Henry White, David White's father, born about

1780, was recorded on the 1850 Missouri Federal Census as born in Virginia.

Ref. 3: Testimony of Roxanne Horton Price to the author at the Price Reunion, 1959

Ref. 4: *Confederate Records Collection*, Texas State Archives, Austin, Texas

Ref. 5 : Letter, Mrs. Evelyn Price Brazil

Ref. 6: *Confederate Records*, Florida State Archives, Pensacola, Florida

Ref. 7: File 478, Gillespie County Probate Court, Fredericksburg, Texas

CHAPTER THIRTEEN

Ref. 1: E-mail to the author from Patti Kimple dated December 7, 2009

Ref. 2: *Ibid.*, May 16, 2010

Ref. 3: Interview with Kevin Brazil, May 23, 2010

CHAPTER FOURTEEN

Ref. 1: Mrs. Margaret Bay Robinson of 102 Jamison Drive, Pennington, New Jersey. Letter to Bracewell dated April 26, 1971. She was born in 1901 in Harford County, Maryland.

Ref. 2: Grace P. Butterworth, Office of the Secretary, Princeton University, to Miss Edra Keeran, 4823 Iroquois Avenue, San Diego, California; Letter dated August 6, 1963

Ref. 3: Smith, Anna Lee Kirkwood. *Bethel Presbyterian Church at Madonna, Maryland, 1769-1969.*

Ref. 4: West, Tommy L. *Some Members of the 18ᵗʰ Century Colonial American Bay Family.*

Baltimore, Maryland: Gateway Press, Inc., 2004.

Ref. 5: Peden, Henry, Jr. *Early Harford County, Maryland, Countians 1773-1790.* Westminister, Maryland: Family Line Publications, 1993.

Ref. 6: Herford County Will Book AJ-C, p.411

Ref. 7: Andrew Bay's Revolutionary War pension application #S 2940, National Archives, Washington, D.C.

Ref. 8: North Carolina State Archives, Raleigh, North Carolina

Ref. 9: Genealogical Society Microfilm #570808, *A Historical Sketch of Wilson County, Tennessee* by J.V. Drake. Nashville: Tavel, Eastman, & Howell (1879)= Genealogical Society Microfilm #570808

Ref. 10: *The South Bank of the Cumberland* from a local Wilson County book

Ref. 11: *Wilson County Marriage Records*

Ref. 12: *Ibid.*

Ref. 13: Thomas Bay's bounty land application, Certificate 51421-160-55, National Archivcs. Washington, D.C.

Ref. 14: Jackson, Marquis. *The Life of Andrew Jackson*

Ref. 15: Testimony from Hattie Bay Hoke, a granddaughter of William Harrison Bay, recorded by this writer in 1965

Ref. 16: *Ibid.*

Ref. 17: Records of Montgomery County Probate Office, Conroe, Texas

Ref. 18: The obituary of Thomas Bay was written by J.G. Johnson of Anderson, Texas, in the March 28, 1861, issue of *Texas Christian Advocate*. The newspaper has been preserved by the Bridwell Library of Southern Methodist University, Dallas.

Ref. 19: Montgomery Probate Office, *Ibid.*

Ref. 20: *Ibid.*

Ref. 21: Hattie Bay Hoke, *Ibid.*

Ref. 22: Bony Bay's testimony to this writer in 1965

Ref. 23: Eli Kattes in Nevada City, Nevada, letter to his Mother dated 1851

Ref. 24: Author interview with Lucy Kattes Bay

Ref. 25: Lucy Kattes Bay, *Ibid.*

Ref. 26: Lucy Kattes Bay, *Ibid.*

Ref. 27: Author interview with Laverne Stovall Shelton, c.1960

Ref. 28: *Confederate Pension Application* #6772, dated March 19, 1900, Texas State Archives

CHAPTER FIFTEEN

Ref. 1: David Bracewell shared his own story with the author by E-mail in 2010.

INDEX